HELEN HAYES

Also by Kenneth Barrow

FLORA:
AN APPRECIATION OF
THE LIFE AND WORK OF
DAME FLORA ROBSON

MR. CHIPS:
THE LIFE OF
ROBERT DONAT

HELEN HAYES

FIRST LADY
OF THE
AMERICAN THEATRE

KENNETH BARROW

DOUBLEDAY & COMPANY, INC.
GARDEN CITY, NEW YORK
1985

LIBRARY OF CONGRESS CATALOGING IN PUBLICATION DATA
Barrow, Kenneth.
Helen Hayes, first lady of the American theatre.
"A Dolphin book."
Includes index.
1. Hayes, Helen, 1900– . 2. Actors—United States—Biography.
I. Title. II. Title: Helen Hayes.
PN2287.H35B37 1985 792'.028'0924 [B] 85-4540
ISBN 0-385-23196-2

Design by Beverley Vawter Gallegos

for
our mutual friends
FRANCES TANNEHILL
actress
and
ALEXANDER CLARK, JR.
actor and wit
("Alas! poor Alec I know him;
A fellow of infinite jests")
also
for my mother
FLORENCE JOYCE BRAITHWAITE
with my love

CONTENTS

CONTENTS

AUTHOR'S NOTE

IT HAS ALWAYS astonished me that there has never been a standard biography of America's most distinguished actress. True, there were two volumes of Helen Hayes's own memoirs published before she entered what she calls her second career. There was a book written by her mother in 1939 and a recent work which focused on the MacArthur marriage, but no painstaking appraisal of this lovely and lovable woman over the whole of her lengthy career.

I first met Helen Hayes at the home of a mutual friend, the equally distinguished British actress Dame Flora Robson. At that time I was still an actor with no thoughts of pursuing a literary career. By the time of our second meeting I was already working on my biography of Dame Flora and asked Helen if she would care to make a tribute.

I was invited to Helen's home at Nyack one balmy summer's day. We sat out on the veranda looking over the Hudson. I recall she was busy trying to stuff a rather large-looking cushion into a seemingly small cover. Her tiny fingers weren't making much headway, so naturally I lent the aid of my larger hands. The project accomplished, Helen turned to me and with all the warmth in the world said, "Now you have done something for my home you will always be welcome here." It had been a very simple act but she made me feel like a million dollars. And I felt truly welcome.

Whenever she comes to London she gets in touch and we meet for tea. Inevitably, eventually I asked if I could write a book about her. She thought about it for a while and then said, "As long as I don't have to read it." I could have been taken aback; I knew she had liked my first book. But I guess it's perfectly understandable that when you've been a working actress for more than three quarters of a century then you've heard it all before.

For those who haven't heard it all before I set about the task of telling this story. I suspect Helen might just take a peek at its pages from time to time . . .

So, to begin with, forgive the presumption of the Limey in recording these golden days of the American theatre and one of the brightest jewels in its crown.

I am immensely grateful to the many people who have taken the time and trouble to help me in my work. I should particularly like to acknowledge the help of Wesley Addy, Brian Aherne, the late Ingrid Bergman, Alexander Clark, Douglas Fairbanks, Jr., Sir John Gielgud, Lillian Gish, Julie Harris, Katharine Hepburn, Myrna Loy, Mary Martin, Vincent Price, Ronald Reagan, the late Dame Flora Robson, James Stewart, Brian Stonehouse, and Frances Tannehill among others.

I am indebted to Dorothy Swerdlove and the staff of the Theatre Collection at the Library of Performing Arts at New York's Lincoln Center, where the bulk of the Helen Hayes Collection is lodged; also to Linda Harris Mehr and the staff of the Margaret Herrick Library at the Academy of Motion Picture Arts and Sciences in Los Angeles; to Wallace Munro and the Actors Fund of America; to Lord Harewood and the management of the English National Opera (ENO) whose 1984 United States tour afforded me the opportunity of extensive research; to Pam Reeve of the Spotlight Enquiry Service, London, England; to Nicole Clark for her invaluable assistance with the photographic pages; to Frances Tannehill and Alexander Clark for their unfailing support and generous hospitality in New York, similarly to Dick Elliott and Dave Schmidt for hospitality in Los Angeles.

Every effort has been made to trace the owners of copyright material included in the text or on the photographic pages.

I am grateful to Mary Martin for permission to quote from a letter written by her to Helen Hayes in 1955; to Walter Kerr for permis-

AUTHOR'S NOTE

sion to quote from his writings; to Harper and Row for permission to make several quotes from *Charlie* by Ben Hecht; for various quotes Copyright © 1938/70/71 by The New York Times Company. Reprinted by permission; to the New York Public Library for permission to reproduce photographs housed in the Billy Rose Collection; to Metro-Goldwyn-Mayer/United Artists for stills from the MGM release *The Sin of Madelon Claudet* © 1931 Metro-Goldwyn-Mayer Distributing Corporation. Ren. 1958 Loew's Incorporated, from the MGM release *The White Sister* © 1933 Metro-Goldwyn-Mayer Distributing Corporation. Ren. 1960 Metro-Goldwyn-Mayer Inc., from the MGM release *What Every Woman Knows* © 1934 Metro-Goldwyn-Mayer Corporation. Ren. 1961 Metro-Goldwyn-Mayer Inc.; to MCA Publishing Rights for permission to reproduce stills from *Airport* and *A Farewell To Arms;* to Twentieth Century-Fox for permission to reproduce a still from *Anastasia.*

Several publications have been useful in preparing this biography: *Letters to Mary* by Catherine Hayes Brown (Random House, 1940); *Charlie* by Ben Hecht (Harper, 1957); *A Gift of Joy* by Helen Hayes with Lewis Funke (Evans-Lippincott, 1965); *On Reflection* by Helen Hayes with Sandford Dody (Evans-Lippincott, 1968); *Twice Over Lightly* by Helen Hayes and Anita Loos (Harcourt, Brace & Jovanovich, 1972); and *Front Page Marriage* by Jhan Robbins (Putnam, 1982).

Finally I should like to express my gratitude to David Bonitto and Michael Frary for the ways in which they helped bring this project to fruition.

KENNETH BARROW,
London,
Spring 1985

HELEN HAYES

PROLOGUE

DUST TO DUST

IT WAS A SURPRISINGLY SUNNY DAY for September in London. The small woman in kingfisher blue made her way down the steps at the front of St. Paul's Cathedral, where a year before the Prince of Wales had presented his new bride to the world. Clutched in her arms was a collection of souvenirs of her visit, among them that inspiring photograph of the dome of St. Paul's standing resilient and proud above the flames of a blitzed and war-torn city. "I remember London after the war," she said, "all that waste and devastation. And the rationing. I stood in line with everyone to collect my egg." As she approached the curb and her awaiting car, a scruffy lad of about eleven years of age detached himself from a crowd of fellows standing nearby and gingerly approached her. "You Miss 'Ize?" he demanded.

"How would he know me?" Helen later asked in some bewilderment. She had acted on the London stage once only and that, in all probability, long before the boy's mother had been born. Earlier that day, as she was walking around the restored old Covent Garden market, a woman had challenged her with "You're one of the Snoop Sisters," reminding Helen of a television series she would prefer to forget. I suggested the boy possibly knew her from the same series (it had, after all, been popular in Britain where we easily warm to such eccentrics) but that it was more likely he knew her as the

PROLOGUE

elderly stowaway in the first of the *Airport* films which is perennially shown on television.

In a career that has spanned some eighty years it is perhaps chastening to have her celebrity reduced to such minor triumphs. There again, in a television age where a swift rise to prominence can quickly be succeeded by an even swifter descent into oblivion, to be remembered at all is a signal honor! "Nowadays they know me only for my second career," Helen mused.

What would an eavesdropper, casually passing by, have made of that last remark? What kind of past might this diminutive woman with her still bright eyes and gently plumpening waistline have known? Perhaps she was a children's nurse or nanny, or a librarian, an archaeologist or a schoolteacher. Or perhaps she wrote mystery thrillers, or had been a celebrated pastry-cook. For once in her life she doesn't look the part. Perhaps that is why the honorary title which has attached itself to her more than any other actress over the years, that of "First Lady of the American Theatre," should sit on such reluctant shoulders. Yet it is deserved. She was one of the first and foremost actresses of her time, too tiny to be designated tragedienne, too versatile to be limited to comedy. And so consummate an artist and a human being that it was impossible for her not to become a star and from all stars to become First Lady. Had an accident of history caused her ancestors to remain in Britain and her path to the footlights brought her to the London stage, she would undoubtedly have been created Dame Helen Hayes.

But it was on Broadway that her destiny lay, a way of life which suddenly came to an end one day in 1971. After thirty years of one ailment after another for which no particular cause could be found a doctor made a surprising diagnosis. "Isn't it looney," was Helen's comment, "to learn after a lifetime in the theatre that I have an allergy to theatre dust?" It was in the theatre that she found greatness (two theatres have even borne her name), yet in the accumulated sweepings of decaying buildings and flaked size and paint lay a poison which would end her life as an actress. Or would threaten to.

It was certainly a propitious invitation which took her to the home of friends in the late sixties. Ross Hunter, the film producer, asked her hosts to remove all the books from her room, leaving just one—Arthur Hailey's *Airport*. After a few days she said, "You know, if ever they make a film of this, there's a part in it I could play." Her interest aroused she readily agreed when Hunter offered her the part.

Like a cross-fade in the theatre when the light dims on one scene and another lamp illuminates a new area, so one career ended and another began.

To her great surprise and to the delight of the many who had seen her performance as Ada Quonsett in *Airport,* she was awarded a Best Supporting Actress Oscar. "How wonderful," thought many an observer, "that this little old lady should be rewarded for her life's efforts with an Oscar." And yet it was her second Academy Award. Her first was won over fifty years ago. "Fifty years ago? But that's almost prehistory," suggests our eavesdropper. "How did she come to that? And what happened to her in between?" "Ah," sighs the minstrel, "that is a long story . . ."

First there was Graddy and her gallivanting mother and then, but that was later, her beloved Charlie, and Mary and Victoria, and that other Mary, her own poor tragic Mary, and . . . Perhaps in that flickering interval as the first light fades, all who want to see can glimpse some of the elements that made the actress. To begin with, it was in her blood . . .

ONE

LIKE MOTHER, LIKE DAUGHTER

1900 – 1913

1

TO BEGIN WITH, IT WAS IN HER BLOOD, if, in fact, any talent can be conveyed from generation to generation simply through the act of procreation. Perhaps it is a vanity that we imagine that the essences of our beings and the roots of our personalities will automatically pass to our children, thus extending our selves into future time. In times to come, Helen Hayes's delight in theatre would pass to a further generation, once through a direct blood line and once not. It is more likely that she, like her adopted son after her, at an early age learned to thrill to the things that thrilled the two generations before her.

If it was in her blood, then it was through her mother, Catherine Estelle Hayes Brown, actress failed, and her mother's great-aunt Catherine Hayes, the celebrated "Swan of Erin," and goodness knows who else before. However it got there, Helen soon found she had the talent for conveying laughter or tears and the gift of sharing her joy. Was it in response to her mimicry, or that shy tilt of the head, or that endearing emphasis on a particular word that led to "She's a born actress" from one, "She should be on the stage" from another, and from a third, "It's in her blood." If she wasn't born with acting in her blood she soon learned that she ought to have been. And when just six weeks and a day after her ninth birthday she first set foot on a Broadway stage, it must have felt as though she were coming home.

That first Catherine Hayes earned her illustrious title with a lilting soprano voice which made her the darling of the Emerald Isle and led to celebrity at the Royal Albert Hall in London. Such was her professional standing that she turned down an offer of fifty thousand dollars from Barnum to tour under his management. Many preferred her talents to those of her contemporary Jenny Lind, for though her voice had similar finesse she had the advantage of a dramatic ability which Lind lacked. Her fame has been eclipsed by Lind merely because Catherine died early, aged only forty-one. Though the Swan found favor with a public in both the Old World and the New, she found markedly less, as is so often the case, with her own family. She had renounced her Catholicism and this proved the stumbling block when she tried to adopt her nephew Patrick. The family wouldn't hear of it. Her great-niece, who, from an early age, had nursed pretensions to a social milieu of elegance and style far removed from her working-class origins, learning that this entrée to a glittering world had been denied her father and, more importantly, herself, would never forgive the family or the Church to which all of them clung. Patrick Hayes aged into a penny-pinching tyrant who brought nothing but unhappiness to his progeny, driving one son to drink and an early grave and his daughters to the graves of early marriages. Fleeing from reality, Catherine Estelle ("Essie" to her family) turned to her mother who, though she would not always indulge her daughter's fantasies, would never ridicule them as others most certainly did, even playing along with her when the occasion demanded. Together they shared a world of dreams in the galleries of neighborhood theatres.

Like mother, like daughter. Mrs. Patrick Hayes, "Graddy" to her granddaughter Helen, who couldn't quite say "Granny," loved the theatre. However, her interest was simply as a member of the audience. She had no ambition whatsoever to tread the boards herself. With Essie she saw play after play. Whatever money could be saved by buying the cheapest cuts of meat and bruised, rejected vegetables would be spent on theatre seats. Ambitions of a career in the theatre soon burned in Essie's soul. She would certainly have preferred to go without food altogether rather than miss a single play. Hers was a different kind of hunger and she avidly devoured everything that was set before her, longing to be a part of it all. In this there was no ambition particularly to master an art. What she wished to be a part of was the grace and elegance of the ladies and gentlemen onstage and, as she imagined, the society to which they had access offstage. But her menu of theatre did not consist solely of glamorous trifles. On one memorable occasion the star actress was none other than Mme. Sarah Bernhardt. Essie would return home floating on a cloud of wonderment to give her own rendition of everything she had seen to an audience of brothers and sisters. The first time she stood before an audience of strangers was when, in her teens, she was offered a part in *Damon and Pythias* with a local stock company in her home town of Washington, D.C.

But the theatre in those days, or such was the common belief of the envious, harbored only degenerates. There was the example of the renegade Swan before her, and Patrick Hayes would countenance no such thing as his daughter's taking up such a way of life. She fled into her early marriage when she met Francis Van Arnum Brown, the most amenable of the five middle-class Brown boys. He married Essie for love. She married for escape from the intolerable life her father had prescribed for her. But she soon discovered that Francis Brown had his own ideas of married life. She wanted nothing of the domestic bliss he had in mind. As far as she was concerned it was as emotionally restrictive as her home life had been. Scrimping and saving every last penny she could, she managed to enroll as an acting student at the Robert Downey School. Again she was frustrated in her ambitions when she found herself pregnant. But, the baby born and settled with her mother, she joined a touring company, the Liberty Belles, through a connection she made at the Downey School. It was scarcely the world of Bernhardt, but an actress must go where an opening offers. It was, at least, professional theatre, but professional theatre of the least. The Liberty Belles played only in third-rate theatres; no openings into fashionable society here. However, Essie was in her element as the comedienne of the company, finding a secret enjoyment in situations which forced her and her fellow thespians to leave expensive hotels under the cloak of night to avoid paying the bill. It was all part of her rebellion and her delight to be part of the world of rogues and vagabonds her father despised and had forbidden her to join.

However, gradually the truth began to dawn. As Essie herself recalled, "I had a great sense of mimicry and amused my brothers and sisters with a perfect imitation of the star in the afternoon's play. Because of this my mother thought I would be an actress some day and I, flattered by this thought, made up my mind I would be. Years later, I was to find out the difference between an imitation and a God-given gift."

By this time she had discovered a God-given gift in her own daughter and resigned herself to seeing her own dreams brought to reality by Helen. The realization that her role in the world of the theatre would place her not in the ranks of performers but in the company of that other theatrical profession, the stage mother, was something which became clear to her over a period of time. She would see glories heaped upon Helen's slender shoulders, and for a time it would bring her happiness. But as is so often the tragic case when ambition is blighted and longings for a personal fulfillment are finally frustrated, Essie would eventually opt for the oblivion to be sought at the bottom of a glass.

2

HELEN HAYES BROWN, named by her mother for Helen Gould, a leading socialite of the day, already at birth a nascent wish-fulfillment, came into the world on the tenth day of the tenth month of the first year of the twentieth century. She has always felt that having been born with the century she will leave with it.

Her earliest memories are of the constant disappearances and sudden reappearances of her mother. Suddenly Essie would turn up, a giddy effervescence concealing the depression she felt at her tour's end, and whisk her from Graddy's house to their own home. Sometimes her father would be there and sometimes not. He was away on his own kind of tour, for he worked for a wholesale meat and poultry concern and spent much of his time on the road. Life was sometimes full of fun because Essie had a lively gift of humor and there would be plenty to laugh about. At other times Helen would hide from her mother's rages. Tormented by her failure to belong to that world of ease and elegance of which she longed to be a part and the feeling that she was trapped by a dull marriage and a daughter of dependent years from fully pursuing a path to her goal, she would be overcome by black moods of despair and fly into irrational tempers. After one such display Helen yelled, "Don't come near me. You are not my mother. A real mother couldn't be so cruel." She informed Essie she was going to leave, never to return. Essie, her anger tempered by amusement, held open the door for her and wished her well on her journey. Moments later there was a knock on the door. Helen needed five cents for her carfare, as her real mother lived some distance away. Solemnly Essie produced the nickel she needed and again bade her farewell. After about half an hour Essie began to worry at her continued absence and went out to look for her. Helen had not got far. The glimpse of a white ribbon peeping over the top of a bench about a block away relieved any anxiety Essie might have felt. She walked casually by and said, "I'm going to the grocer's. Would you like to come along?" Without a word Helen joined her. When they reached the grocer's Essie pretended she hadn't brought enough money. Helen's fingers relaxed to reveal a tightly clenched nickel in her palm. "Buy whatever you want with my five cents," she said.

In her memoirs Essie suggested that Helen was a lonesome child who chose not to play with children of her own age, finding them too noisy. Perhaps the truth was that Helen, never knowing when her mother might take off again in pursuit of "her rainbow," made the most of the time she was home staying close by her side. When her mother was happy she was in seventh heaven. Then she would become aware that a new kind of vivacious merriment was taking over and Essie would pack her trunk and set out on the road again. With what anguish Helen would look on. How could a small child possibly understand the motives which allowed her mother to desert her with such joy sparkling in her eyes? Years later she would come to appreciate that her mother was having a much-needed last fling, but at the time it can only have seemed that her mother was constantly rejecting her.

However, the place to which she was relinquished was warm and cosy and ever welcoming, filled with familiar and comfortable colors and aromas. Helen adored her grandmother. Indeed she has claimed that Graddy was the last of the generation of real grandmothers, those who made "a special grace of age." Be that as it may, with such an example behind her, when it came her own turn to be a grandmother, how could she fail to be that warm and loving creature herself? Helen had as much need as her mother before her to escape from the reality of her life and Graddy also welcomed her to her world of fantasy. Graddy was tall and held herself properly erect, never in a hurry like her busy, bustling daughter. When she and Helen went out together she would wear a heavy black silk gown which touched the ground and a black bonnet with ribbons tied under the chin. How Helen would love it when she was asked to tie those ribbons and straighten the coral pin which held the white ruching around her throat. Together they would visit the nickelodeon, and upon their return, as Essie had done after her childhood visits to the theatre, Graddy would relive the films they had seen for an excited audience of whoever would care to listen. Some of Helen's happiest moments of childhood were spent in spellbound fascination when she implored Graddy to tell her the tales of a childhood spent in the docklands of Liverpool in England when the sun always shone as it never seems to do nowadays.

Then Essie would be back, stifling her sadness with a deep intake of breath and a merry peal of laughter and Helen would be whisked back to her life of uncertainty. But Graddy was not the only constant in her life. When he was home there was that kind and gentle man who was her father. Placid as his wife was volatile, unadventurous as she was ambitious, he was at his happiest in his garden or in other quiet pursuits. He was comfortably fat and always fun to be with. There were surprising things about him too. When Helen accompanied him to the ball park she found him no shrinking violet. He would holler with the best of them much to his tiny daughter's amazed embarrassment. Had Essie known of it she would have been appalled by what she would have termed "low behavior." As with many a father and daughter, there were good, happy secrets shared only by Francis and Helen. His was a healthy, stabilizing influence on her early life.

Slowly the onstage lights of Essie's life began to change. Her ambitions for a stellar career as an actress began to fade. Yet she still ached to attain the heights of society which could be achieved by prominence in the theatre. One day she took Helen on a visit to an art gallery, ever anxious that she should learn to appreciate the finer things of life. One of the paintings over which they lingered was of a naked lady surrounded by attendants. Helen asked the name of the painting and her mother told her it was "Cleopatra in Her Barge." Some time later Helen, by now four and a half years of age, was found by her mother reclining in her tub, a towel draped around her head, languidly swatting at herself with a rattan fan. "And who do you think *you* are?" asked Essie. "I'm Clee O'Patrick in her bath!" she blithely announced.

Perhaps it was at that moment, or perhaps that was the culmination of many such moments, but as the old light faded, the new lamp which lit the new area in Essie's life was a spotlight with a golden glow, and little Helen Hayes Brown was the one caught in its radiance.

3

AND SO ESSIE embarked on her grand plan. To begin with, her future star needed some rudiments of education. Enrolling her at a public school would mean a vaccination against smallpox. Somehow the fear of smallpox was minimal compared with Essie's fear of the needle which she imagined harbored untold other germs which could maim or mutilate. Now completely cynical about the Catholic faith it might seem uncharacteristic that she enroll Helen at the Holy Cross Academy, but because it was independent of the Board of Education and consequently required no vaccination, she allowed Helen the lesser of the two evils—being brought up in the faith.

This, for two reasons, was to prove a happy twist of fate. Eventually Helen would find solace in the religion her mother might have denied her and would value the roots of it in her early life. Secondly she would discover, as does everyone in whom the spark of creativity through the drama has been kindled, that the church with all its ritual and mysticism is the closest kin to theatre. Like many another small girl Helen was deeply affected by the romantic aura carried with them by the nuns. She longed to be one of them and her devotion to her prayers wore threadbare knees in her stockings. Apart from the implicit theatricality of the cloistered life there were opportunities for the pupils to perform. Thus it was at the tender age of five years that Helen Hayes made her first venture into Shakespeare and her dramatic theatrical debut as "good Master

Peaseblossom," one of Titania's fairies in *A Midsummer Night's Dream*.

Helen's devotions were rich in the innocence of childhood fantasy. Apart from imagining herself robed in the glamorous habit of the nuns she also saw herself as an angel. One day Essie asked her if she would like to learn to play a musical instrument. "Oh yes," she replied, "I would like to play the hark." Essie managed to persuade her that at her minuscule height a harp (for that was what she intended to say), would be rather difficult to carry around, let alone play. However, Essie was convinced that this indicated some musicality in Helen and that she truly wanted to be able to play something. If the truth were known it was simply because Helen visualized herself being angelic on a fluffy pink cloud; but no such thought entered Essie's head. She suggested Frank Brown buy the tiniest available violin so that Helen could exercise her hidden talents.

Though Essie's motives might have been misguided, to some measure Helen was fortunate in having a mother like her. She didn't as such point Helen in the direction she felt she ought to take but rather took her by the hand and led the way. Thus the worlds of art and music, the opera and the drama were opened up to the child who might have passed her entire childhood and youth in complete ignorance that such things existed. The reason Essie took her to the art gallery and the opera house was because she imagined that the fashionable lived their lives that way. She probably seldom saw the paintings she was looking at or heard the music which surrounded her, but she was able to see exactly who was there and how they were dressed. Helen, on the other hand, while having these trivialities pointed out to her, *saw* the paintings and *heard* the music. Essie lived in the world she had created for herself. The truth was something she avoided if it didn't conform to her own image of herself. In her memoirs she insisted that Helen came from "a very middle-class family." As Helen has pointed out, *My darling mother would never admit that her class was wild, scamp, working-class Irish.*

Theatre was still the most accessible entertainment for Essie. She and Helen would wait in line for hours for the doors to be opened to the unreserved seats. When, at last, the doors were flung back, the midget daughter would dart between the legs of those ahead and fling herself across the two best seats until her mother arrived at the back of a column of fuming patrons, shutting her ears to their invective. Such visits were a joy to them both. Through all her early years Helen had known nothing but uncertainty as her mother vanished and reappeared. No wonder the child leaped at sharing something like this when it brought so much pleasure to her mother. Helen's delight at theatre and her subsequent enjoyment of acting seemed to do the trick of keeping her mother at home with her. It is only reasonable to suppose that far beneath the consciousness of either of them there was a kind of implicit mutual emotional blackmail at work.

To fit Helen for the society to which Essie was determined she should become accustomed, Helen had been sent to the Misses Hawke's dancing class that she might learn elegant deportment and social poise, and correct a tendency to turned-in toes. In addition, the Misses Hawke gave an annual May Ball for charity at the Belasco Theatre, where their pupils could be shown off. For Helen's first appearance her Aunt Mamie, Essie's sister, made her a green satin dress with spangled shamrocks in which to execute an Irish reel. The Hawkes's choreography always began with a couple of skipping circles. The music cue came and on Helen whirled. All at once she stopped, pensively tapped her forehead and then walked back into the wings, to Aunt Mamie's great disappointment. She had completely forgotten the rest of her routine, no doubt suddenly aware of the vast cavern of faces looking at her. Her composure restored, she said she would go on and do it again, but the next turn was in progress and she had to be content to wait until the next year. Decked out in the costume of a little Dutch girl complete with lacy cap and wooden clogs, she rendered a song about a little girl left by the Zuyder Zee when her sweetheart had gone to America. Her mother directed her to have tears in her voice as she was singing, to sob at just the right moment and, with her apron, to dab her nose at the end. This received the delighted approbation of the audience and Helen became one of the school's star pupils.

The following year, Essie rehearsed her in an impersonation of the Gibson Bathing Beauty Girl which she had seen Annabelle Whitford perform in the *Ziegfeld Follies*. Aunt Mamie made her a sleeveless black taffeta bathing suit and her hair was piled high on her head. In as blasé a way as possible she sang

Why do they call me the Gibson girl,
The Gibson Girl,
The Gibson Girl.
What is the matter with Mr. Ibsen
Why Dana Gibson?
Just wear a blank expression
And a monumental curl
Walk with a bend in your back
And they'll call you
the Gibson Girl!

This song was somewhat incongruously fitted into a show called *Jack the Giant Killer* under the direction of Miss Minnie Hawke. In order to supplement the scenery for her production, Miss Hawke had borrowed an arbor covered with flowering vines from the company which was presenting *The Girl Behind the Counter* at the same theatre during the evenings. In return the show's star was asked as a courtesy if he would care to attend the afternoon show. Extraordinary as it might seem, Lew Fields, of the famous vaudevillian team Weber and Fields, took his place in the auditorium at three-thirty on January 22, 1909. Here he saw the tiny girl with her even tinier voice performing her Gibson Girl routine. What she lacked in projection she made up in personality and pantomime. At the end of the song, as her mother had directed her, Helen strolled off the stage in the same world-weary manner she had adopted for the song. The audience would not let her reach the wings, demanding of the eight-year-old vamp seven or eight of her calculatedly perfunctory bows. Fields laughed until the tears rolled down his cheeks. Afterward he wrote to the manager of the theatre that if ever the parents of Helen Hayes Brown should consider allowing her to go on the stage he wanted to be the first to see her.

One parent had already considered it. How her heart must have blazed! The first important step had been taken.

4

CERTAINLY, given the encouragement of Fields's letter Essie might have whisked Helen off to New York forthwith. Frank Brown, however, did not share Essie's conviction of the course of Helen's future.

It is only reasonable to suppose that he would have been aware that the mother was attempting to fulfill her own fantasies through the child and might have wondered how much she really cared for Helen's happiness. He knew how liable Essie was to leap before she looked and knew that it was up to him to anchor her adventurous spirit for the good of them all. Such a damper on her creative impulses must have seemed highly frustrating to Essie, but Helen truly benefited from having her mother's recklessness tempered by her father's prudence and having her father's pedestrianism challenged by her mother's ambition. To some extent it was a case of "Essie proposes and Frank disposes," though Essie would ultimately, with her greater steel, get her own way. After the "hark" episode Frank did not immediately rush out and buy the first violin he could find. Sometime later Essie took Helen to hear the violinist Mischa Elman in concert. With the flourish of an "I told you so" Essie pointed out Helen's face to Frank when they returned home. Her eyes shone and her skin glowed with what Essie imagined to be the awakened passion of an artist who had come face-to-face with her destiny. "I told you she had music in her soul!" she pronounced. The ever-practical Frank took one look at Helen and realized the truth. She had contracted measles. There must have been a small gleam of triumph in *his* eyes. Nevertheless, shortly afterward he bought the violin just the same.

It was about this time that the Liberty Belles echoed in their lives. Fred Burger, Essie's former producer, was now running a company at the Columbia Theatre in Washington. But this time no offer came for Essie; it was Helen whom Burger wanted to play the role of Prince Charles Ferdinand in Robert Marshall's *A Royal Family* with the Columbia Players. Helen was thrilled at the opportunity and Frank was won over. Again Essie rehearsed her before she went into rehearsal with the company. Suggesting one piece of business, Essie was surprised when Helen interrupted her saying, "But a boy wouldn't do it that way, Mother." Her own sense of artistry was emerging. Essie had to agree that she was right. Helen made her professional debut in this role on May 24, 1909. It was a busy week for her, because the following day's performance coincided with the Hawkes's annual May Ball, and that evening she appeared in both the play at the Columbia and at the Hawkes's show at Chase's Theatre in which she did an impersonation of the Nell Brinkley Girl.

HELEN HAYES

After Helen's success as the young prince, Burger cast her as the five-year-old Claudia in Edward Peple's *The Prince Chap*, which opened on May 31. This time a small part in the play was taken by Catherine Estelle Hayes Brown, as she herself recalled, "making a fool of herself." She was now under no illusions as to her limitations as an actress. Previously Helen had always insisted that Essie stand in the wings where she could see her while she was performing. Essie asked her if she would do the same for her in case she had any pointers to make on her performance. In her scene, Essie, in the distress of dire poverty implored the hero to take her child and raise her as his own. Having secured the promise, the mother died and was carried to a couch by the Prince Chap as the curtain fell. Helen was ready to make her entrance as Essie left the stage. "You cried beautifully," she told her, then added, "but you shouldn't wear silk stockings if you are so poor." Essie was duly chastened.

One of the most regular members of her audience was Graddy Hayes. She would sit on the second row at every matinee in which Helen appeared. Her entrance onto the stage would always cause Graddy's tears to flow. Blowing her nose and wiping her eyes, she would turn to everyone around about her and say, in a whisper that echoed round the auditorium, "That's my granddaughter." After the performance she would regale the two with all the comments she had heard from other members of the audience. She had a real pride in her granddaughter's achievements and Essie perhaps felt vindicated at having failed to become the actress her mother hoped *she* might be. Frank Brown was also, in his own way, not unimpressed by Helen's progress. A member of the Elks, he wanted to enlist her talents for the annual Elks Benefit; but Essie would have none of it. So far as she was concerned such entertainments were the province of amateurs and Helen Hayes Brown was now a professional actress. The generally mild-mannered man was infuriated by his wife's attitude and there was more than one argument about it. But Essie would not relent.

Helen made a further appearance with the Columbia Players as Patch in Edward Kidder's *A Poor Relation*. Essie was again cast in a small role in a company which boasted Julia Dean and Ruth Chatterton among the players. The play was directed by Frederick A. Thompson. Fred Thompson it was who persuaded Essie that Helen was wasted in Washington and that she should be taken to New

York to be shown to the important producers. Somehow an opposed and reluctant Frank was persuaded to come up with the fifty dollars necessary to make the trip and the two set off for Manhattan and Mrs. Martin's theatrical boardinghouse, recommended by Thompson. After a sleepless night in one of Mrs. Martin's cheapest rooms, Essie, rather unnerved by the big city and not in her element as she had imagined, timidly set out with her exuberant and excited daughter to do the rounds.

Fifty years later Helen would recall, *How incredible it now seems and what passionate courage—the naïve, brisk little woman and the skinny, innocent child, essaying to storm, without equipment, preparation, or knowledge, the established battlements of the commercial theatre. We didn't even know how to get around, but we learned.* Talented though Helen might be she did not present the image expected of a child actress. Her talent came from within, but child talent was sold on what could be created from without. No one seemed the least bit interested in this slight, provincial child with her pensive face. After a few days Essie began to despair. Treated by Thompson and his wife to a farewell dinner at Lüchow's (years later Helen would luxuriate, *What pot roast!*), Essie was berated for not approaching Lew Fields, who had, after all, seen Helen's work, recognized her potential, and taken the trouble to express his enthusiasm only a few months earlier. In the interim, it seems, Essie had lost interest in putting forward Helen, with her newfound dramatic abilities, for the kind of musical comedies with which Fields was associated. However, Thompson was able to persuade her that Fields's association with the Shuberts might open many doors for Helen. Helen herself was very keen to meet Fields; her mother was nervous of attempting to gain an interview. It would seem at this point that she was more deeply affected by the constant rebuffs Helen was receiving. The child had a natural resilience to rejection, learned at her mother's knee, which Essie lacked.

Finally she agreed that they should go to Fields's office. They were told he was in conference when they arrived. Essie, nervous that this might prove the final disillusionment to them both, was all for leaving immediately, but Helen, infused with the confidence Essie had evidently lost, was determined that they wait. Eventually Fields emerged in animated conversation with the celebrated beauty Lotta Faust. Having escorted his visitor to the elevator, he returned to be confronted by a distraught and anxious woman thrusting in his face the photograph of a small girl decked out in a black taffeta bathing suit. "Do you remember this child?" she demanded.

Perhaps when Frank had presented Essie with the necessary fifty dollars, which represented to him one whole week's pay, he imagined it might put an end to all the nonsense about putting Helen on the Broadway stage. As a traveling man he might have suspected that New York might overwhelm Essie and that she would return to Washington duly chastened, and allow the family to achieve a more normal way of life. But it was not to be. The die was cast. In her hand Essie flourished the contract for thirty-five dollars a week ("Almost as much as your father earns!") which she had signed on Helen's behalf for her to appear in Fields's fall production of Victor Herbert's *Old Dutch*. Her perseverance had paid off. Frank must have known from this moment that his wishes in the matter must from then on take second place. Perhaps it was in memory of the Swan of Erin, perhaps in honor of Graddy, but what an incalculable sadness there must have been for Frank Brown in seeing his contribution to his daughter's name dropped when Helen Hayes made her Broadway debut.

5

LEW FIELDS was a great comic and he knew another when he saw one. Wearing his regulation derby and his oversized checked pants, he led the tiny child into her first rehearsal of *Old Dutch*. Essie, unaccountably shy of the dazzling personalities she had longed to meet, hung back several paces. However, she was close enough to see the puzzled expressions on most of the faces of those to whom Fields introduced his protégée. Among the company that day were the show's composer, Victor Herbert, Ada Lewis, John Bunny, Alice Dovey, and a tall, handsome young man who spoke with the accent of a British sophisticate. His name was Vernon Castle.

Essie was slightly apprehensive. She could not for a minute figure out what Helen's reception meant. Only later did she learn that word had traveled ahead of them that Fields was bringing into the show the greatest child comedienne he had ever seen. What the stars of the show saw was a serious-faced little girl who looked too shy to speak, let alone stand before a hard-bitten Broadway audience and reduce them to helpless mirth. Was Fields out of his mind? Where was the precocity and pizzazz of the usual moppet? As the days passed, Helen's professionalism and performance completely vindicated Fields's judgment.

Already Helen was developing a talent which set her apart. Years later she was to claim to Douglas Fairbanks, Jr., that, like Laurence Olivier, she worked from the outside in, that when she had found the way the woman looked, moved, and spoke she could then find the feeling and the motivation. In those early days, in roles which had little richness or depth, she was always serious in her approach. Another child might have been content to develop the outside, making sure she was dressed prettily and could repeat the rehearsed inflections of an imposed comic timing. Helen Hayes approached her performance with a seriousness totally unexpected of an actress of her years. The best comedy is that based on truth, and the true approach is to play the reality of the situation with just the awareness that it is comedy coloring the moment. It is a very subtle balance to achieve. The talent seemed to come naturally to Helen.

For the most part, her life had been spent in the company of adults. She had never had any interest in playing with children of her own age and had never developed the method of communicating with adults which relies on that kind of cloying precocity which most children employ when trying to make an impression. In a very short time she had formed a relationship founded on professional equality with virtually everyone in the company. And as her performance grew, so did the size of her part. Fields added page after page to the slim original.

Victor Herbert himself conducted the orchestra. With his walrus moustache and massive, leonine head, he looked as if he were meant to be a musician. He personally coached me in my one rather odd musical number. The Gerry Society allowed a child to talk on a stage or stay up all night at rehearsals, but no minor was permitted to sing or dance. Since I was a born mimic Lew Fields assigned to me, along with an undersized boy who was twice my age, to stand on one side of the stage and while the prima donna and tenor went into the second chorus of their love song we were to imitate their gestures and mouth the words as if they were coming out of our throats. Thus I would be within the law of the Gerry Society. Victor Herbert taught me the exact rhythm and instructed me so that my pantomime was a humorous comment on the singer's style.

"In this clever tot Mr. Fields has the greatest leading woman of her size," claimed Charles Darnton in *Evening World*. "With a youngster only a head taller than herself she tumbles the house into laughter as she goes through the soulful pantomime of a sentimental song which two lovers are voicing on the other side of the stage. The longing in her dreamy eyes and the yearning in her outstretched arms make her seem more than seven (sic). The kiddie knows a thing or two."

That season in which Helen Hayes made her Broadway debut, billed thirty-first in her role as the Little Mime, was enriched by the work of several celebrated actresses. The New Theatre was opened by Julia Marlowe as the Queen of Egypt in *Antony and Cleopatra*, Laurette Taylor starred in *Mrs. Dakon*, Ethel Barrymore was to be seen in Pinero's *Mid-Channel*, Marie Tempest in Maugham's *Penelope*, and Mme. Sarah Bernhardt would bring her French company to the Globe in *L'Aiglon*. *Old Dutch* would settle into the Herald Square Theatre for eighty-eight performances.

Each evening Essie and Helen would arrive at the theatre well in advance of anyone else. This was because Helen always insisted on applying her own makeup, a long and laborious process practiced with painstaking skill. As each of them arrived other members of the company would find an excuse to pop into the dressing room to enjoy her studious industry with an amused wink at Essie. The stage manager had rigged up a tiny proscenium-arched theatre with which she amused herself during the performances. Although there were about ten other children in the show, she saw little of them. These children were employed only for "atmosphere" and they excluded Helen from their games because she was a principal and therefore from another social stratum. Again she was forced into the company of adults. Her outlet for play was largely the play in which she was performing. There were always games of "catch" to be enjoyed, but these were with Lew Fields's brother Charlie, who was appointed to see the child prodigy and her mother safely to the streetcar after the performance. When the winter snow fell, the huge fat man and the tiny girl would pelt each other with snowballs while Essie followed at a safe distance. Fields himself was plagued by children encouraged by ambitious mothers to find favor with him. Helen, on the other hand, apart from the shyness which prevented her from any overfamiliarity, had been taught to avoid demonstrative behavior. Charmed by her reticence, Fields sought her out. The minute he saw her he would rush forward and swing her up to his chest and give her a huge, warm hug.

Helen was naturally fascinated by all the colorful people in the company. She loved to listen to the silly banter of the actresses; to watch Billie Coupier as she donned her "diamonds and furs" ready to greet the stage-door Johnnies who were always there waiting for her; to nibble the sticks of fruit from her champagne cup and sample the chicken-à-la king she would have served. Champagne and ⌐hicken would remain for many years the symbol of a status Helen longed to achieve. Scarcely a performance would go by that Helen could not be found in the wings watching her favorites, noting a new piece of business even the actor might not have been conscious of himself, always at pains to discuss and advise on anything she saw when, as frequently was the case, she was invited to comment. There was only one member of the company who chose not to befriend her, apart from the caste-conscious children, and that was the fat and jolly comedian of the show. John Bunny, who had come to Broadway from the British music hall, would eventually find fame as the fat man in more than a hundred and fifty silent film shorts, mainly with Flora Finch. Offstage, as is so often the case, he was as morose as he was jolly onstage, as sullen as he was funny. He invariably overate and slept off his dinner between scenes, inevitably needing the assistance of the stage manager to rouse him in time to meet his cue. Sometimes the stage manager would pretend to forget and Helen, who was always around at the time, would "save the show" by reaching out trembling fingers ⊦⊃ wake him.

This was a child who had sufficient professionalism to earn the respect of seasoned artists. Yet she was immature enough to be terrified of the obnoxious Bunny. It may seem extraordinary that at her diminutive height she could be thought of as anything but a vulnerable child. However, she projected a startling maturity which belied her nine years. This odd dilemma was to lead to a conflict between her perceivedly adult mind and her wildly childish emotions and it would bring heartbreak in its wake.

6

VERNON CASTLE is known to recent generations solely as the character impersonated by Fred Astaire in the last of his RKO screen musicals with Ginger Rogers, *The Story of Vernon and Irene Castle*. Astaire proved ideal casting for this charming and elegant man, himself strongly influenced by the debonair Anglo-Saxon manner. The tall, skinny actor was charmed by Helen at first sight and she was charmed in her turn by his gallant good manners toward her. Much of the makeup she used came as gifts from him. He would knock at the door of her dressing room and instead of the usual "Are you decent?" he would inquire of the diminutive miss, "Are you visible?" One day he quipped at her in French he imagined she would not understand and was astonished by a perfectly pronounced reply in the same language, the result of lessons from a visiting French governess who had answered Essie's quest for culture and from whom she had learned unselfconscious speech. Sometimes Castle's "Rosebud" would come offstage to be greeted by his dresser who, with all formal ceremony, would hand her a note from Vernon. These notes from trivial early beginnings grew over a period of time into an elaborate and rather odd loveplay. No doubt Castle's motives were entirely innocent. During the run of a play what is not exactly boredom but rather a sense of "marking time" sets in for actors and gives rise to all kinds of silliness. Castle was enchanted by the replies he would receive to notes written in the guise of a jealous husband who had noticed Helen dallying with Fields or the repulsive Bunny. However, it was somewhat insensitive of him not to realize that this child, who took everything seriously, would take seriously his pretended professions of love. Perhaps the seriousness of her replies, which so delighted him and the other members of the company, appeared to be the clever artifice of the mature imagination they knew she possessed and which she demonstrated in her work. No one seemed to understand that she was emotionally underdeveloped and that she took Castle's protestations of love with a seriousness which was not feigned. Perhaps it was only natural that, denied by circumstances a fully developed relationship with her father, whom she hardly knew and seldom saw, she would seek a father figure in the attractive men she met in the theatre. Helen has said that she somehow aroused a paternal instinct in all the men who developed her career in the early days. Perhaps this was because she exhibited such a need and because Essie seemed so inadequate as a parent. A charming figure such as Castle who was, at the same time, a talented fellow professional must have seemed to fulfill everything Helen felt she needed in her life.

After the close of *Old Dutch* in New York, the company took it on tour, returning to the Broadway Theatre with *The Summer Widowers* on June 4, 1910. Helen was cast as Psyche Finnigan, an ebullient and cocksure little girl. At one point she had to address a line to a maid and, obviously at Vernon's prompting, the line was delivered in French. Beautifully spoken, the line brought down the house. There was also the famous scene in which she was partnered by a tiny actor named Will Archie, who was dressed as a little boy. "Look at this lovely raspberry tart I've been given for going an errand," he would say. "That's not a raspberry tart," Helen would reply, "anyone can see it's strawberry." To prove that it *was* raspberry Archie invited her to take a bite which only proved to Psyche that it was blackberry. By the time she admitted it truly to be raspberry she had eaten the whole tart! Helen was directed after this to brush the crumbs from her hands, but inspiration led her at one performance to wipe her hands on Archie's sleeve thus lending greater piquancy to his line, "You can't never trust a woman . . ."

In her offstage affair it was the man who could not be trusted. One evening during the show Helen asked her beloved if he ever intended to marry. "Not until I marry you," was his unwittingly cruel reply. Helen, of course, imagined they were engaged from that moment. After the close of *The Summer Widowers* there was a short layoff before the tour began. Billie Coupier had decided not to go on the road with the show and was to be replaced. Called early to rehearsal before the commencement of the tour, Helen and her mother waited in a box as the company assembled onstage. Vernon appeared and called, "Where's my girl?" At Helen's reply he continued, "I have a surprise for you" and began to make his way up to the box. The thrill of joy she felt turned to numb disbelief as Vernon introduced her to the dazzling young woman beside him. "Here's someone you're going to adore," he said. "This is Irene Foote. She's taking Billie's place in the show and she's promised to marry me." As though this were not pain enough to break Helen's heart, Castle had arranged for Irene to share a dressing room with her. His reason

was that his fiancée had no experience of theatre and needed someone to show her the ropes. Not only had Helen to endure a rival and
share a dressing room with her but Vernon had chosen to marry an
amateur!

It was a bitter time for the nine-year-old. She threw herself into
her performance with an even greater gusto in order to show Vernon
how more greatly talented she was than the lady with the ugly
name for whom he had jilted her. Perhaps Castle realized too late
the impression his pretend love affair had made on Helen. Both he
and Irene went out of their way to be kind to her, but Helen treated
Irene with cold contempt. That is, until later in the tour when Castle
had asked Fields to audition him and Irene in a special dance routine
the pair had worked up together. For some odd reason Fields placed
nothing but obstacles in the couple's way, and when he finally
agreed to see them he made them do their act on a bare stage lit only
by a single light bulb. Perhaps Fields thought Castle, who had built
up a fair reputation as a solo performer, was wasting his time in
creating this new act, and was trying to convince him that he was
making a mistake. Helen, realizing how important it was for the two
of them to succeed, stood in the wings willing them *both* to win
through as they did their beautiful routine around the shadowed
stage. "He'll be sorry," she heard Irene mutter as Fields made his
protest by walking out before they had finished. From that moment
she had a new friend in Helen, who delightedly watched over the
subsequent years as Vernon and Irene Castle danced to international
celebrity. Vernon met an untimely death. During World War I he
flew photo-reconnaissance over enemy lines for the British Flying
Corps and was killed in a U.S. airbase crash in 1918. Helen would
treasure a photograph which Irene sent her of the two of them dancing. "To Helen," it was inscribed, "with much love from both."

7

UPON THEIR ARRIVAL in New York Essie had tried to enroll Helen at
all the best convent schools, finally placing her at a Dominican convent on East Sixty-eighth Street, the only one prepared to take a
"stage child." The reluctance of the others to take her on was perhaps understandable, as theatre tours would constantly interrupt
her education. Apart from these there were other calls upon her

time. Fred Thompson, the director from the Columbia Players who had been instrumental in persuading Essie to bring Helen to New York in the first place had moved into film production, and was now directing with the Vitagraph Company, which operated in a studio in the Brooklyn area. To Essie's horror he suggested that Helen should appear in one of his films. No theatre actor worth his salt would condescend to work in this new medium. In England perhaps Sir Herbert Beerbohm Tree, Marie Tempest, and their ilk would appear before the cameras, but in New York it was considered degrading. However, Essie owed a debt of gratitude to Thompson and she agreed with trepidation to allow Helen to make her first, and hopefully her last, film.

The venture was kept secret from everyone at the theatre. To her alarm, as Essie nervously shepherded Helen onto the studio lot, whom should she encounter but John Bunny. Imagining him to be merely a curious visitor she implored him not to let anyone know he had seen them there. "If you don't tell on me," replied Bunny, obviously as disconcerted as she at being found out, "I won't tell on you."

Helen Hayes's debut as a moving-picture actress was in support of a collie named Jean and actor Maurice Costello unwisely consenting to appear both with a child and a dog. The scenario involved Helen's falling into a ravine to be rescued by her father, who was brought to the scene by the faithful Jean carrying in her mouth the child's calico doll. Essie attempted to disguise her moppet with curled hair and a strangely made-up mouth but the subterfuge was in vain. One evening some weeks later someone at the theatre suggested Helen might enjoy the film showing across the street. When the two arrived at the nickelodeon there was the name of their film *Jean and the Calico Doll.* Surreptitiously they crept into the darkened cinema. Despite the attempts to alter her appearance, there was Helen, larger than life, up on the screen. *(Unmistakably me, but me looking very odd indeed . . .)* They were both shamefaced as they arrived at the theatre that evening, and indeed Essie was severely criticized by several members of the company for so recklessly jeopardizing Helen's career. Vernon Castle tried to soften the humiliation by suggesting that Helen was a far better actress than the dog! Notwithstanding the censure this venture had aroused, Essie was not discouraged from organizing various further clandestine forays into the world of the Vitagraph two-reeler.

Visits to the theatre continued. A printed card bearing the legend Miss Helen Hayes, management Lew Fields would often earn free seats at matinees. Savings on food in the best traditions of Graddy Hayes's housekeeping would buy tickets which could not otherwise be secured. At the old Metropolitan Opera House, able to afford only seats whose view of the stage was severely limited by the pillars that held up the roof, Essie and Helen *heard* but seldom *saw* the likes of Jeritza and Caruso.

During the run of *The Summer Widowers* Helen bade farewell to much of the happier aspects of her early life. Graddy had often thrilled her with robust and highly colored tales of the supernatural, particularly with one along the lines of Poe's "The Premature Burial" in which a bride at the altar had fallen apparently dead but had revived as her groom was about to bury her. "People," she had informed her wide-eyed granddaughter, "are being buried alive all the time." Now, at ten years of age, confronted by death for the first time, Helen had to look upon the dead body of her dear Graddy laid out in her coffin. "Sit up, Graddy. Please sit up *now!*" the bewildered little girl cried. The old lady's friends sat about appalled by the behavior of the "little actress." Actress Helen certainly was, but there was nothing feigned in her deep love for her grandmother. Gone with her was a whole sensation of past associations. However, the heritage that had passed from Graddy through Essie to Helen would be developed into a gift of which Graddy might justly have been proud. Like mother, like daughter, like granddaughter too.

For her part, Essie had altered. It seemed there was no place for her in that glittering world she had longed to make her own. It became painfully obvious that she had nothing more to look forward to than being seen as a barely-to-be-tolerated adjunct to Helen Hayes. Lew Fields would completely ignore her as he rushed to take Helen in his arms. She would become known as "Stage Mother Brown." Though Helen has retained great respect for her mother's counsel, for the guidance she received from no one else, she has found her mother guilty of overprotection. Naturally it must have also occurred to others who sought only the best for Helen in her early years.

Though Mother never read any of the textbooks, she could boil down

Stanislavski's teachings into one sentence. She would pick up ideas and inspiration from watching actors and directors rehearse, storing everything away against the time they might help me. She once heard a vaudevillian refuse to do a second chorus because he believed an actor should "always leave them wanting more." Mother taught me restraint and taught me to simplify and never let me fall into the trap of mannerisms. It was she who taught me to dig deep to find the truth and then project it. This was and is hard work.

After several appearances with the Columbia Players, one of which saw Helen in the title role in *Little Lord Fauntleroy,* and two further Fields musical comedies, she found herself at the awkward age of twelve washed up as an actress, and the two of them returned home to Frank Brown. During the next two years there were only infrequent appearances with the Columbia Players to remind Helen of her vocation and to remind Essie that she had ever escaped from the unremitting boredom of her domestic life. Her excesses of energy now had to be channeled once more into domestic tasks and all the petty social events to which a woman in her position had access. What probably exacerbated her frustration was that now she had been disillusioned of the dreams which previously had supported her. The black moods returned, and with no hope in sight she succumbed to the disease that plagued so many of the Hayes family before her, the attempted escape from pain through the blurring influence of alcohol.

As is ever the way when drink takes a hold on a member of the family it was the others who suffered the most. For them there was no escape as Essie selfishly pursued oblivion. Helen, who had hoped her mother's crazed torment was a thing of the past, found little compassion for her now and began to despise her for the weakness which impelled her to live her life through her daughter. As for Frank, he would only repeat with Chekhovian stoicism, "In a hundred years no one will know the difference."

One day when Helen returned from the convent school she found Frank in tears. The anger that had been seething inside her came to a head. She found Essie, roughly grabbed hold of her and shook her as hard as she could. "Go inside and say you're sorry, do you hear?" she spat at her. "Say you're sorry to my father." Both stood simply staring at one another for the longest time. Helen refused to give way, to disallow her eyes their rage. Eventually Essie's stare wavered; she turned and went inside to do as she was bidden.

There had been a fundamental change in their relationship. Though Essie had been shaken into submission by her little girl in a display of uncharacteristic spirit, it was a young woman who had held her in her gaze. Helen Hayes Brown had, at thirteen years of age, been forced into adulthood.

TWO

DEAR LITTLE GREAT ACTRESS

1913 – 1918

1

THOUGH HELEN WAS GROWING UP emotionally she still looked three or four years younger than her true age. Inevitably producers only saw her as a child. There had been great success with the Columbia Players' production of *Little Lord Fauntleroy*. Under the harsh tirade of the grandfather in Act One she was sufficiently convincing to elicit from a small boy in the audience the cry of "Why does he have to be so mean to someone as nice as you?" After the laughter from the audience had died down, there was a pause after which Helen could not resist a *sotto voce* aside to the boy. "Just wait a little longer," she advised. "He becomes very nice in the next act." The charm of the situation excused the breach of theatrical etiquette. All who saw her remarked on the child's naturalness in performance. One of her fellow players in that play had been Jessie Glendenning. Many noted the resemblance between the two, a similar coloring and the same tone of ash blond hair. Apart from this Miss Glendenning recalled at the best possible moment "the light shining within the child."

Essie was entertaining a group of friends at bridge when a tele-

gram arrived. She was instructed to bring Helen to the Empire Theatre Building in New York to read for a part in a play with John
Drew. Drew! Fifty years later, were a young actress summoned to
audition for a part in a play with Laurence Olivier, the prospect
could not have seemed more dazzling. *Mother saw a light at the end of
the tunnel and she regained her balance immediately. We were entering the
world of John Drew and Charles Frohman and the Empire Theatre. With
the air of a queen mother delivering the princess royal to her rightful
domain, Mother stepped aboard the Congressional Limited bound for New
York.*

After a night without a wink of sleep they arrived promptly at
eleven o'clock at the office of Alfred Hayman at the Empire Building. Accustomed to the courtesy of the Fields company, where all
the men would doff their hats the moment Helen appeared or suffer
a stern reminder from Essie, they were both startled by his gruff
"What do you want?" and nervously crossed the seemingly tennis-
court-sized space between the door and his desk. He told them a
child was needed for the first act who could plausibly "grow up"
into the person of Jessie Glendenning for the later acts. "Can you
act?" he barked at Helen. Her answer was simple. "Yes," she said. A
kind of terror had set in and Essie was fortunately constrained from
going into her stage-mother routine. Impressed by the simplicity of
the child who made an unaffected little curtsy as he drew her toward him, Hayman had no hesitation in sending her down to the
stage where Drew was rehearsing. "Go down and tell him you're his
new leading lady," he said, to which she curtsied once more and
with Essie left the room. In a moment Hayman was on the telephone
to the stage. He told Drew, "This child has been sent from heaven."

Helen has described Drew as being "larger than life—a Victorian
overstatement like the Albert Memorial." As she made her demure
curtsy to the seemingly gigantic and consummately elegant figure,
she was saved from terror only by the twinkle in his eyes. After she
had read her part for him he introduced her to his producer-partner
Charles Frohman, who was as small and round as Drew was tall and
aquiline. She was in the midst of her reading for Frohman when a
luminously attractive young woman rushed up to him with a
"Hello, C.F. How are you, darling?" Frohman asked her if she would
wait a moment while the young lady finished her reading, at which
the visitor apologized for the interruption. As Essie walked her back

to the hotel Helen was in a thrill of excitement. "Imagine," she marveled over and over again, "Mr. Charles Frohman called me 'young lady' and Miss *Billie Burke* apologized to me for interrupting!"

Although it was a milestone in the career of Helen Hayes, *The Prodigal Husband,* which opened at the Empire on September 17, 1914, held little significance in the history of the theatre. Drew had, in fact, resisted Frohman's earlier attempts to interest him in the play but had unwisely changed his mind. His role as a playboy who, having adopted the daughter of his concierge, falls in love with her later in life and is reformed from his hedonistic ways by the purity of her love, was not the kind of role with which audiences popularly associated him. He was not a great actor in the sense of possessing the power and depth of interpretation with which to breathe fire into everything he played. His was the school of acting which with impeccable stage manners and dress sense could, in a suitable vehicle, sweep an audience along in a mood of gentle gaiety. Patrons emerged from an evening with Drew thoroughly entertained but seldom intellectually stimulated.

The first-night audience for a Drew play was of the most sparkling. Essie was overwhelmed at the sight of so many luxurious furs and diamond-circled throats and wrists and was sick to the stomach with nerves. Helen was saved from butterflies herself in dealing with Essie who babbled so uncontrollably she had to be removed from the dressing room to spare the other occupants. She was only conscious of the thoughts of "little Simone" as she made her way onstage for the scene in which she invited Drew to join her on the floor with her dolls and toys. As still happens in the opera and ballet, curtain calls, in those days, would often be taken between the acts. Such was the reception after two or three calls together that Drew insisted Helen take the remainder alone. In dizzy excitement Essie lost count of the number of calls she took. Helen asked if she could stay to watch the rest of the play, but Drew insisted to Essie that she take "the childey" home to bed. "Tomorrow she will be famous," he added.

The play was not a great success. However, Drew was right and Helen won great praise from the critics. Wisely Essie always kept her press from Helen, simply informing her whether or not she had provoked a favorable reaction. Criticized for this by Drew, who felt that the praise would encourage Helen, Essie retorted that she had progressed this far without that kind of encouragement. The new father figure in Helen's life shared Fields's disapproval of Essie. Each evening he would send his valet to Helen's dressing room with an invitation for his "Childey" to join him in the star dressing room. The invitation never extended to Essie. Try as she might have done to rationalize such rejection, Essie could never appreciate the effect she had on others and was inevitably hurt. Some days before the play had opened the two of them happened to see Frohman coming down the street toward them. Essie was all for speaking to him, but Helen, already learning to be embarrassed by her mother, pulled her to one side. However Frohman saw them, greeted them, and congratulated Helen on the way her performance was growing.

After eight weeks Frohman decided to take the play off and send it on the road. Jessie Glendenning chose not to tour and Frohman decided to use the Swedish actress Martha Hedman, who was already under contract to him and also in a play about to close. Alf Hayman suggested that Essie might take Helen to see Miss Hedman in her play one evening after Helen had finished her scene in *The Prodigal Husband* so that she might learn the Swedish accent. After the performance, when Helen said her usual goodnights to Drew as on every night, he said, "Goodnight, Childey. You are going straight home to bed now aren't you?" "Oh no," she said on this occasion, in great excitment, "we are going to the theatre!" Having demanded the reason from Essie he telephoned Hayman in front of them all and said, "The childey is not going to imitate anyone. Let Martha imitate the childey. This is final and I'm sending her home to bed where she belongs." The disappointed childey had to make do with a later matinee performance instead. "Never let anyone change your voice or your style of acting," Drew advised Helen.

It was a happy tour, for Drew was a genial star who ensured that audiences away from New York saw actors of as high a standard as had been seen in the Broadway production. By keeping these standards up and drawing full houses the morale of the company remained high.

In Pittsburgh we were eating dinner at the William Penn Hotel. Mr. Drew was also in the dining room with his niece, Miss Ethel Barrymore. He invited us to meet her. Awed, Mother could not move. I propelled myself over, somehow, and got introduced. Miss Barrymore seemed to have more than glamour, more than beauty, and a voice that shook you to your shoetops. She was everything a great star should be. I gaped. Then I went upstairs to scrutinize myself in the bedroom mirror. I saw a frail, pasty-faced girl, little, always little. I tried stretching my neck and succeeded only in practically dislocating it. I did not dare hope to approach her, ever. I lacked the lung power, the beauty, the impressive height, the presence. Not many decades hence Broadway would boast a brace of theatres each honoring the names of two living actresses. To Helen's incredulity the one bore her name, the other the name of Ethel Barrymore.

Only one incident marred the tour. Frohman had gone to Europe on a business trip and cabled that he was about to return. Drew wired back that he should stay where he was because of the increasing danger of German aggression. However Frohman insisted that he embark on the next ship. "If the Huns sink you," Drew cabled back angrily, "I'll never forgive you." His words would haunt him the rest of his life, for Frohman set sail on the *Lusitania.* His death was reported on the front pages of every newspaper. That evening Drew played his role as usual but, as Helen noted, he was nowhere on the stage. Next day she sobbed to a reporter from the New York *Tribune,* "Charles Frohman was a dear man. He was so kind. He taught me so much. I'll never forget him." An extraordinary rumor grew up that Helen was really the love child of Frohman and his mistress, Maude Adams. No one really knows where this rumor began but it would persist for many years to come. On one occasion Essie overheard someone inform her companion of this relationship as they stood in front of the theatre in which Helen was appearing. Essie was about to contradict the story when she caught sight of herself in the glass in which Helen's portrait was displayed. Deciding she looked a mess and far from the way a star's mother should, she decided to leave them in ignorance! Years later Charlie MacArthur would tell Ben Hecht, "Now I know why Helen is so out of the ordinary. Having been created by two sets of parents, she belongs in Ripley's *Believe It or Not!*"

2

THE TOUR OF *The Prodigal Husband* over, Helen returned to school. Shortly before the Sacred Heart Convent closed for the summer recess, she took part in a debate on the practicability of the Panama

Canal. Her argument won her a handsomely bound volume of Tennyson. The Mother Superior begged Essie to allow Helen to attend college to study law, so astonishing had been her ratiocination and the extent of her knowledge. However when Essie broached the subject with Helen she was told, "Mother, I don't know any more about the Panama Canal than you do." She had learned her entire speech from books on the subject and then given a performance! Ever the actress.

The Columbia Players were by this time disbanded but another group had been organized in Washington by a Mr. Poli. Helen was asked to join the new company. Naturally she was delighted to be considered but made it clear that she now felt it was time to move out of the child-playing category and into older ingenue roles. However, though she was by now fifteen, it was difficult to see her as anything but a child. Nevertheless after being cast as a maid in one play she was given the opportunity of the more challenging role of a sophisticate in the next. The text demanded that she smoke a cigarette. She rehearsed lighting one and smoking it at home to the utter disgust of her father. In the comparative secrecy of her bedroom she would practice manipulating a cigarette, afraid to light it in case Frank became aware of the smoke. Consequently when she came to rehearse the scene, although she was able to handle the cigarette with nonchalant ease, she could not stop coughing. Directed to cross her legs she did her best, but as neither foot touched the floor when she was sitting down it proved rather difficult to effect. The director took the part away from her after three days, promising her a better ingenue role as soon as he found one. When no such opportunity arose she eventually agreed to play a ten-year-old in a piece called *The Dummy*. It was not the kind of work she wanted to do, but by this time almost thirteen months had elapsed since the end of the Drew tour and she was aching to get her feet back on the boards.

It seemed that Broadway had forgotten her when a call came which proved that Alf Hayman hadn't. There was the chance of a part for her in a play with that splendid actor William Gillette. Though she wore a pair of high-heeled shoes to the audition to give her an advantage should it prove an ingenue role, Hayman was disappointed to discover that Helen had grown so negligibly in the intervening months. Even a hasty pinning-up of hair in Ethel Barrymore's dressing room between keeping Essie from snooping around Miss Barrymore's closets did not do the trick. "I hear you're a great actress," Gillette told Helen, "but I'm afraid I'm too tall to play opposite you." To soften her disappointment he told her he would have a great part for her one day. Hayman was furious when the reaction was reported to him. "Helen Hayes could play Lady Macbeth right now if she wanted to," he protested. It was frustrating for the actress. She could work to develop her talent but there was nothing she could do to increase her height.

Two and a half years passed between the end of the Drew tour and Helen's next major opportunity, though there were several productions for Poli. It was in one of these that she was seen by a scout for agent Chamberlain Brown, who arranged for her to read for George C. Tyler. Although it was for a child part it was the first leading role to come Helen's way and she felt her usual confidence as she stepped out of the iron cage of the elevator to Tyler's office over the Amsterdam Theatre. A column of smoke from behind his ancient rolltop desk was wafted aside as the squat figure of Tyler waved them into his tiny room. Framed photographs of legendary actors beamed down at them. Tyler's jovial face lit up and he exclaimed, "So here's my Western Pollyanna." Patricia Collinge had portrayed Eleanor Porter's "glad girl" on Broadway and was to tour the role in the East while Helen took the play to the Far West and the Deep South. Perhaps Helen reflected with concern that at twenty-four the diminutive Miss Collinge was still playing child roles. Helen was twenty-three days short of her seventeenth birthday when she first set foot on stage as Pollyanna Whittier at the Lyceum Theatre in Rochester, New York. Tyler told her he foresaw a great future for his new star. Over the next few years he would spare no effort in fulfilling his own prophecy.

3

HER NEWFOUND STATUS as the star of her company had a salutary psychological effect on Helen. For the first time in her career the press rarely referred to her as a child. Even though she was playing a little girl, she was perceived to be the leading lady of the company. Consequently she was greatly encouraged and her self-esteem was strengthened. Though there was comedy in the play there was true pathos as well. Helen had never had any trouble making an audience laugh but she had had little opportunity to truly move them.

On one occasion she was bewildered by the audience reaction. The auditorium of the little Montana theatre was packed with the toughest looking cowhands. There were the strangest sounds from them during the play. Some of the "gladness" in the character was pretty hard to take for some audiences and when, with both legs broken, she was carried on crying hysterically, "I'm glad I'm alive, I'm glad I'm alive!" the strange sounds increased. She was convinced that it was this audience's way of booing her. When the curtain fell and the auditorium lamps were brightened, she ventured to take a peep at them. Virtually every last flinty character was blowing his nose in an attempt to conceal the tears which had accompanied each stifled sob.

Helen was grateful for Patricia Collinge's advice, "You must learn to play the part without crying." Audiences often fail to cry themselves when they are confronted by an actress in tears. It is a rare talent that can draw emotion through identification with the actress as well as the character and it would be several years before Helen had developed the technical poise to achieve this herself. "Her impersonation," claimed one critic at the time, "was superior to that of Patricia Collinge . . . in that it was more restrained and better poised and seemed more sincere. She made the 'Glad Game' seem more appealing and more of her own speciality than did Miss Collinge, who allowed one to get the impression that it was the playwright's device that she was operating."

I have always been of a happy nature, but not until I began to play the glad girl did I realize how helpful the happy-natured may be by exerting their influence on others. Most people who are happy have an unconscious effect on those about them. The greatest joy in life is in making others happy, in doing so intentionally. Although this philosophy, expressed a few years later, was sincerely meant and would remain basic to Helen's character for the rest of her life, it was only one side of her feelings about playing Pollyanna. To other interviewers she said she would scream if she ever heard that word "glad" again. She would gleefully tell the story of a little girl brought backstage to see her. "Now, tell Miss Hayes how much you loved her in the play," cooed the mother. "Shan't neither," snapped the little girl, scowling terribly, "I hate her, she's so blame good she never swiped a thing."

During the tour she began to experience the burden of stardom. One thing a star must make is a commitment to health. No audience likes to arrive at the theatre to be told that the leading player will not appear. It becomes the solemn duty of the artiste never to permit this disappointment and many have to be dragged to a sickbed kicking and screaming. In addition to professional integrity there is the ever present ego and lack of security. One morning in a small Midwestern town Helen woke without a voice. The doctor diagnosed laryngitis and forbade her to appear that night. However Helen overruled him and her mother. Her understudy was very pretty. One day she had seen her rehearse and thought she played the part well. Helen was terrified that she would make a success and replace her in Mr. Tyler's affections. The doctor stood by with Essie in the wings to spray Helen's throat at each exit, both convinced there would be no voice glad or otherwise. But onstage Pollyanna's voice rang out, though Helen's voice gave out in the wings. The actress's innate professionalism asserted itself.

The tour eventually arrived in Los Angeles and at the first opportunity Helen and Essie motored over to Hollywood. Since the days of her Vitagraph two-reelers Helen had ventured before the cameras only once and then in a leading role just before the commencement of the *Pollyanna* tour. She was cast as Peggy in *The Weavers of Life*. The role was that of a young saleswoman who agrees to her fiancé's wealthy father's demands that she live two months as a member of the family before undertaking marriage. She soon sees the shallowness of them all and when she departs to marry a young man "of her own station" she leaves them with a new realization of their own selfishness. It was a good preparation for Pollyanna but as a film it was a turkey. *It was probably the worst film ever made—so bad that it was actually shelved in days when everything was shown! However, three years later, when I had my name in lights on Broadway for the first time, the producers dug the old film out and played it at a theatre across the street.*

By the end of 1917, nearly every major company or producer had a studio somewhere in the environs of Los Angeles. But Los Angeles was far from being the metropolis it would eventually become. Much of Beverly Hills was wild bush country. The studios themselves were just great long barns. Through an introduction to William S. Hart, the screen's favorite cowboy, Helen was tested by the Fox Studios on their lot on Western Avenue. How this test turned out she never knew. Though she supplied her itinerary for the following few weeks, the studio never contacted her. It is perhaps surprising that when Hollywood was in its ingenue era with stars such as Mary Pickford and Lillian Gish filling cinemas all over the world, a promising ingenue such as Helen was overlooked. Helen never went to look for work in pictures again. Eventually Hollywood would come in search of her.

4

THE COMPANY OF *Pollyanna* was playing in Biloxi, Mississippi, when a letter from Frank Brown caught up with his wife and daughter. It enclosed a letter from Alf Hayman. "Dear little Great Actress," the letter began, "Where are you?" The gist of the following was to inform her that William Gillette wanted her for a role opposite him in a play by Sir James Barrie, fulfilling his earlier promise. "How long are you to be under Mr. Tyler's management?" the letter continued. "Let me hear from you at once!!!"

Because of her commitment to Tyler, Helen sent the letter off to him. It was somewhat dampening to her excitement when she received his reply. "I expect you to remain with *me* for the next fifteen years. You are going to be well taken care of next season with an increase in salary, and you are going to have a play all your own (I hope before the year is out). Don't ask me what it is going to be, for I don't know myself—but it *is* going to be, if I live." The disappointment at not being able to play with Gillette was worsened by the prospect of a play to herself, if Tyler lived. She didn't know whether she was ready to shoulder the responsibility of a starring role on Broadway. As if to temper her disappointment, the promised increase of salary was brought forward and her next paypacket contained not her agreed one hundred dollars but the incentive of an additional fifty. Further evidence of the value Tyler placed upon her was the bonus of a drawing room for her and Essie on the occasions when an all-night train jump was necessary. Mother and daughter were in a thrill of delight at such luxury and burst into hysterical laughter as the porter closed the door of their own drawing room on them the first time.

Having lived to the end of the *Pollyanna* tour, Tyler presented Helen with the script of a Booth Tarkington play charting the escapades of the scamp *Penrod*. To Helen's relief there wasn't the starring role she had been promised. Rather she was cast as Margaret Schofield, the "love interest," which pleased her greatly. At last she was to be seen as a young woman and not a little girl. She was, after all, almost eighteen.

Margaret was not the usual wet young thing with which most young actresses try their wings, but a spirited individual of the kind which would a few years later come to be known as a flapper, a character-type with which Helen would, for better or worse, and mostly the latter, become associated. However the focus of the play on paper was taken from her by the title role of Penrod. The focus of the play onstage was taken from Penrod by a bright imp who played the black boy Verman. No one knew where Tyler had found this young rascal, who was never there when he was wanted and came out with a strange kind of mumbo jumbo instead of his written lines when he was supposed to speak. In any other circumstance the actor would have been fired, but the boy was so endearing and he was so absolutely right for the character that he was allowed to get away with it. Naturally he was warned and admonished, and his chaperone in the shape of his doting grandmother threatened, "I'll bash yo' head against the wall if yo' don't behave yo'self," but she and the rest of the production staff were reduced to helpless mirth by each successive misdemeanor. Opening night of the tryout in Atlantic City went surprisingly smoothly. Second nights tend to be a bit flat, nervous energy being replaced by complacency, but not with this company. In one scene Verman was supposed to crawl through a hedge on all fours. On this particular night rather than crawl through head first as he had been directed he crawled out backward. Turning, he revealed that during the time he had been hiding in the hedge he had coated his face in thick white flour! Everyone broke up. The audience collapsed in a riot of laughter and the actors broke up too as the little woolly head grinned from ear to ear and bounced up and down. Andrew Lawlor, who played Penrod, moaned as helplessly he tried to control his mirth.

The play was not the success it might have been when it opened at the Globe Theatre on September 2, 1918. It was too large a house for such an intimate little play and a transfer to the tiny Punch and Judy didn't save it. Helen won a healthy amount of praise. She also learned to control onstage giggling so that she didn't break up as easily as the rest of the cast at the continued antics of the company bright spark. This talent was to save her from many such situations in the future, for she had a ready humor which saw the funny side of things quickly. The play closed prematurely as a result of the terrible influenza epidemic of that year.

Before the closure Helen had received a special-delivery letter from Alf Hayman suggesting she come and see him. The role of the girl, coincidentally also called Margaret, in the Barrie play was still open. It seemed that he could think of no one but Helen for the role. She and Tyler had no contract, indeed Tyler always worked without contracts. "My word is sufficient," he would say. Essie was all for Helen telling him that she wanted to do the part whether he wanted her to or not. However, Helen already felt a great loyalty toward him. Her word, she insisted, was sufficient too. Apart from this, Tyler was not the kind of man you argued with, and timid little Helen did not have the courage to stand up to him. In as quiet a way as possible she told him she would dearly love to play Margaret. He read the script and immediately recognized the potential advantages for his rising star and contacted Hayman. He told him Helen would be available to play the part at a salary of three hundred dollars a week. Helen was aghast. No one would pay that amount of money. It was twice what she had earned on *Penrod*. She would surely lose the part. However, Hayman agreed, a great boost to her self-confidence. "I'd have waited until doomsday if necessary," Hayman told her. "I think Sir James Barrie had you in mind when he wrote it."

5

THE ROLE OF MARGARET, the dream daughter in Barrie's *Dear Brutus*, could certainly have been written for Helen. Her natural freshness can still be seen in her early sound films. Though these were made some twelve years later, her qualities of uncloying charm and originality are matched by no other actress of her day. These qualities, coupled with the vulnerability of youth made an indelible impression on all those who saw her in *Dear Brutus*. Even the hardboiled and cynical Dorothy Parker was moved to tears. "The ladies' cup goes to Helen Hayes," she wrote in *Vanity Fair*, "who does an exquisite piece of acting. Hers is one of those roles that could be overdone without a struggle, yet she never once skips over into the kittenish, never once grows too exuberantly sweet—and when you think how easily she could have ruined the whole thing, her work seems little short of marvellous. I could sit down right now and fill reams of paper with a single-spaced list of the names of actresses who could have completely spoiled the part . . . *Dear Brutus* made me weep—and I can't possibly enjoy a play more than that."

It's such a relief not to have to be glad anymore. Even if she is only a might-have-been-daughter, Margaret is a regular girl who goes without her rubbers and rips the hem out of her skirts climbing around woods. I shall never be glad again! She was certainly ecstatic, if not glad, at her success in the role. However, for a time, it seemed as though she might have to withdraw from the part.

To begin with, the rest of the cast, if not English by birth, were British by ancestry and came naturally to Barrie's dialogue both in accent and intonation. Though Helen was emotionally and temperamentally perfect for Margaret, she was let down by the Washington drawl in her accent. Iden Paine, the director, was constantly checking her speech and correcting her pronunciation. But accents cannot be learned in bits and pieces. The actor can never successfully project a different nationality merely by getting his words to sound right, but must learn the ethnic attitude. Speech patterns and rhythms come from personality rather than from syntax. William Gillette came up with the answer, suggesting that Helen read and learn Shakespeare's sonnets. For days she compared Essie to a summer's day and admitted no impediment to the marriage of true minds and eventually the false notes began to disappear and she moved toward a more natural expression of Margaret's thoughts.

However, it seems that Iden Paine was so preoccupied with the externals of Helen's performance that he failed to give her the full benefit of his direction and she felt she was getting nowhere with the part. Again Gillette came to the rescue. After rehearsals he would secretly usher Helen and Essie to Alf Hayman's office at the top of the Empire Theatre and work with her on her scene. She appeared, in fact, in only one scene, and with Gillette, so it was easy for them to work alone. Under his inspiration she felt her understanding of the role growing. However it would have been most impolitic for her to go into Paine's rehearsals and introduce new business and new interpretations that he had done nothing to produce. So Helen had to continue to learn the performance Paine expected and the performance Gillette had inspired side by side. Occasionally some of the new work slipped out in the regular rehearsals and she was admonished by Paine. How was she going to do the role the right way, she inquired of Gillette, if every time she introduced the new business Paine told her to do it the way he wanted. Gillette suggested that she continue to play the role the way Paine inter.ded it in rehearsal and save their own work for the opening night.

One day—it was November 11, 1918—there was an extraordinary commotion outside the theatre. Everyone rushed out of rehearsal to see what was going on. The Armistice had been signed! Helen had celebrated her seventeenth birthday during the *Pollyanna* tour in Fort Keogh, Montana. She had been treated to a birthday cake by a company of soldiers about to embark for France. "You make it all worthwhile," the sergeant had told her. "This is what we are going over there for—so wonderful children like you can continue to be." An extraordinary sadness had overwhelmed her as she bade them farewell. Consequently, now it was all over, amid the throngs of cheering happy people, the tears welled up and she cried like a child. Grabbing hold of Essie's hand she pushed her way through the crowd. At Forty-second Street the going got harder, as everyone was standing still. Then they heard a beautiful voice. It was Caruso, in his sixth-floor window in the Knickerbocker Hotel, giving vent to his passionate joy with George M. Cohan's "Over There."

When the song ended, a hush descended on the crowd; the moment was too solemn for applause. I elbowed my way toward Fifth Avenue, wanting to be among the first to reach the altar at St. Patrick's. But when I got there it was already jammed to the doors and I could only kneel on the steps outside along with thousands of others.

The tryout for *Dear Brutus* opened in Atlantic City. On this longed-for but dreaded first night there was a telegram from Tyler: NOW FOR YOUR BIG OPPORTUNITY. HERE INDEED STARTS IN EARNEST THE REAL BEGINNING OF A CAREER THE GREAT AND TRIUMPHANT SUCCESS OF WHICH THERE IS NOT THE SHADOW OF A DOUBT. I WOULD BE WILLING TO STAKE MY SALVATION ON IT. Encouragement, certainly, but Helen was lacking in self-confidence, not knowing how much of which performance to give. And indeed, caught in this dilemma, she failed to fulfill the character. With Essie she walked up and down the boardwalks trying to put her finger on what had gone wrong. It was nice of Gillette to be waiting for her back at the hotel to give her the news that Hayman was "prouder than ever of his great little leading lady" but it failed to reassure her that she was ever going to be able to do his faith justice. Naturally next day there was a whole set of "don'ts" for her in Paine's notes session. He had seen barely a vestige of the performance he had rehearsed and saw nothing of value in its place. However someone must have had a word with him, Hayman or Gillette or both, and he began to leave her alone to develop her performance along her own lines, simply from time to time correcting her position on the stage. Consequently she began to feel her way into the part through that week and the subsequent week in Washington where her proud father was able to see how she had grown as an actress. *Father always seemed to be waving goodbye at the railroad station, getting smaller and smaller in my life, his brave smile blurring more and more as we chugged away.*

Opening night at the Empire Theatre was the night before Christmas Eve. In her dressing room high up in the theatre Helen received the first of many such notes from Gillette via his oriental man-servant. "Dream of My Life," it began, "It is important that I come up at once. It will be impossible for me to play the second act unless you let me come—for my mind would be distracted and harassed. It must be *at rest*. Make it so by saying to the Japanese one that I may come for a moment. I am relying on you for this." It was signed, "Your Hallucination Daddy." The reason for his urgent visit was to tell Helen that she would be magnificent.

As the third-act curtain fell we stood up to a formidable crashing roar, a Niagara Falls of sound. I had never before heard anything like it. Mr. Gillette refused to take a curtain alone. He held me by the hand. We took twenty calls! I suffered tortures. I felt that the calls were for him and that the audience would assume that I was staying on, hogging the scene. No matter how I tried to free myself from Mr. Gillette's grip, I could not wrench loose. Then I figured he was so nervous he was unable to let go of my hand. After the final curtain he released me. Looking down from his great height he said, "You didn't think I was going to take those curtain calls alone did you? Those curtains were for you."

Next morning Heywood Broun wrote in the New York *Herald Tribune*, "Miss Helen Hayes is as eager as a Christmas morning and as dazzling as a Christmas night. It may be that nobody will ever call her the great Miss Hayes, but if not she will have to grow out of an amazing equipment of natural charm and technical skill. She was on the top of the tree last night."

He was wrong in one respect. The day would come, and it was not too far distant, when many would speak of the great Miss Hayes. She would scarcely ever leave the top of the tree. But what a great Christmas present! To have Broadway at her feet.

THREE

A STAR ON
HER FOREHEAD
1919 – 1928

1

"LITTLE MISS HELEN HAYES . . . an extraordinarily gifted and skil-
ful actress . . . is (of child actors) the one most generally suspected
of genius . . . Her 'technique' is so remarkable that older actresses
sit open-mouthed and wonder where and how she learned to do it
. . . All this adulation, all these flattering bids for her art, all the
reckless predictions of future triumphs, have come to this girl at
eighteen. Most people think the world lies at her feet, that only her
height—she looks to be no more than five feet—can bar her from all
the great roles of the theatre.

"Some there are, however, who wonder if her triumph has not
come too soon, if she can carry into her twenties the charm and the
power of her teens. At eighteen she is a marvel—no less. What will
she be at twenty five? The Maude Adams of her day, or an obscure
and happily married woman, unknown to fame? In 1926 shall we all
be besieging the box-office of some Central Park West theatre buying seats for Miss Hayes in *The Ray of Violet,* or will one of us be
saying, 'That little Hayes girl who used to play in those Tarkington

comedies—she was a wonder wasn't she? I wonder what ever became of her?' "

Thus wrote that bombastic, egocentric Alexander Woollcott in *Everybody's Magazine* some nine months after the opening of *Dear Brutus*. Woollcott was not new to her work. Then a critic of barely seven
months, he had reviewed *The Prodigal Husband*. However, it is some
indication of Helen's newfound success that in this long article
about what kind of future could be anticipated for the child actor of
the day that he, of all people, would go out on a limb to single out
Helen for his laurel crown.

Helen was trying to stop reading about herself. William Gillette
had warned her never to read her own reviews, as it so often could
affect one's work. Occasionally a critic will single out some particular line-reading, an inflection, an emphasis, a clever piece of business, of which the actor himself might be unconscious. Having had
that moment raised in his consciousness it could never be recreated
as naturally again. For better or worse, however, Helen had read all
her reviews for *Dear Brutus* and perhaps, for once, it was wise. At
such a point she needed that charm of self-confidence to carry her
forward. There was scarcely a critic mean in praise of her and it was
good to know that she had arrived. Such was her new status that Alf
Hayman chose to call Essie and Helen into his office to warn them
about her being seen too much in public places. Stars, he argued,
should never be seen eating in public restaurants, as a public who
could see their favorites free would eventually not bother to pay to
see them. Fortunately Essie argued with him that Helen was scarcely
a star as yet and had little enough diversion in her life as it was. The
day of the aloof and mysterious otherworldly, illusionary figure of
the actress was becoming a thing of the past. And besides Essie
wanted to be seen around with her!

The elderly Gillette became very fond of Helen. He was impressed that she always spent the first act in the wings, ready and
made-up, to soak up the atmosphere of the play before she went on.
As time progressed she would quit the side of the stage just before
the curtain came down and dash back to her dressing room. The
reason for this was that many of the cast would gather in her dressing room to smoke, as the fireman never bothered to check there,
and Helen loved to hear their chatter and the horror stories of theatre life which actors love to swap. One night Gillette told her he

had missed her in the wings and she confessed the reason. To her dismay Gillette said he would like to join them. She imagined this would throw a damper on the proceedings. However, when the note came addressed "Dear Vanishing Dream," she could do nothing but tell the Japanese messenger that Mr. Gillette would be most welcome. And so he was on many subsequent evenings when he added his own colorful stories to the fascinated ensemble, each time prefacing his visit by a note to his "Hallucination dear" or "Dear Wraith of my Heart" and signed sometimes "Your Shadow Dad" or "Snooze Dad." Consequently he was bitterly disappointed when Helen told him she was leaving the cast. It had always been understood that Helen was just on loan to Hayman and that Mr. Tyler should be able to reclaim her services when he had found another play for her. Helen, too, was deeply upset when he decided she should join a repertory venture he was undertaking in Washington. Essie again pointed out that there was no contract between them and if she wished to remain in *Dear Brutus* she should tell Mr. Tyler just that. However, Helen insisted that Mr. Tyler was looking toward her future good and she must honor the commitment she felt she had made to him. Rather than have Gillette hurt by hearing of her departure formally through Mr. Hayman, she found a quiet moment to tell him herself. On the last night Gillette angrily confronted Essie, demanding to know what on earth Tyler had done for Helen. Essie found herself thrown on the defensive, defending Tyler when really she would have been happier for Helen to stay. He had been kind to her was her suggestion. "In what way have *we* failed to be kind to her?" demanded Gillette. Clutching at a straw, Essie cited the raise in salary and the provision of the drawing room on train journeys. "You should be very happy," he cried in exasperation, "to have sold Helen for a couple of Pullman tickets!"

It was with heavy hearts that the two of them left the theatre that night. Their hearts were even heavier when less than a month later the Washington season had collapsed, a financial disaster when audiences failed to appear. Helen appeared in only one undistinguished piece, *On the Hiring Line,* as a flapper. The only noteworthy circumstance of the production was that it afforded her a first meeting with a warmly attractive young actor named Alfred Lunt. He had rather more to occupy his mind for, in the second play, in which

Helen had no part, and which, in fact, closed the season, Lunt met for the first time an actress named Lynn Fontanne.

Helen was not to be long on the hiring line as Tyler decided to mount a similar venture in Atlantic City where he presented Booth Tarkington's *Clarence* and another play called *The Golden Age*. Both plays were a great success and Helen and Essie set off to Lake Placid for a well-deserved rest when the season ended. The Lake Placid days marked the incursion of troubled waters into Helen's life. A letter arrived from Tyler telling her to stay out of New York. He did not want her involved in the labor disputes aroused by the proposed affiliation between Actors Equity and the American Federation of Labor. Helen knew nothing at all about Actors Equity and was happy to concede to his request. Subsequently he ordered her to return to New York immediately to join the Fidelity League. Fidelity was to the status quo of the producers' autonomy, and the membership of the League among which Helen now was numbered were sarcastically referred to as the Fidos. *Mr. Tyler's flat insistence that I not join the union began to alienate me from all of my friends. I felt like a traitor. My chums weren't angry but they were all disappointed that I wouldn't stand up to Mr. Tyler. But I hadn't been encouraged to stand up to anyone in my life.* It was to be three years before she would pluck up the courage finally to speak to Tyler on the subject. In that time her friends made every effort to make her understand their point of view. Margalo Gilmore, Humphrey Bogart, and Helen Menken each had their say. Helen even resisted the arguments of her idol Ethel Barrymore, who made a special point of trying to woo Helen to the actors' cause. She was caught in a dilemma. For the time being her loyalty, which had been won by fear, lay with the man who had promised to shape her destiny and not with her peers. Perhaps this is understandable. Nevertheless, as she was to recall fifty years later, *I found it impossible to live with myself.*

2

THUS IT WAS that when George Tyler assembled the cast for the Broadway premiere of that summer's tryout play, Booth Tarkington's *Clarence*, Helen was the only member of the cast not to be a member of Equity, now affiliated to the American Federation of Labor and having won all their demands. No one seemed to bear too much of a grudge against Helen. Everyone seemed happy to put the summer of unrest behind them and get to work on this delightful play. It concerned a slow-going philosophical doughboy, played by Alfred Lunt, who attracts the attention of an industrial millionaire by a supposed ability to drive an army mule without swearing. He imagines that such self-control might help sort out the problems of his family, his unhappy second wife, his son who has been expelled from school, and his daughter, who at sixteen has informed the rest of them that she is to marry a divorced man. Within three weeks and four acts the stepmother is happy, the son accepted again by his school, the governess betrothed to the divorcé, and the broken-hearted daughter ready to go to boarding school.

It was a much funnier play than a bare synopsis can suggest, relying on the comedy of character. His role as Clarence would make Lunt a star, especially the scene in which he had to play a saxophone. There was one high note he often failed to achieve. He joked that it was the spirit of Adelina Patti coming back for yet another farewell performance. The pronouncement "Patti's in again" would reduce the entire cast to hysterics throughout the rehearsal period. Helen's role was that of Cora, the daughter in whom "youth had awakened with a bang." Her best scene came when she was forbidden to see her divorcé ever again and she burst into hysterical weeping, asserting her despair in a passionate flow of language, interrupted occasionally by her governess correcting her grammar. In the midst of this her father came in and instead of offering her his solicitude gave her a withering look and snorted, "Go upstairs and wash your face." As one critic noted, "The memory of Cora's baffled gaze, the memory of her dead, tragic accent as she repeats, incredulous, the words: 'Wash my face?' will linger with us for months to come." The play, which opened at the Hudson Theatre on September 20, 1919, would run for a total of three hundred performances, though Helen, at Tyler's insistence, would leave the cast after three months. Three months was time enough for her to fall in love. *I was nineteen, with no social life. The theatre seemed world enough for me. It was normal that I should turn my youthful imaginative thoughts toward our handsome, bachelor leading man. In retrospect I realize I was in love with Alfred Lunt. Laurette Taylor was starring across the street. With her, in an insignificant part, was a young English girl who, as soon as she had finished her bit, always rushed over to our theatre to wait for Alfred. Seldom have I seen a more awkward, skinny creature. For some reason she always wore a hat with dangling bedraggled plumes. I squirmed with jealousy and, as I had with Irene Foote, resented her fiercely. To get to his dressing room she always had to walk past me and Mary Boland and one or two of the others as we waited to go onstage. Years later, Lynn Fontanne—for it was she—told me, "The hardest thing I ever did in my whole life was to walk past the gauntlet of your eyes. They bored through my back. My feet felt bigger and my plumes grew limper."*

Helen possessed few social graces at this time. Indeed she was incredibly shy for someone who spent her life in such worldly company. Whenever she met people for the first time she would become tongue-tied. Her experience of life was so limited that she could think of nothing that might make a conversation. Rather oddly she decided to make a hobby of Japanese prints. She felt that as the subject was so unusual she would rarely find anyone who knew more about it than she and that it was sufficiently feminine not to scare off the men. She spent hour upon hour in the New York Public Library looking at books on her chosen subject. However there was one great drawback to her conversational aid, the problem of the Japanese names. She tried and tried but could not get them to stick in her head and eventually gave up the whole project as a bad job. In an effort to help her with strangers, Essie suggested that she try to find something nice to say about each one that she met. It all sounds a bit Pollyanna-like, but it was a remarkable talent she developed over the years, finding just the right compliment or warming comment which put herself and her new acquaintance immediately at ease.

Helen's personal reviews for Cora were a delight. Woollcott likened her to Marie Tempest and claimed she had the world at her feet. Each evening as she emerged from the stage door a young sailor tossed rose petals at her feet. This continued until he was seized by the Shore Patrol for being AWOL.

Perhaps it was in the nature of the play, but as the run went on her performance became mechanical, lacking her usual spontaneity. The "Wash my face?" line was the show-stopping moment until suddenly at one performance it met utter and absolute silence. Each of the other actors onstage imagined they had done something to spoil it, but on each of several subsequent nights the laugh failed to come. One night Mary Boland took her to one side and said, "Once when I was with Mr. Drew, dear, I was made very conscious of just how funny a certain reading of mine was. That, dear, is sheer death. I beg you, forget how the audience laughed before. Forget how funny it all is. Play it as seriously as you and Cora feel, and the laugh will come back, I promise you, because you'll be spontaneous again. Just stop *trying* to be funny, dear. It worked for me!" Helen asked Essie to watch the performance from her usual vantage point and tell her where she was going wrong. Essie reported that she was, indeed, overworking and laboring what had been the brightest moments on opening night, so she set about trying to eliminate the stolidity from her performance. Suddenly one night she found the key and the laughter spilled forth again. However, Helen had finally realized that though her mother's teaching and guidance had been of the greatest value to the child actress, if she were going to grow she needed professional training. Essie was horrified at the idea imagining she might lose her natural freshness and reminded her of the warnings given her by Drew. For the time being she did not pursue the subject further, but the seed of the idea began to germinate in her mind.

Again Helen was sad to leave the cast of a play in which she had had such happy times, not least of her reasons being parting from Lunt. However, Tyler argued that she must not be content to stand still. Edward Childs Carpenter had seen her in *Dear Brutus* and decided that here at last was the actress to portray the title role in an adaptation he had planned of Mary Roberts Rinehart's subdeb *Bab* diaries. It was again light comedy and the role was that of a girl who invents a lover in order to convince her family she is grown-up. Helen was longing to grow up as an actress and told Tyler that though she would be delighted to play Bab she wanted him to find her something meatier. During the out-of-town tryout of *Bab* she told a reporter: *I am to realize my greatest ambition—to play tragedy right here in Boston . . . I am only nineteen and so far they have kept me in foolish roles. The comedienne always longs to shine as Camille or Lady Macbeth. I can't quite see myself as Camille and I don't think I shall ever be a second Ethel Barrymore. However, we are rehearsing a tremendous thing by Eugene O'Neill which is just as tragic as I could hope for. Then comes the real test of what I am worth. Afternoons, except matinee days, I shall give special performances in a tragic role that will simply half kill me to play. And in the evening I shall go on in an almost farcical role. I hope I shall be equal to the test.* Eugene O'Neill noted, "Tyler is thinking of putting on one single matinee of *The Straw* to see if she can play the part. He claims she is going to become *the* great emotional actress of the future." As it transpired, the director decided that Helen was not ready for the role and the project was abandoned. Tyler eventually presented the play with Margalo Gilmore in the part. Twenty years later Helen would play it on the radio and receive from O'Neill his congratulations. "I have always had a sentimental spot for this play," he wrote.

Essie was relieved to see Helen taking an interest in the opposite sex, worried that she might have chosen to be wedded to her career. Helen had taken to using the lunch allowance her mother made her to buy a gardenia from the florist and pin it to her dress, hoping that other members of the cast would imagine she had a suitor who sent her flowers. Here was life imitating art. And life pursued art in Boston, where many of the young men from Harvard imagined Helen to be truly Bab and courted her favor. She was the belle of the ball and enjoyed every delicious minute of it. *I was in seventh heaven. As Bab, I was having my first burst of personal popularity, and I impatiently awaited the confidence that should have gone along with it. For the first time, boys were competing for my attention. Babism had taken over Harvard. In every subject the boys were cutting classes in order to attend repeated matinees. They were failing test after test in order to see her. It was divine.* One of her suitors was bizarrely Mary Roberts Rinehart's son Alan, who felt himself madly in love with her. They made an extraordinary couple, since he was extremely tall and skinny and when they were dancing on a crowded dance floor, recalled Helen, he appeared to be dancing alone! He saw the play twenty-five times and asked her to run away with him to Peru. Another less fanciful suitor informed his Beacon Hill dowager of an aunt that he intended to marry Helen. Essie and Helen were duly summoned to tea. It was the scene from half-a-dozen plays and movies where the aristocratic lady with infinite charm wished to make it firmly but politely known that there was no possibility that she would permit an alliance between her darling nephew and an actress. All the niceties of a gracious hostess serving tea only served as a prelude to "Mrs. Brown. Let us come to the reason for this meeting. What do you think of this romance between my nephew and your daughter?" But Essie had her own dialogue for the scene which had not been rehearsed by her hostess. "My dear madam," Essie began, "the sooner my daughter forgets about your nephew and the sooner we can leave Boston the better." The elegant face blanched above her tea-cup. "My daughter is an artist," continued Essie quietly. "She has a future in the theatre. I *cannot* have it threatened by a meaningless little romance. And now I am afraid we must thank you and leave. Helen needs her rest before her performance." With which mother and daughter departed.

The play did not open to success on Broadway. Woollcott praised Helen's comedy, but Heywood Broun felt there were moments when she played for the easy laugh. Other critics were even less kind. Helen knew she had not been at her best, and she knew why. Contractually Edward Childs Carpenter's name could not be billed without Mary Roberts Rinehart's name in tandem, and considering that the title of the play consisted of but three letters the names of the authors above the title outside the theatre would have looked preposterous. Tyler decided the lights should read HELEN HAYES in BAB. Essie was furious with him, believing Helen had not yet arrived at the point in her career where she was sufficiently a star to support an entire Broadway play. This was an extraordinary woman. Having fought long and hard to bring her daughter to prominence, she nevertheless had the good sense to attempt to delay a moment of which she had dreamed for twenty years. In her first and only confrontation with Tyler, she pointed out that Helen's name would have to compete with John Barrymore in *Richard III*, Ruth Chatterton in *Mary Rose*, George Arliss in *Poldekin*, and John Drew in *Catbird*, among others. But Tyler would not back down and terror set in as Helen stepped onto the stage. Her need for training seemed even more apparent.

However, she and Essie had shared with mixed feelings that poignant and joyful moment when they had first arrived outside the Park Theatre. Standing on the island in the middle of Columbus Circle they stared up at the legend on the five-story-high sign. Tears welled up in Essie's eyes, pride overwhelming her anger. Several days later a sign appeared, HELEN HAYES in THE WEAVERS OF LIFE, outside a nearby cinema. She was a star indeed. But the star of a brace of flops.

3

MOTHER AND DAUGHTER were now living at the Great Northern Hotel on Fifty-seventh Street. Near neighbors were another mother and daughter, the latter being Ruth Chatterton, whom they had known since the days of the Columbia Players. One evening they were invited by Ruth to an after-theatre party at Henry Miller's apartment. Helen sensed the minute she arrived that most of the guests agreed with the critics about *Bab*. She decided to confide her anxiety to Miss Chatterton, asking her exactly what was wrong with her performance. "Okay Helen," Ruth began, almost as though she had hoped to be asked. "I've never thought for a moment that you didn't have talent. That's obvious. But"—indicating not one quarter of an inch of space between her thumb and forefinger— "you don't have *that* much technique." Helen asked, "How do I get it?" A quick discussion followed between Miss Chatterton and Ina Claire whom she had seen nodding in agreement. In no time at all Miss Claire was on the telephone to Frances Robinson-Duff, the eminent drama teacher, and the next afternoon Helen began a course of correction of the various aspects of her technique. It was a wonderful, stimulating time. The concentration on the use of her diaphragm to control her breath, the control of her body to simplify expression, and so on taught her to take a good look at her overall talents as an actress. She found she liked very little of what she saw. *By the time I was twenty-one I had learned to overact frightfully and to use all the cute tricks that had stood me in good stead—you know, jumping about, the never-sit-on-a-chair, always-jump-on-it-and-kneel bit, or sit on tables if there's one handy, all the little things which in that period were supposed to be cute-little-girl things. I had just had one role after another that suited the small capacities that I had developed—that little thing that I brought originally, that fresh sense of make-believe that children have—and they were using it over and over again. I was charming, that's what I was, charming. Eventually I learned that the actor's life is just one long search for the ability to be absolutely truthful.*

The final curtain fell on *Bab* at the Park after only eighty-eight performances, but a successful tour followed. Tyler seemed to have sensed Helen's quest for self-improvement and suggested, nay, *ordered* her to go on a vacation to Europe. He booked first-class tickets on the SS *Olympic* and ordered a suite at the Crillon in Paris. He did all the booking but Helen was expected to pay. After *Dear Brutus* her pay had reverted to one hundred fifty dollars per week; it was just about enough for her and Essie to live comfortably in New York, but there was little saved. When Essie questioned the extravagance, Tyler retorted that now Helen was a star she must be prepared to live like one. The trip would leave their cupboard bare, which might have been acceptable had it proved the glorious adventure it should have done. When the *Olympic* docked at Cherbourg, Helen and Essie were met by Tyler in the huge white Mercedes in which he had motored from his own vacation in Egypt. A tour through the French countryside could have been delightful had Tyler not insisted that they tear along the quiet lanes at breakneck speed. Paris could have been thrilling had she not been whisked from place to place and banished to bed, more often than not to cry herself to sleep, just at the hour when the young Parisians were stepping out to enjoy themselves. After two weeks of this Tyler left them in the charge of his general director who was to see them to England the next day. With Tyler gone, Helen announced that she wanted to spend another week in Paris. Thus she was able to wander where she pleased and stand and stare, to visit the Latin Quarter and the Folies Bergère, blushing at the comedian's jokes which Essie, next to her, could not understand. Perhaps she lived to rue this extra week, for when they arrived in London she found that Tyler had arranged meetings for her with many important people and her late arrival meant she had stood up the likes of George Bernard Shaw and Sir James Barrie. To a great extent she was relieved as she knew she would have been desperately tongue-tied in their presence. Shaw she would meet at a later date, but in years to come she would regret that her personal experience of Barrie, the man who created two of her favorite roles, was limited to a long-distance view of him taking an afternoon walk. However, in London she was to discover what would remain her favorite of all cities. She discovered it in her own way in an easy perambulation around its streets and alleys. The young actor who would be her co-star in her next play showed her his London from the top of red double-decker buses. Though he was of Hungarian origin, her guide was to become the image of the quintessential Englishman. His name was Leslie Howard. With his wife and child he traveled back to America with Helen and Essie on board the *Adriatic*.

After *Penrod* and *Clarence* this was to be her third Booth Tarkington play and he had written *The Wren* especially for her. *In* The Wren *I play a very bossy young person who can't help managing and mothering all the people round her; she's always settling everything. I'm not that way a bit in real life. I can't settle anything. I'm helpless when it comes to doing anything but act. When I was in* Bab *Mother had to go away for three days. I nearly died. The first day I missed my train! Everything went wrong the entire time she was away.* Franklin Pierce Adams coined a famous brickbat when he observed that Helen in this play "suffered from fallen archness." Woollcott was, on the other hand, charmed by Helen's playing though he was at pains to point out that when she and another actress made their entrance after tramping the wild countryside the shoes of both were spotless. "Of course," he commented, "both ladies may have walked on their hands." He considered the play lightweight and so it proved with audiences. Helen hated playing in it. Although she claimed to be nothing like the character, Tarkington had intended it as a portrait of her, and as though to emphasize it as a special gift, the play had opened on her twenty-first birthday, October 10, 1921. To Helen's relief it ran only for twenty-four performances. However, by the time it closed she was already busy in rehearsal for *Golden Days* which, under the title of *The Golden Age*, had been the second great success of the Atlantic City season.

One of the company was a handsome young man who was the son of a foremost musical comedy comedian, Alexander Clark. Alexander Clark, Jr., would be a frequent fellow player and a friend for the rest of their lives. "Helen was about the nicest young woman I ever knew," Alec recalled, "I don't think I've ever met a nicer. She was pretty, not beautiful, but very pretty, with the widest-set eyes. A natural way with which she comported herself. Her sense of humor was superb. When later she came across the likes of George Kaufman and Marc Connelly and Moss Hart, all the big writer comedians, she more than held her own. However, she always thought of herself as the little simple girl. She played those kind of parts and that brushed off on a lot of people. She was certainly not simple— she had a marvelous sense of humor and would laugh and laugh at any good joke. But when she met a big critic like Woollcott she'd always have the feeling that she was only a little girl, still a young ingenue, not in the Ethel Barrymore class. She had utter naturalness as an actress, lacking the qualities that made other people seem phony." The company was largely made up of young people, and Helen, who now enjoyed the society of people of her own age, was relaxed and happy. But the play was not a success. "It is a pity," considered James Whittaker, "that you and I and Helen Hayes cannot get to the third act without going through the two that precede it." However, he added, "Since Maude Adams left them to their barren, unsentimental selves, stockbrokers, policemen, and hardened burglars have been secretly pining for another girl to make them cry. I think Helen Hayes is their girl." Forty performances of the play were followed by a short tour. The last night occasioned several pranks from the fun-loving young cast. Helen and Brownie, as the younger players had chosen to call Essie, spread the sandwiches for the party scene with cold cream. Alec Clark put alum in the punch bowl and waited with glee for the mouths of his fellow actors to pucker up!

A boy that I knew came to see me in Golden Days *and told me that it surely did not demand that I look such a fright in the first act. "I was ashamed of you," he said, "I had told my friends that you were pretty." I explained carefully that I had to look plain in the first act so that the transformation in the second act would work. "Well," he answered, real sulky, "if I had anything to say about it, I shouldn't have it." "But you haven't," I cheerfully replied. But what would happen if I had a husband who talked like that? He would make me change it or bother the life out of me. Oh, lots of husbands have spoiled actresses' careers, so I'm never going to have any.* The interviewer hearing this asked, "Any career?" "No," cut in Brownie, "any *husband.*"

4

FEARS THAT TWO FLOPS might mean a barren season for them with all their savings gone on the European flight of folly were allayed when Brownie and Helen were informed by Tyler that he had commissioned George Kaufman and Marc Connelly to write a play for her before *Golden Days* had opened. Mr. Tyler announced that the two writers would be coming to their new house on East Nineteenth Street. Helen moved their sparse furniture around the huge, forty-foot living room so that they would not look quite as impoverished as, in fact, they were. Before Kaufman started the reading he asked

Helen, "Of course, you play the piano." There was no piano in the room. "Of course," replied Helen with a sweet smile and a tilt of the head. "You sing an old spiritual and accompany yourself on the piano, you see," he added. Then he began to read. Helen's eyes met Brownie's. She had never played the piano in her life. Brownie hoped the play was going to be a stinker that they could easily turn down. But as the story unfolded of the young man who learns an after-dinner speech from a book of sample speeches only to have his rival recite the same speech immediately before him, to be saved by his wife, who gets to her feet and stumbles through an impromptu speech on his behalf, each of them knew that as soon as the writers had gone they would have to go out and buy a piano and hire a teacher's time. That is exactly what they did. That very afternoon they walked out of Wurlitzer's Music Store the owners of a seven-hundred-fifty-dollar piano, owing seven hundred dollars. Six weeks later Helen could play and sing the spiritual.

During the tryout week in Rochester, Kaufman and Connelly constantly wrote and rewrote scenes. By Thursday they left for New York with the instruction "Change nothing." Saturday morning a batch of telegrams greeted them. "PLAYED ELSIE LAST NIGHT WITH A SCANDINAVIAN ACCENT. VAST IMPROVEMENT. AUDIENCE QUITE WILD. HELEN HAYES" "CHANGED LAST HALF OF FIRST ACT, MAKING THE AUTO HORN EFFECT MUCH EARLIER THAN YOU SAID. IT WAS A RIOT. SECOND SCENE OF SECOND ACT CHANGED FROM A BANQUET TO A PICNIC IN FIREMAN'S GROVE. A SCREAM LAST NIGHT. ALL GLAD YOU LEFT. SUCCESS. OTTO KRUGER." "PLAYED SCENE WITH HELEN HAYES IN THE THIRD ACT STANDING ON MY HANDS. JUST WHAT WAS NEEDED. GEORGE HOWELL." Percy Helton, who had been begging daily to have a certain line about a fire exit incorporated into his part cabled. "SLIPPED THE FIRE-EXIT LINE IN TONIGHT AND KNOCKED EM DEAD. RECEIVED ALL SORTS OF OFFERS FOR MY NEXT PLAY. HOPE YOU ARE HAVING A GOOD TIME WE ARE." Norma Mitchell, solving a problem line, wired, "BLACKED UP AND SANG MY EXIT LINE. IT WAS A RIOT. THREE SCENE CALLS."

The good spirits of the cast were conveyed to the audience on the opening night of *To the Ladies* at the Liberty Theatre on February 20, 1922. It was a delightful and witty play generally considered to be Helen's best opportunity since *Dear Brutus*. Having survived three flops in a row, Helen relaxed into her longest run since *The Summer Widowers*. Mother and daughter breathed a sigh of relief. They would be able to pay for the piano.

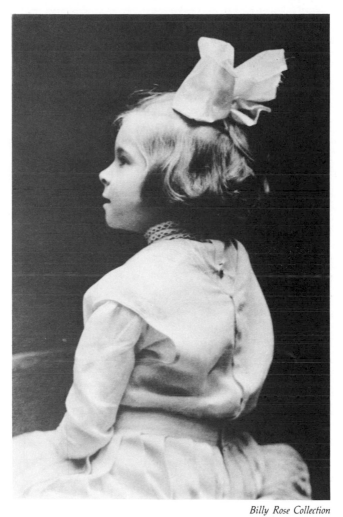

Once upon a time . . .

At nine years of age she made her Broadway debut in *Old Dutch* with Bobbie Fuehrer.

Sarony/Billy Rose Collection

As a child she was frequently cast as a boy.

Billy Rose Collection

Her dramatic debut on Broadway was in *The Prodigal Husband.* With Jessie Glendenning who played the same character grown up.

Billy Rose Collection

Her first great role was as Margaret, the dream girl, in Barrie's *Dear Brutus.*

As the Egyptian queen in
Caesar and Cleopatra,
clearly yearning for
biological suitability. With
Lionel Atwill as Caesar.
Billy Rose Collection

Percy Hammond first
called her First Actress in
1927 when she played in
Coquette. Here with Elliott
Cabot and Charles Waldron.
Vandamm/Billy Rose Collection

There could be no lovelier act of God than Mary MacArthur.

Her Academy Award winning role in *The Sin of Madelon Claudet. MGM-UA*

She failed to be carried away by Clark Gable, with her here in *White Sister. MGM-UA*

Gary Cooper was a different matter! The Legion of Decency didn't want America to see this scene from *A Farewell to Arms,* her finest film. *Paramount*

The First Lady with her First Gentleman.

A charming moment from the film of *What Every Woman Knows,* with Brian Aherne.　　*MGM-UA*

Broadway's shortest leading actress brilliantly portrayed history's tallest queen. As *Mary of Scotland.*
Vandamm/Billy Rose Collection

When eventually *To the Ladies* went out on tour, Helen was interviewed by the Chicago journalist Ashton Stevens. During the early part of their conversation she gave her usual guarded impressions of her life and work. At some point, however, Brownie stepped out on an errand and Helen relaxed. *I know I am hopelessly moral. The great actresses tell us it was their hectic lives that made them great artistes. And I haven't the first talent for being hectic. I guess I've got no temperament. I was reading Emma Calve's book the other night. Her lover had written that all was over. And she got in a gondola and went up and down the streets of Venice all night singing at the top of her voice to relieve her agony. I don't think I could do that. One of the shames of my life is that I've nothing to be ashamed of. I don't know whether it is good policy of me to expose my blameless life. I hate the things I have to play. I get so weary of being sweet . . . and dear . . . and pure. I'd like to have just one chance to be brilliant. And in this sophisticated day a woman doesn't seem to be brilliant on the stage unless she's been wicked. I want to be wicked—on the stage of course. Not that I wouldn't want to be wicked off the stage if I really wanted to. But I have no inclination to be a bad woman in my private life. There's something terribly wanting in me.* Brownie's reactions on reading this piece are not recorded.

When the tour ended Mr. Tyler told Helen there was no new play for her and ordered her to Europe again in pursuit of culture. This time he organized a trip to Florence via Paris, where he would meet her with transport and motor her through the Swiss and Italian Alps, taking in Rome and Mont Blanc, each to flash by her in bewildering geography as on the previous trip. Helen and Brownie insisted on a smaller ship for the crossing and a cheaper cabin. Eventually Mr. Tyler left them to their devices on condition that they arrive in London by a certain time to confer with writer Israel Zangwill about a play he was writing for Helen. They arrived at the appointed time. Zangwill produced a pile of manuscript. "I didn't know you had completed the play," said Helen in some surprise. "I haven't," he replied. "What you see before you is simply the perfect first act." Immediately he began imperfectly to act out the act before them. Two hours later they were still waiting for the curtain to fall. As they departed, Zangwill informed Helen that she must cable Mr. Tyler and tell him she thought the play magnificent. "I can't say I like it until it's finished," protested Helen as demurely as she was able. "Tch, tch," remonstrated Mr. Zangwill, "I am a great writer,

Miss Hayes, and you may be sure it will be a great play when it is finished." Lying through her teeth, Helen promised to send the cable.

As a character with the appalling name of Appolonia in a play called *Loney Lee* Helen opened and closed a tryout tour in three weeks. Almost three months elapsed before Mr. Tyler presented her with the script of a play called *We Moderns.* This, in Woollcott's words, "slightly stale and sophisticated" comedy was the perfect play now completed by Israel Zangwill. When it opened at the Gaiety on March 11, 1924, audiences found it perfectly awful. Zangwill's masterpiece played a total of twenty-two performances.

Helen began to wonder if Tyler in fact had her best interests at heart. She was certainly not being seen to her best advantage in such plays. Also she continued to feel embarrassed about her fidelity to the "Fidos" and her alienation from her Equity confrères. John Halliday took her to lunch one day in an attempt to get her to change her mind. "You belong with your family, Helen, the other kids who are struggling," he pleaded. "I want to, Jack, oh, how I want to," she sighed, "but Mr. Tyler would never let me." "Then do it anyway." Helen shrugged. "But he's been so good to me . . ." Jack Halliday then proceeded to tell her just how good Mr. Tyler had been. It seemed that George M. Cohan had wanted Helen for a play called *In Love with Love* and had asked Tyler to let her play it opposite Jack. Instead Tyler had ordered her off to Italy even though she had told him at the time how desperate she was for good work. Lynn Fontanne had been given the part. "I hardly think you have to worry about loyalty after *that,"* concluded Jack.

It was a different Helen that walked into Mr. Tyler's office than on the day the nascent Pollyanna made her entrance. A terror-struck Brownie waited in the hallway. "Mr. Tyler, I am going to join Equity," she announced. When she rejoined her mother she said, "He told me that if I walked out of the office there would be no turning back. I said nothing. And out I walked." *Mr. Tyler had been my theatre parent. He loved his business and used his own bank account to finance his productions. His gift to me was in stretching my efforts, making my reach exceed my grasp and forcing me to more ambitious parts. He was a nineteenth-century gentleman and he lost me to the twentieth. Before he dismissed me, he had made me one of the leading young stars in New York.*

It was a painful separation, but George C. Tyler had done such a good job that my career could now soar without him.

When Tyler's producing days were over and he fell on hard times, Helen and the Lunts repaid his faith and foresight by supporting him through his declining years.

5

BEFORE HER CAREER could soar she had to eat humble pie. There was no chance of work that late in the season anyway. She joined an actors' and artists' cooperative at Woodstock for no pay in a production of Lady Gregory's *The Dragon* in which she acted with an unknown Broadway actor called Edward G. Robinson. It played in a half-completed barn which wasn't waterproof. After only one performance the heavens opened and "rain stopped play." It had, however, been a refreshing vacation. This was followed by the role of Constance Neville in special performances of *She Stoops to Conquer* for The Players club, a signal honor which could not have been won while she remained outside the ranks of Equity.

She was not idle long. In July there was a telephone call from Atlantic City. Edgar Selwyn asked her to come out to see his try-out of *Dancing Mothers* in case she would be interested in taking the leading role on Broadway. She was not keen on the part: it was yet another flapper. Brownie suggested that they ask for a prohibitive salary as the easiest way of getting her out of the part and so asked for seven hundred fifty dollars. Without hesitation Selwyn agreed, and Helen opened at the Booth Theatre on August 11, 1924. The play concerned a neglected wife who to win back her erring husband and wayward daughter abandons propriety and goes out on the town. To begin with the play did badly and the cast were asked to take a drop in salary. Helen agreed on condition she would be able to leave the play if other work presented itself. She was fed up with flappers, longing to play Shakespeare's Shrew or Juliet or Shaw's Cleopatra.

Her social life was nonexistent; her only constant companion was her mother. Though Brownie made it clear in her memoirs that she was relieved at seeing Helen enjoying the company of the opposite sex in Boston, she seems conveniently to have forgotten her opposition to its going any further. When she had announced to the Beacon Hill socialite that she was not going to have Helen's future ruined by a meaningless little romance, she meant *any* romance. It was fine for Helen to flirt, but for her to love was out of the question. Forever with Brownie in tow, Helen had little opportunity of meeting men on her own terms. Certainly she was shy, but the constant chaperone fostered her shyness and welcomed the dependence which meant Helen missed trains when Mother was not there to organize her life. One cannot admire Brownie for this, but one can pity her that her own life was so utterly dependent on maintaining the status quo or suffer the alternative of despair. But her stance was taken on quicksand. Helen was burning with love, longing to be given and return affection. Nevertheless it would take a miracle for her to be able to do anything about it. Then the miracle happened.

It was November 1924. Helen had just left the cast of *Dancing Mothers,* which would complete a run of more than three hundred performances without her. Walking on Fifth Avenue, she heard someone call her name. It was Marc Connelly, co-author of *To the Ladies.* He was in love with Margalo Gilmore and wanted to buy her a beautiful gift. He enlisted Helen's aid. Later, with the present, a Tenniel original of *Alice in Wonderland* in a brown paper parcel under his arm, Connelly guided a reluctant Helen to Fifty-seventh Street and Seventh Avenue and the studio of Neysa McMein. Between four and seven every day the "glitterati" of New York's celebrity register would foregather here. Woollcott and George Gershwin, Harpo Marx and Robert Benchley would climb the flight of stairs to the second-floor studio in the corner of which on a raised dais, wearing a smock, a beret pulled over her rumpled, tawny hair, sat the hostess at her easel, working on her magazine covers as though completely unaware of the crushing throng of wit and egotism that sounded off around her. Connelly and his companion arrived when this particular party was well under way and his arrival was greeted with gusto. Helen, not noted for exuberant wit was acknowledged and quickly ignored and she happily slid along the wall until she found a place where no one might see her. Connelly joined his partner George Kaufman. Helen sipped ginger ale and listened as Irving Berlin played one after another of his melodies on the piano. She hoped she could get away with being thought "a good listener" should anyone foolishly engage her in conversation. This was not the time to talk about Japanese prints even were she able to remember the names of the artists. By the time she had thought of a witty retort the one who had made the mistake of speaking to her in the first place had excused himself and moved to more stimulating society at the other side of the room. How long would she have to endure this before she could make good her escape? Then she was rescued from her plight and from a lifetime of celibacy.

Irving Berlin, still at the piano, was playing his "Always" with one finger, like a little boy, and that lovely melody drifted toward me over the din along with the most beautiful young man I'd ever seen. He stood looking down at me with hazel eyes dabbed with green. His hair was curly, his ears pointed. This was a mouth designed exclusively for smiling. He looked exactly like a faun, though Brownie later informed me that from what she heard—and it was the most reliable of sources—he was worse; he was a "satire"!

"Do you want a peanut?" this enchanting creature asked. It wasn't enough that he poured the peanuts from a crumpled paper bag into my trembling hands. He had to add, "I wish they were emeralds."

6

"EVERYONE WHO KNOWS Charlie MacArthur," Alexander Woollcott once said, "always lights up and starts talking about him as if he was a marvelous circus that had once passed his way." The circus parade of his life began on November 5, 1895. "I don't think God is interested in us after puberty," Charlie claimed. "He is interested only in our births, for this requires His magic. Our dying requires only His indifference." God's particular interest in this birth would have been invoked by the boy's father, the Reverend William Telfer MacArthur, evangelist. Watching the threshing machine on his Pennsylvania farm go up in flames he ordained himself on the spot a minister, borrowing twenty-five dollars from a Chicago storefront bank's manager on pain of "hellfire and damnation." "The Old Pollywog (the joker son's name for his dour Scots tyrant of a parent) roared at us from morning to night," recalled Charlie. "He was constantly uncovering some new streak of wickedness in us. He would line us up at night, all still hungry as wolves, beseech God in a firm voice to forgive us, uncover our backs, and whale the hell out of us. He kept a strap soaked in vinegar to make it a finer instrument of the Lord." When an unknown covert sin manifested itself in the shape of a huge festering boil on the side of the boy's neck, the avenging angel decided to make it an example of the Lord's mercy. Each night for a week the faithful flock would implore of the Almighty His forgiveness of this great sin. The innocent sinner would stand the while in the fiery brilliance of naptha flares. After seven days of reverent supplication the Lord replied. Hallelujah, an ooze of pus loosened itself from the hideous bulge. The hero of the expiation was brought home in triumph. An older Charlie would often grin when, whilst shaving, the light hit upon the mark of Satan which remained branded on his neck.

The gentler side of the MacArthur ménage, born Georgiana Welstead, sister to eighteen other brothers and sisters, sprang from English military stock. She bore the reverend seven children—Alfred, Marguerite, Telfer, Helen, our hero, John, and Roderick—and bore the marks of poverty, hardship, and childbirth which had transformed her youthful beauty to careworn, premature age. "My mother was an ingenious woman," said Charlie. "She had to be. We were very poor, but she always found ways to put food on the table. Some days the larder was so empty that she had to tie a piece of cabbage onto a string and dip it into a boiling pot of water. She would then serve us 'soup à la cabbage.' I remember that on many nights I couldn't fall asleep because my hungry stomach made so much noise."

As so often happens, those raised in a restrictive religious environment seldom choose to follow the paths of righteousness for the rest of their lives. It was to the Reverend MacArthur's acute sorrow that six of the seven chose more worldly paths. The youngest son Roderick met premature death when, in a shotgun accident, half of his head was shot away. As Georgiana nursed the bloody mess of her dying son she heard a commotion outside the house. In came several of the faithful flock bearing the reverend on a shutter. He had broken his leg. Georgiana would not outlive her youngest son by long. Before winter set in she planted tulip bulbs, falling exhausted on a sickbed at the end of her labor. "The flowers will be up in the spring," she told Charlie. "I'd like to see them." But when they bloomed she was gone.

Recalling Charlie, Ben Hecht wrote, "I remember him at the beginning. Muscled arms and heavy fists, a lean, longish face, untelltale eyes, gypsy hair with a widow's peak, a pointed nose with an oversensitive tip, a mouth clown-turned at the edges, the neckline of a hungry man, slow moving and as full of graceful posture as an artist's model, unable to dance, sing or pay long attention to anything, smiling when others laughed, still drinking when comas took his companions, uttering brief lines from Rossetti, Swinburne, Matthew, Mark, Luke and Job, and as detached from world problems as a man basking on a pier—this was our young friend, fresh from the mint and beckoning like a gold piece."

Charlie MacArthur's path into the world led him via Mexico against Pancho Villa with the Illinois militia under Colonel Milton Foreman, through the battlefields at Cantigny, Château-Thierry, and the Argonne in World War I, to the minefields of Chicago as a reporter on *The Examiner* under its legendary editor, Walter Howey, who would stop at nothing to get a story. One night he telephoned his new reporter. "A little girl with golden curls has disappeared from her home near Moline," he cried excitedly. "I have it on good authority that she's locked in a safe in the Moline station. The stationmaster closed it without noticing the child had stepped in." It seemed the old safe had been left open for ten years and no one knew the combination. The use of dynamite was completely out of the question. "We have exactly five hours to get her out alive!" howled Howey.

"We need a cracksman," yelled back Charlie. "The state prison at Joliet is full of them. Can we spring one or two?" Howey kept a drawer full of letters of resignation. None of them were signed by Howey but carried the signatures of every state official and man of importance secured from each of them on pain of disclosure of every last bit of dirt he knew about them. A couple of calls to pertinent politicians secured the necessary clearance and Charlie was on his way to Joliet where great excitement broke loose at the promise of free pardons. Howey organized transport in exchange for sparing the disgrace of a railroad president and rushed medical staff to Moline. The mother of the golden-headed babe with several members of her family were placed near the safe as photographers flashed the arrival of Charlie with his pair of villains pushing their way through the gathering crowd of onlookers.

Sandpapering their fingers, the two set about the safe under the light of an arc lamp. The minutes ticked inexorably by as the deadline of all deadlines approached. The child's mother shivered in the anticipation of terror. At last the click, ten minutes from time. Two railroad officials moved forward and swung back the heavy doors. Necks craned to look inside. There, nestling inside the dusty depths lay a heap of old suitcases and discarded ledgers. The little golden-headed babe was nowhere to be seen.

Two disgruntled convicts were led back to their cells. A bewildered crowd dispersed. The child was discovered in the attic at home sulking over some slight. Charlie telephoned Walter and told him the worst. "That's a terrific story," cried Howey. "I told you there was *no* little girl!" shouted an exasperated Charlie. "We don't need a little girl," chanted an ecstatic Howey. "The story's about humanity; the goodness in people's hearts. I'll give you a headline—IT'S A WONDERFUL WORLD. Now *write that story!"*

Charlie's path to the future led him through barrooms and brothels. Invited by a Chicago politician to the infamous bordello run by Madam Farrington at Twelfth Street and Michigan Boulevard he was told that anything he would care to choose would be paid for by the politician. "Anything?" he asked with a twinkle in his eye a closer acquaintance would have recognized as a gleam of wickedness. "Yes," promised his host. Charlie carefully scrutinized the array of girls set before him. "I'll take . . . ," and he paused for a moment. "I'll take the walnut player piano. Please have it delivered to my house." He was a great joker and everyone loved his company. The air lit up when Charlie arrived. His reporting became legendary. Sent to cover a sordid case in which a dentist had been accused of raping a patient he turned in a three-hundred-word story headed TOOTH DOCTOR FILLS WRONG CAVITY.

Ashton Stevens, the dramatic critic of *The Examiner* who, in the not too distant future, would wait until a young actress's mother had left the room before claiming for Walter Howey the lowdown on Helen Hayes, had under his wing at *The Examiner,* the "Little Girl Reporter" Carol Frink, who added the sparkle of her individual reporting to the newspaper's columns. Elfin and pretty with ash blond hair, she was not a million miles in looks from that actress carving herself a niche on Broadway. At the age of twenty-two, Charlie MacArthur married Miss Frink. The newlywed husband insisted that his wife give up journalism and concentrate on fulfilling what he considered her genius in the great novel she was nursing in her creative breast. She was packed off to Michigan with a new type-writer. Whenever he showed an editor her work it was turned down. His, on the other hand, would be accepted. Needing more cash to support two households, Charlie bade Chicago farewell and New York hello, starting work with *American Weekly* for the Hearst Press.

A couple of weeks later he made a barroom buddy of a man who had recently perfected the formula of a rejuvenating cream, the main active ingredient of which was distilled from the sex organs of a South American snake. Miriko, it was claimed, could restore the full bloom of youth. His imagination working overtime, Charlie became a partner in the venture. He engaged two chorus girls whom he instructed in history so that they could answer any question relating to their lives based on the phony birth certificates he obtained placing their births in the early 1830s. He invited his boss, Morrill Goddard, to interview the two nonagenarians in the hope that *American Weekly* would launch the preparation as a sensational scoop. In the middle of the interview an irate woman in her middle thirties rushed in. "So this is where I find you," she cried, "in a hotel room with two men!" "What do you want with these two old ladies?" inquired Goddard. "Two old ladies? Why, is that any way to speak of my daughters? I've been looking for them for a week." With which she escorted them from the room. The resourceful Charlie somehow extricated himself from his boss's wrath.

Carol became enraged at the childish behavior of her spouse. Distance had lent disenchantment to their relationship and she decided to call it a day, though it would be many days before divorce was discussed. Charlie saw no particular urgency. Once bitten by marriage he was twice shy of treading that path again. It would have to be a very special person to make it seem worthwhile. For the time being he was content to play the field.

By now he shared an apartment on Madison Avenue with a fellow writer whom he had met at a stuffy society soirée. "What do you think of our hostess?" a boring fellow guest asked a bored Charlie. "Not very much," was his reply. "Don't you find her charming?" countered the guest. After a moment's consideration Charlie replied, "She's too enthroned." A round-faced, rotund stranger stepped up to him. "Sir," said he, "that's the first time I ever heard language at a society event. The name is Benchley. If you're ever looking for anywhere to live I have an apartment you'd be welcome to share." "I'm a late sleeper," answered Charlie. "You will have to be very careful to boil your eggs very softly and not to scrape the toast."

Robert Benchley and Charles MacArthur became the new double-act-about-town. In time Benchley invited Charlie to join him and his coterie of acquaintances at his lunchtime retreat in the Red Room at the Algonquin Hotel. At its famous Round Table Benchley would sit with Alexander Woollcott, Ring Lardner, George S. Kaufman, Dorothy Parker, Robert Sherwood, Franklin Pierce Adams, and Edna Ferber. Occasional guests at the table included Harpo Marx, Noël Coward, Paul Robeson, Marc Connelly, Nunnally Johnson, Alfred Lunt, and now Charlie MacArthur. He bowed low when he was introduced to the group. "I was warned to watch out for your fangs," he declared, "but now I realize that was only a myth. No fangs are visible. Only sabers."

"On that very first day," recalled Woollcott, "I realized that Charlie was a confusing mixture of Satanic mischief and childlike comic blundering. It was as if he had escaped from Robin Hood's merry band and was vaguely headed for the Holy Land on a pair of rubber-bladed ice-skates." Woollcott soon was trying to pair off Charlie with Dorothy Parker who was more than willing to be wooed. Apart from weeping at plays Miss Parker was a tough cookie with a hard line of wit. "You can lead a whore to culture," she would tell the American Horticultural Society, "but you can't make her think." At a Halloween party where the guests were "ducking for apples" she announced, "Change one letter in that phrase and you have the story of my life."

Along with the rest of his chums he would often turn up at the studio of Neysa McMein at Fifty-seventh Street and Seventh Avenue. One day in late November 1924 he was quipping his way through the assembled throng. Suddenly he spotted a slim little thing with ash blond hair sitting quite by herself sipping a ginger ale. Someone approached her. She looked up startled and then smiled a sweet, shy smile. Her head cocked on one side she listened to what was said, nodding occasionally, smiling nervously. The man in front of her hovered uneasily, then made an excuse and elbowed his way to the other side of the room. The young woman seemed to breathe a sigh of relief and went back to her ginger ale. Irving Berlin was plucking "Always," as ever with one finger, from the piano. Charlie drifted over toward her. "Do you want a peanut?" he asked. She glanced a nervous look at him, followed by a warm smile. He was enchanted by that smile. He poured rather too many peanuts from the paper bag he was holding into her hands. "I wish they were emeralds," he added.

7

THE LIGHT WAS DIFFUSED, everything in a kind of soft focus, her brain not quite registering her actions. One moment they had been at Neysa McMein's, the next they were trotting round Central Park in a horse-drawn barouche. And then he was gone. She chattered, how she chattered, to everyone she knew. "Charlie MacArthur this, Charlie MacArthur that . . ." "That satire," interpolated Brownie. "I hope he'll call me," sighed Helen. She had told him she was in the book. "Why doesn't he call me?" "Will he ever call me?"

He never did call. However, quite by chance when she and Brownie were out walking, they bumped into him. Helen could barely stammer out his name. "This is the Mr. MacArthur I told you about," she added. He was obviously pleased she should have been talking about him. As they walked away Brownie said, "So that tramp is the one you've been raving about." Helen had seen only his curly hair and engaging smile. Brownie had seen only the dirt on his collar and his filthy hands. "But, Mother, he's one of the most brilliant men in New York." Brownie snorted. "How do you know? Just because he said he wished peanuts were emeralds? He probably heard that from someone else and seeing how green you were threw it to you." That night he turned up at their apartment bathed and clean enough for Brownie. "If Helen hadn't been so enraptured," she was to recall later, "I could have liked him better. As it was I could almost see horns sprouting and a cloven foot."

One Sunday evening the following February found Helen escorted by a new acquaintance to Alexander Woollcott's for a gathering of the usual. In walked Gershwin and Benchley, Harpo Marx and Berlin. Connelly and the Kaufmans were not far behind. Jeanne Eagels arrived late. For once in her life Helen had a good joke up her sleeve. "We haven't seen you for a while, Helen . . ." "No, well you see, I've been in *Quarantine.*" The play had been no joke, however. Heywood Broun had claimed that the woman behind him had remarked "Isn't she just too cute?" twenty-one times. While disagreeing with the woman, he was afraid that Helen was just on the brink of too-cuteness and that it was time she began accepting challenges. A timely warning.

The play the partygoers were all talking about was *What Price Glory?* "I'm willing to bet five hundred dollars," roared Woollcott, "that *What Price Glory?* will be playing to infatuated audiences one hundred years from now!" Benchley chirped up, "I'll take the bet! That's if you promise to be buried with the money in your teeth, so I can get at it easily." Helen's one prepared joke played, it took a cocktail to inspire her to the best unprepared cue-line of the evening. Helen, anxious to be rid of her *To the Ladies* piano, announced, "Anyone who wants my piano is willing to it." Back came George Kaufman, "That's very seldom of you, Helen." With which she found her way to the place she preferred at parties like this—the corner where no one might see her.

This time George Gershwin had beaten Irving Berlin to the piano and was finishing beating out some catchy new tune when, in a moment of *déjà vu,* Helen heard a strange but familiar voice. "Hello, Helen," said the voice. There was the faun with the hazel eyes dabbed with green. "Hush everybody. We must have quiet," bellowed Woollcott. Paul Robeson was about to sing. "Let's get out of this fish trap," suggested Charlie. "But I'm here with someone else," she stammered. "I'll not hold that against you. Come on." As they slid out of the house, Helen attempted conversation. "I'm about to rehearse in Bernard Shaw's *Caesar and Cleopatra.* We're opening at the new Guild Theatre. I'm playing Cleopatra." "I wish I could play the asp . . ." Into a taxi and off into the night. His hand grabbed hers, her lips received their first offstage kiss. "That satire," warned Brownie at the back of her mind. Helen turned her head and looked out of the window for the rest of the journey to the house on 15 Park Avenue. "What's your phone number?" Charlie asked as she climbed out of the cab. "It's in the book," said Helen, and then remembered that the last time she had told him it had produced little in the way of results. "Would you like to come and see me in the play?" she blurted out. "Love to," said Charlie, "I'll be there." And his cab was gone.

"It isn't the thing for a young star to do," Ftatateeta scolded.

"What isn't?" asked Cleopatra. "To count the house every performance. It looks awfully mercenary." "Oh, but I'm not counting the
house, Miss Westley, I'm just checking to see if someone's out in the
audience." Helen Westley gave her a knowing look. "Oh, and does
he come *every* night? How nice." Helen's face fell. "He hasn't been
here at all. Yet." "But you've been looking through that hole in the
curtain every night for two months! In my day we called the fellow
up and kept on at him until he showed." Helen sighed and went
back to her dressing room. She knew she couldn't do that.

Brownie had almost lost her the role of Cleopatra. The offer had
been a complete surprise. Helen had been called to Theresa
Helburn's office where the offer was made. "Oh, that's been the
dream of my life. I know the part perfectly. In fact, I know everyone's part. When do we begin rehearsals?" The meeting had been to
sound out her interest, as the new Guild Theatre on West Fifty-
second Street would not be ready to house the production for another three or four months. Salary, Miss Helburn said, would be
discussed later. There was no discussion. Brownie hung up the telephone without a word when $250 and 2 percent over $8,000 was
offered. "They cut us off," said Miss Helburn when she rang back.
"No they didn't," said Mrs. Brown coolly. "I hung up. There was no
answer to such a ridiculous proposition." Helen was distraught, furious with her mother. A part like Cleopatra which could turn the
tide of her career could not be set aside so lightly, apart from the
fact that it was her dream role. "The Guild aren't poverty-stricken
and there is no reason why we should be," remonstrated Brownie.
Helen left the house and called Miss Helburn from the corner drugstore. Eventually Brownie settled for $350 and 3 percent. "You do
understand, don't you Mother? I just had to play Cleopatra if I ever
got the chance." Brownie arched an eyebrow. "Of course," said she,
"but we still have to eat. And you have now gotten yourself a
seven-hundred-and-fifty-dollar appetite."

*Nobody was going to stop me from playing Cleopatra, not even Brownie.
There were doubts on Broadway that my sheltered life and obvious innocence
qualified me for the role of the feline young queen, but I was an awakening
female and, by this time, I was also an actress. It was difficult to cross
Mother, but I had to play that part.*

Sadly it was not the success she might have wished. Heywood
Broun offered his usual criticism. "Somebody in authority ought to

tell Miss Hayes every night, 'Don't be as cute as you can.' From my point of view I should have preferred a Caesar slightly more humorous (than Lionel Atwill) and a Cleopatra less so. Helen Hayes is probably the most carefully trained and expert of all the younger actresses in America, but I wish she would forget some of her tricks. Her Cleopatra is certainly a half-sister of the little girl in *Clarence* who would not wash her face."

One Saturday night Helen was sitting still dressed in her last act costume of flimsy black chiffon listlessly letting the Nile and Egypt slip away from her before she went back to her Sphinx of a mother. Then her dresser announced that her Mark Antony was outside. Charlie hadn't seen the show but was passing the theatre. He couldn't take his eyes off the bodice of her gown. It left little to the imagination. His appetite was keen. "How about supper?" he asked instead. "I can't," she sighed. "I have to go home to Syosset, Long Island. We've borrowed a house for the season. It's such a long drive . . ." Her voice trailed away. Here he was, at last, and there was nothing she could do. Then she heard herself say, "Why not come out to Syosset? We can have supper there. You can pick up some things and stay the weekend. Of course, Mother's there . . ." Charlie grinned. "I'll risk your mother, and I don't need to pick anything up." She telephoned ahead. Brownie's voice was cool. *She had thought Charlie was out of the picture. But after that weekend, he was never to be out of it again.*

8

THAT SUMMER WAS a time of joy. Helen invited all of Charlie's friends out to Syosset so that he would be happy and relaxed and not deterred by Brownie's stony silences or cutting remarks. Charlie would arrive with a toothbrush and a grin and there would be laughs aplenty from the minute his impish face appeared. Forgive the biographer if he draws the reader back to Broadway for a spell, but an actress must work, especially if she sinks all her savings into a summer of entertaining folk of extravagant tastes. The Brown bank balance was extremely low and Helen was forced to take a poor piece called *Young Blood* which opened at the Ritz, November 24, 1925. She was cast yet again as a flapper with a do-gooder mentality. Audiences had seen it before and let her know by staying away. After two months the play closed and she went with it on a short tour.

It was one of the things an actor dreaded—being left high and dry two thirds of the way through the season. The bank balance had been low and was not extensively replenished. Someone suggested she would find it cheaper to pass the summer in Paris and that if one crossed by freighter expenses could be kept to a minimum. Helen set out to try to book passage for herself and Essie. While she was gone a call came through from the William A. Brady office. Would Helen be interested in a revival of Barrie's *What Every Woman Knows*, which he was to stage at the Bijou Theatre to use up the end of his lease there, about three or four weeks playing. Brownie said she would have Helen call him back the minute she returned. Helen came in weary, having trailed around several companies without any luck. At first she was not very keen on the idea of playing Maggie Wylie, as the role was so closely identified with Maude Adams and she would be treading on a memory. Then again, she was superstitious about turning down a Barrie role. Perhaps the thought of a possible bonus of two thousand dollars toward their summer helped make up her mind to accept the offer. She was given a run-of-the-play contract for five hundred dollars per week.

One thing which worried her was the Scots accent. She learned that Maude Adams had played the part without the Scots burr and to begin with she followed suit. However she felt that in contrast to the character actors with their rich Scots burrs, she and Kenneth McKenna, who was cast as John Shand, seemed colorless. She persuaded McKenna to join her in learning the accent and they found a Scots actress turned fortune-teller. As well as instructing her in a creditable accent she told Helen's fortune. Helen dismissed her prediction of a long run. "Had she told me I was going to cross the water, I might have believed her," she laughed. The play opened April 13, 1926, at the Bijou.

John Mason Brown claimed, "In playing the elfin child of that lovely fantasy *(Dear Brutus)* she revealed less an art than an instinct, less a person than a personality. Since there are, unhappily, no laws on the subject, she was permitted to roam abroad on her notices, invade the flapper field, and populate the stage with several years of younger generation ladies . . . In Maggie Wylie Miss Hayes has grown up, and has recaptured the grace, the charm, and, though I be excommunicated for saying it, the wistfulness of a Barrie heroine. It lights up the whole play and brings out of it the enchantments of pure magic. Although this hoarse and slightly tonsilar voice is lifted in praise, others have hinted that Miss Hayes is less than she ought to be, and that Miss Maude Adams was more humorous and deft. Concerning the which this reporter begs leave of the assembled gentlemen to point out that Garfield was the twentieth President of the United States. At least I hope he was." (New York *Evening Post*) Thirty years later Mae West would quip, "I knew Helen Hayes was the most when she starred in a piece called *What Every Woman Knows!*"

This play gave Helen her first really long run. The fortune-teller had been right. After the first four weeks it continued a further fifty-eight before an additional tour. Helen would be tied up with Maggie Wylie until June 1927. Charlie too had had a success. The air was certainly charmed, for on February 9, 1926 his first play, written in collaboration with Edward Sheldon, had opened. *Lulu Belle* had, what seems amazing today, a cast of 115. One hundred of the actors were black, and a look at the play today would suggest racism in the extreme, with every "nigger" expression ever coined. Years later Charlie apologized to Paul Robeson, adding that in those days that was the way everyone spoke.

With the public side of their lives taken care of we can now look at their budding romance. To begin with, as soon as marriage was mentioned, everyone was against it. "Charlie MacArthur is a well-known skirt-chaser," warbled Tallulah Bankhead. "He has roamed around New York with Bea Lillie, Dorothy Parker, and dozens of other well-ripened females. I surely thought naïve little Helen was saving herself for the boy next door." Benchley chimed in, "Charlie's a man of the world. Helen makes Pollyanna seem like a painted hussy." No one went quite so far as to say it, but Helen was considered a colorless milksop. When she was about to play Cleopatra, George Jean Nathan had even stated in print, "While we think Miss Hayes a good actress, we do not think she is biologically suited to the part." Charlie's father took the opposite view when he was introduced to his prospective daughter-in-law. "You are a sinner," he thundered at her. "No son of mine will ever marry an actress." Neysa McMein told Helen that once Beatrice Lillie, the successor to Dorothy Parker in Charlie's affections, was back from England, then

Helen would be set aside. Alice Duer Miller added, "You're out of your depth, Helen—Lady Jane Grey in the royal henhouse. Steel yourself for the tenth day." Apart from what Benchley said behind their backs, to Helen's face he said, "You're one of the marrying kind. You want to live with Mercury? Just try putting bedroom slippers on those winged feet." Dorothy Parker, she was told, had been driven nearly to suicide by him. Mrs. Parker wrote a story where she described herself sitting by the telephone waiting for his call. When Charlie took Helen to look in on the Algonquin Round Table there was a sudden break in the barrage of witticisms. Dorothy Parker turned to a terrified Helen, "And what do you think, Helen?" she purred. Everyone gave everyone else a knowing look. Harpo Marx said (for he spoke offstage), "Do you want to think up a plot and backer for a movie starring Valentino and Baby Peggy?" George Kaufman added, "It's a plain case of miscasting." Her father confessor told her the doors to the Catholic Church would be barred to her forever if she even thought of marrying a divorcé who, Heaven forbid, was a Protestant. He was not yet even a divorcé. Now that Charlie was a successful playwright, Carol MacArthur was making divorce proceedings difficult. Woollcott who enjoyed encouraging *amours*, especially if there was a wicked side to them, was repulsed by a consummation and did everything he could to put asunder those whom he had joined together. "Can you live on the razor's edge, Helen? Do you really think you can hang chintz curtains on the lip of Vesuvius and call it home?" Helen let the conversation subside for a moment. "I know I can't give Charlie excitement," she said slowly, "but Charlie has enough excitement for everybody. What I can give him—or die trying—is contentment and some degree of peace."

"My disapproval of the marriage is one thing!" protested Woollcott. "But I won't tolerate anyone else's interference." The object of this particular outburst of displeasure proved Helen's greatest obstacle. The opposition of friends and colleagues was trivial compared with the disapproval of Brownie. Brownie had not only given Helen birth in the physical sense, but had been the instigator of everything she now called success. She was her mentor, her teacher, her traveling companion, her banker, her manager, her agent. Until the party at Neysa McMein's, Brownie had been half Helen's life and Helen had been all of hers. "You're making a fatal mistake," she said.

Helen spoke softly. "I love him, Mother." Essie's eyes blazed, *"Love! What about your career? The first thing you know you'll have children. What then?"* Helen had been readying herself for this. "No, Mother, we're going to wait." Essie howled in derision. "Wait? *Wait?* That's what I said when I married Frank Brown—*and look what happened to me!"* The blood of both of them ran cold as they stared at one another. She had wiped out Helen's life with a single stroke. Each faced the other as she hadn't done since that long-ago day when Helen was thirteen years old.

9

ONE OF THEM had said something which sparked off a minor tiff. Whatever and whoever it was didn't matter. By the time the car pulled up outside Tommy Hitchcock's house at Great Neck neither Helen nor Charlie was speaking to the other. As Charlie stepped over the threshold he yelled at Hitchcock, "I'll wrestle you to the ground!" and felled his host with a flying tackle. The match went on for ten minutes or more, the one throwing the other this way, the other hurtling that. Suddenly Charlie fell in a heap with a loud thwack. Helen rushed to him and crouched by his inert body, stroking his forehead and kissing him. Then he opened his eyes. "Is this the only way I can get your attention?" he asked. Always charming, always endearing, always unpredictable.

All human beings provoke different reactions in different human beings. Each person's assessment of any other selects different qualities. The Charlie Helen saw was more than the light dancing on the wave, she saw also the dark waters beneath and was not afraid of them. *More than anything else Charlie needed someone to listen while he was talking big. That Algonquin crowd were as hard on each other as they were on everyone else. It was dangerous to expose your dreams to the death rays of their sophistication. He needed a starry-eyed listener like me. Few, if anyone, got past his façade. He traveled life with a "no-trespassing" sign on his spirit. He was a private person. His sister described for me the gentle, distant boy who never was quite part of the tumultuous brood of seven that grew up, close-packed in their small house. Even I could never claim I knew Charlie very well, only in miracle glimpses. I can remember every time the guard dropped and Charlie and I touched in complete intimacy.*

Wit is a brittle, glittering quality which has little to do with warmth. Charlie's being comprised both, though he rarely let the warmth show through. Ben Hecht claimed that like Cyrano he would defend a cause with his life but would speak of it mockingly, if at all. "Of our forty years of friendship I can remember hundreds of things he did, but nothing he felt. He never told me." When a schoolboy at the Wilson Academy at Nyack where he enjoyed the nickname "Chick" he was best remembered for the day when each of the students was to offer evidence on the evils of drink. As though to forewarn all of his future life he recited from *The Rubaiyat of Omar Khayyam*, "Come fill the cup . . . ," virtually grounds for expulsion. However one of his schoolfellows, James Nalbud, recalled for Ben Hecht, "Charlie's antics were not always pranks. One day he passed the hat round the students 'for a good cause.' He raised ten dollars, and was off to town. We all thought the 'good cause' was Charles MacArthur, and there was murmuring against his slick ways. A few days later I ran across an item in the Nyack *Journal* of the eviction of a poor family on the outskirts of the town and how some unknown youthful benefactor had secured new quarters for them by a down-payment of rent. I showed Charlie the story about the eviction. He grinned and said, 'Shut up, Dubie.'"

Another illustration of this side of Charlie can be found in his relationship with Edward Sheldon. Sheldon, a relative through Alfred MacArthur's marriage, was an invalid. After a brilliant career as one of Broadway's most dazzling playwrights, he was paralyzed by arthritis. The once handsome man then spent twenty years motionless, laid out on his bed. Though his body was lifeless and he was completely blind, his mind was alert, and he was able to speak in a resonant, seemingly effortless tone. He was seldom alone, as old friends, new friends, and hangers-on would gather there for hours to exchange gossip and to listen to the voice of the Oracle. Everyone brought their problems, but not Charlie. Perhaps Charlie was the only one who heard Sheldon's problems and the problems of others that the invalid could do nothing about. Charlie became Ned Sheldon's mobility and sat beside the bed of the ex-star actress as she screamed and sweated her way through symptoms of withdrawal from heroin, and destroyed the suicide note of another such before the police arrived, thus leaving her reputation untarnished. There were the drunks whose miseries he could hear, the suicidal who he helped see the morning, the down-and-out derelicts he gave hope.

In the age-old rebellion against the previous generation, the preacher's son has so much more scope. If the father propounds the blameless life, the son has all the lasciviousness of the world as his oyster. Charlie, imbued with native curiosity, went out into the world in search of bad company. However, Charlie was handicapped as a hedonist more by an innate humanity and human goodness than any painstaking adherence to his father's dictates might have produced. The enigma of the man was that he was no out-and-out adventurer or playboy, nor a straightforward saint, but rather a great deal of both in a disturbing, ever charismatic combination.

We were one of those couples everyone worried about. They thought of him as a fantastic, wild creature and they said it would never do. But he was a tower of strength who looked enchantingly irresponsible. And I look like a staunch fortress and am a crumbling reed inside.

10

IF *What Every Woman Knows* had placed Helen in the front rank of Broadway's leading actresses, her next play was to win her an even greater accolade. The play had first been submitted to her under the title *Norma's Affair,* a comedy. Two seasons later it came back as *Coquette,* a tragedy. At first Helen was not a bit interested, and who can blame her? How can anyone turn a comedy into a tragedy and still be true to the subject? However, Brownie felt it had merit and persuaded her to read it. She was soon convinced that with a few changes it was an excellent subject to follow Maggie Wylie. Unbeknownst to her she had missed out on another role which might have had a different kind of impact on her life. Edgar Selwyn was looking for someone to star in a new comedy. Alfred Lunt and Lynn Fontanne had recommended Helen. Selwyn had dismissed the recommendation on the grounds that she was still a virgin and couldn't get near the character. And so Helen lost out on the part of Lorelei in the original stage version of Anita Loos's *Gentlemen Prefer Blondes.*

But back to *Coquette.* For her director Helen was delighted to have an old friend, George Cukor, who had been the stage manager on *Dancing Mothers.* She found him a delightful companion. She shared the same sense of humor with the gentle homosexual, and he was the ideal dancing partner, as she was always entirely at ease with him. Perhaps they were too much at ease when rehearsals began because they were seldom able to keep from laughing at some of the Deep Southern dialogue in the play. The rewrites were slow in coming. The play had co-authors in Ann Bridges, whose first play it was, and George Abbott, who refused to come to rehearsals because he had not been asked to direct. In the end it was agreed that Abbott should take over direction, as someone needed to take a firm grasp of the play. After about ten days under Abbott the play's producer decided to take a hand in the direction. The producer was the infamous Jed Harris, another of Broadway's tyrants on whom Laurence Olivier based much of his interpretation of his villainous King Richard III.

Helen's first entrance was about five minutes into the play, though on this occasion she had to wait nearly two hours, as Harris questioned virtually every word spoken. Indeed when she came on and said, "Hello," he stopped the rehearsal again and said, "Now, Miss Hayes, what are you going to do with that 'Hello'?" The usually placid Helen had a ferocious temper when she was aroused. But there was always a stillness before the storm. Quietly she replied, "Just nothing." Insensitively Harris pursued his point. When eventually he let her continue again he stopped her with a dissertation on her interpretation. Suddenly she flung her script to the floor. "Mr. Harris," she screamed, "I didn't realize this was Euripides. I thought it just a simple play about simple people. I will not continue until you get out of here!" For a woman who felt she had no temperament she knew how to use her position as star.

The play flopped in Atlantic City. It had a good first act but the second act disappointed. Norma Besant, Helen's part, was a coquette as the title implies. Her father, believing the man she loves has maliciously fouled her good name, shoots him dead. At his trial he can only be proved innocent of murder by proving that Norma is chaste, but she is found to be carrying the young man's child. Eventually she kills herself. The second-act curtain was shortly after the shooting. Helen told George Abbott, "If my own father killed the man I loved, at that moment I would want to see him hanged. What I would feel later I don't know." Abbott replied that she would lose the audience's sympathy if she denounced the father. "I lost the audience's sympathy tonight," she reasoned, "and the bottom fell out of the play from then on. I'm afraid that if I get bad notices in Philadelphia I shall not take the play to New York."

Jed Harris, now on Helen's side, supported her. In Philadelphia the audience was shouting, "Hayes, Hayes, Hayes!" after the second-act curtain when, beating her fists on the couch, she screamed, "I hope he hangs, I hope he hangs!" The reception was the same in New York when the play opened at the Maxine Elliott on November 8, 1927. Noël Coward summed up everyone's feelings when he said, "Helen Hayes gave an astonishingly perfect performance. She ripped our emotions to shreds."

Helen has always shunned the title "First Lady of the American Theatre." Perhaps this is understandable. Such a claim can be a great burden. As with Laurence Olivier, often claimed to be the greatest actor in the world, there is a kind of unspoken challenge to have to prove that with each succeeding role. It is a title that is not bestowed for the work an actress has done unless she is prepared to live up to it. Elizabeth Taylor for many years suffered the description of most beautiful woman in the world. How understandable that she let herself run to fat. In later years Helen would accept work of diminishing quality as if to try to do the same. Katharine Cornell, she has always contended, was the true claimant to the title. As recently as 1984 she claimed in a television interview that the title had been the brainchild of a publicist for a radio show in which she was involved in the forties. But this is not so. In fact her claim to the title goes back as far as *Coquette,* and it was Percy Hammond who made the nomination in the New York *Herald Tribune.* "It seems we shall have to enlarge the already long list of First Actresses," he wrote, "and so far as this season goes, put Miss Hayes at the top." Whether she realized it or not, she had a talent to be reckoned with. It was inescapable. As Charlie MacArthur once said, she had a star on her forehead.

Perhaps Charlie was reluctant to wed a breadwinner. He was proud of her as an actress but it is reasonable to suppose that he had a resolute pride which would render him incapable of allowing her to support him. His divorce from Carol was absolute. When she had refused to divorce him he had initiated proceedings against her. However, he did not propose marriage immediately to Helen, though he had bought her an engagement ring sometime earlier which she wore on a chain round her neck and out of sight. Helen had made all the first moves at the beginning of their relationship but she knew that the major move must be left to him. He put off the day, saying that it depended on the outcome of his next play. He could not marry her until one of his plays was "really significant . . . a play that changes things."

The Front Page was just such a play. Tennessee Williams claimed that it was the play which took the corsets off the American theatre, making it possible for him later to write his kind of play. Written in collaboration with Ben Hecht, it drew on their experiences as newspapermen in Chicago. The central character of Hildy Johnson drew heavily on Charlie himself. Walter Howey became Walter Burns. There was even a character in the play now much closer to home. Hildy had a line in the play where he said, "I have three tickets to New York for me, my girl and her goddamn ma." The "ma" in question, though she didn't realize it at the time, was none other than Brownie.

Under the direction of George Kaufman, the play opened at the Times Square Theatre on August 14, 1928. *Coquette,* which was still playing to packed houses, was closed for one night to allow its leading lady to attend the most important first night of her life. She sat way up in the balcony, her heart beating so loud she was worried it might disturb her neighbor. Her seat by the fire exit meant that she could give a blow-by-blow description to Charlie and Ben, who were sitting out on the fire escape, too nervous to watch the play themselves.

I wanted Charlie to have a success not only because I loved him but also because my future happiness depended on that night. The curtain went up and it wasn't long before the audience began warming to this rowdy play. But my fears didn't diminish a bit until the great moment when Dorothy Stickney, in the role of the prostitute, roared onto the stage like a high wind and tore into the scene with all her great talent. She made her exit to one of the wildest ovations I've ever heard. People don't carry on like that today— the ovation went on for minutes and minutes and minutes and in that time, while the great music of applause and cheers was circling around my head, I knew that my future was assured. I raced out at the end of the act. The heroes of the night were huddled on the iron steps, all pinched and white in the half-light. Reaching Charlie's arms in two bounds over the rickety fire-escape grating, I babbled wildly about the audience's reaction.

"Helen, will you marry me?" said Charlie. "You took the words right out of my mouth," she replied. Later he would say, "Maybe with me you will never be rich, but I promise that you will never be bored."

FOUR

ACTS OF GOD AND LOUIS B. MAYER

1928 – 1935

1

"Is He a Bridegroom or a Bigamist?" screamed the headlines. Carol Frink had got it into her head that the divorce was not valid and had threatened to take out an injunction to put a stop to Charlie's remarriage. Thus on August 17, 1928, the tie which bound him to Helen for the rest of his life was made in a secret ceremony. By the time the world heard about it Helen was in the midst of her regular performance in *Coquette*. The press was there in force at the stage door when she emerged. Perhaps because in days gone by she had pinned to her dress a gardenia from an imaginary secret admirer before she went to rehearsals, Harpo Marx filled a Steinway piano crate to the brim with fresh gardenias as his wedding present to her.

Shortly before the ceremony, Helen had confided in the worldly Tallulah Bankhead. "There's an intimate question I'd like to ask you," blushed Helen. "Fire away, dahling," gleamed Miss Bankhead. "When a girl gets married . . . what . . ." she began. "What can she do to keep from getting pregnant?" Tallulah laughed her nicotine laugh. "Dahling," she chortled, "just what you've *always* done!" Helen probably got more constructive advice elsewhere, for she managed to prevent conception until Charlie and she had somewhere they could call home. Originally they lived in a hotel, but eventually Charlie found an apartment with a back window facing over the East River. *The Front Page* was still running and *Coquette* was still pulling audiences in, so they could afford to live on smart East End Avenue. Then when Howard Hughes bought the film rights to *The Front Page* their prosperity was assured for some time to come. Charlie's cut of the $125,000 Hughes paid gave him financial stability. The film rights were also bought up for *Coquette*, but they were bought by Mary Pickford for herself. Although the film would win her an Academy Award, the content of the story had to be toned down considerably to make it palatable to "Little Mary's" public and it bore little resemblance to the play which had won Helen an admiring public on Broadway. With no wolf at the door the two MacArthurs could begin to plan a family and soon the third MacArthur was on the way.

Helen was already three months pregnant when the forty-five-week post-Broadway tour of *Coquette* reached Los Angeles. No hotel was needed for her here, as Charlie had rented a bungalow. He had arrived before her, beckoned by the movies. An apartment was found for Brownie, who was still traveling with Helen and acting as her manager. When they were having lunch one day, Helen fainted. Brownie was alarmed. She knew nothing about the pregnancy. The doctor who was summoned ordered Helen to bed, adding that any overactivity could lose her the baby. Charlie called Jed Harris and explained the situation. Rather than replace his star, Harris decided to cut his losses and close the show. Other members of the cast claimed that they were due severance pay. Harris's lawyers argued that under the standard contract they had a right to close the show without payment of salary in cases of fire, accident, strikes, riot, enemy action or, in this case, an Act of God. The case went to arbitration under Equity.

Suddenly Helen's secret became front-page news, her unborn child baptized the "Act of God Baby." The bungalow was besieged by reporters. Charlie managed to fend them off without too much stress to Helen. The doctor said she must be protected from stress. Charlie knew, of old, all the tricks reporters would use to get their stories, and he also recognized that they had a living to make and that it was best to play along up to a point. Things calmed down when the news came through that Equity had ruled against Harris, who was ordered to pay the actors for two weeks' lost work. One newspaper ran a cartoon of a rather smug stork atop a pile of money, supported by the legend, "MacArthur baby not an Act of God." Charlie grinned. "At last," he said, "I'm getting some of the credit."

A solicitous Brownie took Helen back to New York where she could have the baby in some semblance of peace. Charlie was to follow on a later train, but a farewell party given by his cronies turned into a marathon drinking contest which somehow managed to put him on board a ship for New York by way of the Panama Canal. Charlie's hangover lasted until Havana, where he disembarked in some bewilderment to telephone Helen and let her know more or less what happened. He couldn't resist one or two hairs of the dog on the way. Not surprisingly the ship sailed without him. Using the spare cash in his pocket he managed to get to Florida, where he borrowed enough from Anita Loos to get him to New York. In a Manhattan suffering the deepest of deep midwinters he arrived dressed in white flannels, tennis shoes, and a white sweater. Helen bundled her chagrined darling into a warm coat and galoshes and the last leg of his journey proceeded uneventfully.

Charlie kept saying to me, "Make sure it's a girl. You will make it a girl." He said that boys are competitive. They enter at once into competition with their fathers. Girls are a gentler influence in life. So we decided that our baby should be a girl. Visiting Ned Sheldon they were discussing the choice of a name, though girls' names only. Sheldon said, "For a girl there is no prettier name than Mary."

When labor pains began their regular pattern Helen insisted on walking to the hospital, which was eight blocks away. Charlie was already in a state of acute anxiety but walked several paces behind her. "If anything happens here on the street, I'll pretend I don't know you," he murmured. Their little girl was born the morning of February 15, 1930. *Did you ever see a very young baby? The first days or weeks they are so unhappy. They seem to resent being brought into this world. They cry a great deal. Some of them have little, old, wrinkled faces. When I looked at Mary I felt like apologizing to her for bringing her into a world that, manifestly, she did not like. I shall always remember that and never in any circumstances prate about what she owes me. I owe her all the care I can give for bringing her into a world she did not seem to want to live in.*

Charlie brought his Mary her first bouquet, a bunch of violets with a single red rose in the center. "We have given her life and death, Helen," he said. "That's all we can be sure of."

2

Once I took a role that a great many people considered, shall we say, "below my dignity." They wrote me in droves to tell me so. Charlie had a rubber stamp made so I could stamp all those critical letters and send them back. The stamp said, "Go see a doctor."

Jed Harris brought the script of *Mr. Gilhooley* to Helen while she was still in the hospital. She liked it enormously because it presented a challenge. The role was that of an Irish harlot who ruined the man of the title. It was her first opportunity to play an out-and-out unpleasant role. Under Harris's own direction the play opened at the Broadhurst Theatre on September 30, 1930, to less than polite applause. Helen was shocked, for the first time in her career, to see the backs of patrons leaving the theatre as she took her call. The reviews, claimed Brownie in her book, were dire. But she cannot have read all of them. Brooks Atkinson said Helen gave "a shining performance" and John Anderson wrote "Her performance of the street girl is schemed out with such intuition and stated with such clarity that it becomes a major portrait of acting creation." But audiences didn't want to see their fresh little ingenue grow up. Although her role in *Coquette* involved a pregnancy and a suicide, the character possessed all those qualities of innocence which they associated with Helen's playing. In the role of a heartless prostitute she was betraying their trust. She was the daughter who had gone wrong. They would forgive her only if she reverted to her former ways. However, one member of the audience was impressed by the new scope he saw in Helen Hayes. Soon after, Maxwell Anderson would begin work on the play which would break the mold of typecasting for Helen for the major part of her career.

"After her adventure in the heavier *Mr. Gilhooley* in which her lot was not a happy one, it is pleasant to have Miss Hayes back in something resembling her own field," wrote Burns Mantle, echoing the sentiments of most of her public when she opened in *Petticoat*

Influence at the Empire Theatre on December 15, 1930. However, the play had only a moderate run of about three months, though it did mark the beginning of Helen's long and happy association with the impresario Gilbert Miller. It would also be her last appearance at the Empire Theatre, occupying for the first time the star dressing room to which she had been summoned by first John Drew and then William Gillette. Stage Mother Brown had never been inside these hallowed portals and it was a moment of great piquancy when the star invited her mother to join her there. Later when the Empire was torn down, Helen attended the auction. From a tiny scrap of the curtain she made a little pincushion which would become her good-luck emblem. Also she bought a section of the balcony railing over which she and Brownie had hung "in days of glorious poverty" which became part of the structure of the bar at the home which would be hers for more than fifty years.

A new phase of her career was about to begin. Charlie would later recall, "Helen was determined to do movies against my wishes. I knew what harm might befall her. After all it's a dreadful thing to throw this ribbon of celluloid around the world, for even the Chinks in Singapore can say, 'Your wife stinks.' Well, I went out ahead of her and got hold of the script, which belonged in the Smithsonian Institute. It was for the picture *The Sin of Madelon Claudet*—the word 'sin' was supposed to be provocative. I could have torn up the script, I suppose, but I didn't want to win the argument by having my wife cut her throat. So I found myself being drawn into the picture."

In actual fact Helen's enthusiasm was mixed. On the one hand she had always dreamed of going into the movies. In the days when she was an up-and-coming actress the idea of the kind of film stardom enjoyed by Mary Pickford *et al.* must have appealed to her. Even after the test for Fox she had thought occasionally of trying to get to Hollywood. However, everyone she consulted tried to dissuade her. Brownie was certainly dead set against it. Now that Helen was a star it seemed unthinkable. She even turned down several early offers. Then MGM came up with an offer and Helen played hard to get. Now, it seems, she had come to a realization that she hadn't got the kind of looks to be a film star. If this is so it was a shallow reason. She was not a Broadway star because of her looks, but there were many parts she could play where it didn't much matter what kind of face she had. The same might possibly be true of a career in films. As Margaret Case Harriman observed at the time, Helen's face was the greatest asset to the actress in that it was a face that reflected things, rather than a face which was an object of beauty in itself. When an improved offer was made, Helen accepted. The fact that Charlie was already working as a scenarist with Metro no doubt influenced her decision. Also both of them had been worried about bringing up Mary in Manhattan and the clear air of California seemed a better environment.

Charlie was justifiably infuriated by the first project that Hollywood *Wunderkind* Irving Thalberg produced for Helen. It was a script for *The Lullaby*, a turgid melodrama about mother love which had played on Broadway in 1924. Charlie protested that Thalberg wouldn't expect his own wife, Norma Shearer, to play in such rubbish. Thalberg said quietly, "You're a writer, you fix it." Charlie did some good work on it but neither he nor Helen could save it. At its first preview it was a dismal failure. By this time Thalberg was in Europe. Louis B. Mayer, the head of the studio, took a more practical, less esoteric, attitude to the studio's product than Thalberg, his vice president and head of production. The movie must have been truly terrible because Mayer had the softest spot for stories about mothers who sacrifice their lives for their children. He ordered the film shelved and cabled Thalberg that he intended buying up Helen's contract and sending her back to New York. In the meantime Samuel Goldwyn had seen a screening of a couple of the early reels of *Lullaby*, and saw in Helen the ideal Leora Tozer for his screen version of Sinclair Lewis's novel about a self-sacrificing doctor, *Arrowsmith*. Mayer had no qualms about recouping some of his losses with Helen by loaning her to Goldwyn.

The screenplay for the Goldwyn film by Pulitzer Prize winner Sidney Howard was well constructed; the role of Leora offered the actress a development from sweet freshness through loving supportiveness to the pathos of a tragic death; also Helen would have as her co-star the debonair and sympathetic Ronald Colman. She decided to cut *her* particular losses and return to Broadway with at least one film to her credit. The film's director was John Ford. Though the film is overlong and often tediously slow, it still shows great style, particularly in the scene in the tropics where Helen unwittingly infects herself with the bubonic plague virus which will cause her death. Her playing here is simple and understated and she achieves an intense poignancy.

Perhaps her everyday proximity to a writer led her to protest to Ford when he began making wholesale changes in some of the scenes, not realizing that most directors did this in most films. "Who is directing this picture?" was his response to her complaints, "Get back on the set and stick to your acting . . . such as it is." Unlike the occasion when she had confronted Jed Harris, she was completely at a loss for words and stumbled into her canvas chair. When later Ford came over to her and asked if he had upset her she pronounced, "I am not accustomed to being spoken to in that manner," at which virtually every member of the crew fell into hysterics. Helen prayed for the ground to open under her. When it didn't, she too began to laugh and was joined by Ford. She was completely incapable of being grand.

By the time *Arrowsmith* was in production, Irving Thalberg had returned to Hollywood. Running *Lullaby* through, he realized that the film was flawed by two or three scenes only. He persuaded Mayer that the whole project could be saved by some inexpensive retakes. Mayer, always keen to turn a deficit into a profit, agreed. Thalberg called Helen to work on Sundays when she was not needed by Ford—that is, until Goldwyn heard about it. A bitter rival of Mayer, he threatened to take Helen out of his picture until this stopped, so the final work on *Lullaby*, which now had a new name, *The Sin of Madelon Claudet*, was held up until *Arrowsmith* was completed. *I never worked for Mr. Goldwyn again, but I wish I had, darn it. Working for him was the nearest I've felt in Hollywood to being back in the theatre, the good theatre that I'd been working with in those days, the theatre of Jed Harris, of Gilbert Miller and George Abbott.*

Madelon Claudet was rushed out so that MGM could claim the discovery of film talent in Helen before the Goldwyn picture appeared. The early sound films of Helen Hayes are due a reassessment. No wonder the critics went wild about this performance ("Here is the finest exhibition of sheer artistry the cinema has seen in seasons. Possibly it has been equalled. Never has it been excelled." Regine Crewe.) There is one early moment of theatricality when she clasps her hands and looks heavenward, but thenceforward eveything is honest and true and different from anything the cinema had thus far or has since produced. There are no clichés in this performance. Similarly nothing she does has since, by repetition, been reduced to cliché. She seems to find a surprising, new and original reaction to every word and situation. Helen has claimed, somewhat self-effacingly, that anything good in her performance she had found in Charlie's writing. There is a moment when she is released from prison and she instinctively reaches up to touch the branch of a tree. This moment has often been claimed as one of the actress's most real and touching moments. Helen has said it is Charlie's moment, for he wrote it. On the contrary, she fulfilled it. Had Lana Turner or Hedy Lamarr found that moment in their screenplay would it have been played with the same delicacy and feeling? Similarly she fulfilled every line he wrote in her own uniquely individual way. Her performance is in no way dated. Had it been filmed this year it would still be considered great acting.

Movie stars generally have learned to act in movies by watching other movie actors. Hence movies became a glossy regurgitation where only the looks, sometimes the personality, seldom the style, changed. Helen Hayes ably adapted the essences of her unique theatrical abilities and presence into a unique screen persona. She was one of a handful of true originals in the cinema of the thirties.

Recently President Ronald Reagan recalled, "I never had the experience of working with Helen Hayes, I'm sorry to say, but I was acquainted with her—we all knew each other in that Hollywood of the Golden Era. She is ever and always a lady; a lady of warmth and kindliness, as eternally feminine as she was when she captured the hearts of all who saw her on stage or screen. What was her secret? Certainly it wasn't just theatrical artistry although she was a superb actress. There was more to it than that. There was beauty and an inner light that was Helen Hayes herself shining through every role she played. If anyone is looking for sheer enjoyment, tell them to run a Helen Hayes picture."

The film itself is not a great one. Without Helen it would have been a thin affair indeed. But in her hands it is often compelling. The passage of the last decade of the character's life when she is toiling to support her son, who believes her dead, is told by a series of images and events with a sudden sliding shift of frame from the screen. This piecemeal, laborious progression is saved from banality by Helen, who brings delicious invention to the series of vignettes, never, as so many another star actress would have done, criticizing by an implicit moral attitude Madelon's descent into degradation. By whatever method she comes by the money in each of these episodes, whether by theft, by blackmail, by selling herself to a passing drunk, one delights with her in her success, the ends totally obliterating the means. Her descent from simple country girl to naïve socialite, slick call girl, blowsy tart, and wretched hag to ancient derelict is at all stages believable and only in the dénouement in which she is not seen is credibility strained. Years later when Hollywood knew public taste better she would have been permitted the death scene which was her due or, at the very least, a reunion with the son. A failure among producers to appreciate the public's capacity to absorb tragedy without causing the box office to suffer robbed many a film of this era of its natural consummation.

Helen never actually saw the film and has always questioned its success. Two weeks after the film was premiered in New York, October 30, 1931, she and Charlie did attend a performance. However there were such painful memories as scene after scene unfolded that they couldn't keep from groaning. Someone behind them leaned forward and threatened to have them ejected and they left. One unfortunate omission from the film is the performance of Mary MacArthur. She had toddled across the screen and into her mother's arms in the first version, in the role of Helen's tiny son, but, sadly, the scene was cut from the released print.

Until this point in her career the name of Helen Hayes had been known merely to theatre aficionados. Now in every township across America large enough to boast its own cinema and across the English-speaking world, posters proclaimed, "To Fill His Cup with Happiness, She Sank to the Very Depths—But to the End She Kept the Secret Locked in Her Heart. Introducing to the Screen one of America's Greatest Stage Stars."

3

ONE OF THE CONDITIONS of Helen's contract had been that she would be able to return periodically to the Broadway stage, a condition Louis B. Mayer rarely granted, as he preferred to keep his "family" together. His collection of "more stars than there are in the heavens" did not permit stars shooting off whenever they felt like it. After her first six months in Hollywood, Helen made her first six months' return to Broadway in Ferenc Molnar's *The Good Fairy*, which opened at the Henry Miller on November 24, 1931. It was an odd little piece but perfectly in keeping with the Hayes image of old. She played Lu, an usherette in a cinema who believed herself to have been sent into the world to spread sunshine and good deeds. It was her archetypal Tyler role with distinct echoes of *The Wren*. Critics found that she had lost none of her old powers of enchantment. After almost five months at the Henry Miller the play was taken on a brief tour.

Helen's celebrity had never been greater. Even with only *Madelon Claudet* playing in New York she could not walk down the street without being instantly recognized. When *Arrowsmith* premiered on December 7, there were crowds at the stage door of the Henry Miller lining up for her autograph. It was at the same time thrilling and terrifying. *I don't remember that the need to achieve fame was an overpowering private fantasy with which I lived. Even though what fame demands of you is all part of my work, it has never ceased to bother me. I have never known how to do it well—being famous. I was not trained to it because I grew up in the theatre when actors and great stars simply didn't perform offstage for the public. Then one day I was suddenly plunged into the world where an actor is public property. I don't think I've known more than a few people who enjoyed the obligations of fame. I used to think that one of those who seemed to adore the adulation of the crowd was Joan Crawford. However, one day after she and I had been to the theatre together in New York we were confronted by a mob. Joan went quite pale and said, "Oh God, I'm always afraid they're going to say something to hurt me. I'm always trying to placate them, to keep them as my friends." We both knew how a mob can turn on you in a split second.*

She and Charlie took their first vacation together in Europe the following summer. On their first morning at Cannes Helen rushed gaily down the rocks on to the beach. "Hurrah!" she cried. "Peace at last! No footlights, no greasepaint, no curtain calls, no directors, no movies—peace, peace, peace!" Her gay abandon was interrupted by a gruff American voice which barked, "Hey you, get off the set. Can't you see we're making a movie!" How ironic that she should have bounded straight onto the set of Gloria Swanson's latest film!

Back in Hollywood, while Helen was waiting for Mr. Mayer to name her next project, their bungalow suffered the onslaught of a Valkyrie in the shape of Ethel Barrymore. In she roared and grabbed hold of Charlie and shook him. "Do you think you're too good to write for the Barrymores?" she stormed. "You lazy good-for-nothing Broadway hack, you're going to write *Rasputin and the Empress* for us or else I'm going to tear this bungalow apart with my bare hands. Take that!" And she kicked him in the shins. Charlie ran to hide behind Helen as the great Ethel dashed everything from the table onto the floor. "Now, are you going to write it or do I do my worst?" Helen was astounded. "Charlie, I think she means it." "Of course I mean it," bellowed Miss Barrymore, picking up first one thing and then another. "This is for Jack and this is for Lionel, and this . . ." Before she could do any more damage on behalf of any other member of the Barrymore clan, Charlie piped up and agreed to write the picture. It had been Irving Thalberg who had managed to bring all three Barrymores, Lionel, Ethel, and John, together in one film. He had imagined Charlie would be thrilled to write the screenplay, but Charlie was as enthusiastic about the project as he would have been to spend the rest of his life on the wagon. Ultimately it was to cause him more trouble than any film was worth. The three Barrymores fought for the limelight in the film in every scene but not as a united front against the rest of the cast; rather with each other. Here were three giant egos each determined to make a better showing against the others. Charlie had to reassure each of them that he was not favoring either of the others over the one. On one occasion he sent each of the brothers a case of Scotch and Ethel several baskets of roses, each with a handwritten card, "To my favorite Barrymore, C.M." It was a dull film, however opulent the MGM art directors were able to make it, and Ethel Barrymore, whose first talkie it had been, ran back to Broadway, her tail between her legs, not to return for more than a decade.

Charlie received an Oscar nomination for the screenplay. An award might have proved an embarrassment when MGM was taken to court by Prince Felix Yossoupov and his wife, Princess Irina Alexandrovna, the former czar's niece. Because of their positions in the court in the film the seemingly fictitious characters played by John Barrymore and Diana Wynyard could easily be identified as Yossoupov and his wife. Bernie Hyman had ordered Charlie to come up with a scene where the Wynyard character was raped by Rasputin (Lionel). In addition he had ordered a preface to the film which stated that the film concerned the destruction of an empire brought about by the mad ambition of one man. "A few of the characters are still alive. The rest met death by violence." Suits were filed in both New York and London. The London court found for the princess, awarding her $125,000 in damages, and the New York suit was settled out of court for a reported $750,000, though it may have been considerably less. Ever since the action there has never been a picture released without a disclaimer as to the fictional status of the "events and characters" in a film. An interesting postscript to these events came when Helen, on a visit to Monte Carlo, was invited to a dinner where Yossoupov was to be a fellow guest. Her host informed her that this was the man who had killed Rasputin. "Then should I avoid the subject," asked Helen. The host laughed, "If you do, you can be sure he won't." And indeed, the prince introduced the subject himself and they heard all the gory details. It was all the fellow had to talk about.

In his review of *Arrowsmith*, critic Edwin Schallert had suggested that Mayer should bring Helen back to Hollywood with all speed. "In this portrayal," he wrote, "she makes our Garbos, Dietrichs, Shearers and Swansons, clever though they may be, look like amateurs." However Mayer could not understand her appeal and could think of no way of casting her. Had she not been a star of some magnitude there would have been no problem, as she would, in his eyes, have been ideally cast as the perennial friend of the heroine, but as the heroine she had severe limitations. Paramount had prepared a property for Fredric March and Claudette Colbert in Hemingway's *A Farewell to Arms*, but delays had meant that the leads needed to be recast. Mayer was pleased to loan Helen out yet again while he thought further about solving his seemingly insoluble problem. Helen was delighted with the Benjamin Glazer and Oliver H. P. Garrett screenplay in its fidelity to Hemingway's original. Frank Borzage was set to direct. She would have top billing with co-star Gary Cooper in second place.

In conversation with her biographer Helen described their first meeting. I had suggested that actors called each other 'darling' not from any stance of affectation but because often within minutes of their first meeting they would share moments of great intimacy, their strangeness to one another being bridged by the term of endearment. *The first morning I reported at Paramount I was rushed into makeup and my face was hastily applied. That's funny, I thought, but maybe that's the way they do things at Paramount. Then I was rushed into wardrobe where I was hastily pinned into a nurse's uniform. Then they rushed me into the studio. "Miss Hayes," someone said, "this is Gary Cooper. Now, can you get into bed together?" It was all set up for the stills photographers so that they might have a photograph in the newspapers that evening!*

She liked Gary Cooper from the start. At first he was in awe of her. He was somewhat bemused by his own success in pictures as he had no acting background and was suddenly cast opposite one of the most distinguished of Broadway's young actresses. Indeed there is at least one scene in the film where this shows, where he appears wooden and awkward. However her charm and friendliness, which the majority of her co-stars would enjoy throughout her long career, soon helped him to relax. He was greatly impressed when on occasion she would ask his advice on how a scene should be played. Rather unkindly, T. S. Rutherford has claimed this to be the best screen portrayal of a romance between a giant and a dwarf. The disparity in their heights is difficult for the viewer to accustom himself to, especially since Hollywood insisted for decades that whatever their heights off screen all actresses should be four or five inches shorter than their leading men on screen. Borzage chose to be honest here and it is the honesty in their relationship as players that makes such an impact even when this film is shown today. Helen adored Cooper and has claimed that had he but crooked his little finger she might have kicked over the traces, but he never did. Cooper, in fact, possessed many of the qualities which appealed to her in Charlie.

Helen's dressing room was immediately across the corridor from one of Paramount's leading contract players, Marlene Dietrich. On her first day of shooting Miss Dietrich appeared in her doorway and said, "I hope you break your leg." Helen was shocked beyond belief. She had heard of the bitchiness of Hollywood actresses but had never believed that a complete stranger could be so brutal and callous. Later someone told her that in Europe it was considered unlucky to wish someone luck in the theatre and that "Break a leg" was standard form and she realized her mistake. She and Miss Dietrich became firm friends. Every day the German star made a hot lunch for her daughter, Maria, before she left for the studio and always brought a portion for Helen. This was no *femme fatale* but a good-natured *Hausfrau.*

A Farewell to Arms is undoubtedly Helen's finest work on film. Her performance is a piece of perfection. Here there are none of the cooings and purrings or the slick brittleness of other thirties leading ladies, "merely" her honest simplicity. Too bad the makeup department didn't appreciate the natural qualities in her appearance which would have complemented her thought qualities rather than try to make her look like Claudette Colbert. In trying to add a glamour which was not hers they almost succeed in making her appear artificial at the moments of greatest truth. When she has undergone a Caesarean section and is nearing death, her long mascaraed eyelashes, coiffeured hair, and rouged lips belie her performance, especially when she calls for cosmetics to *improve* her appearance before Cooper sees her for the last time.

Borzage's direction is superb, although he decided to take an antiwar stance through the story which was not Hemingway's intention in the original. Otherwise it is remarkably faithful to the book with the addition of one scene only, filmed with such sensitivity that it appears to stem from the original thought. In this scene an Italian padre visiting Cooper in his hospital bed senses the great love between Frederic, the soldier, and Catherine, his nurse, knowing that if they were to be legally married she would be forced by the hospital authorities to return to America. He turns his back on them and in an undertone begins to recite the marriage ceremony. At first the two of them are joking with one another and then they realize what he is doing and allow the "marriage" to take place. The scene was obviously inserted to appease the censors, who would not have approved of Catherine's becoming pregnant outside some form of marriage, even if it were only in God's eyes and not the law's. The love scenes are honestly played and the audience doesn't feel cheated by Hollywood. The more explicitly sexual scenes were eventually cut by the Legion of Decency, though there are existing prints retaining all the original footage.

The studio's inability to appreciate the audience's intelligence in being able to accept a tragic ending led the bosses to insist that Borzage film two endings. In the originally released version Catherine did not die. The two were left smiling hopefully as the bells rang out to celebrate the Armistice. The alternative ending replaced an optimistic musical soundtrack with Wagner's inspirational *Liebestod*. With Catherine dying in his arms saying "I will be brave," Frederic gathers her up in her bedsheet, at once her wedding veil and her shroud, and carries her to the window as doves flutter into the sky. When this version was shown audiences told the executives which they preferred and thankfully the original ending was shelved. "Playing with a haunting beauty that not even she has brought to a role since her unforgettable stage portrayal in *Coquette,*" wrote Richard Watts, Jr., when the film was released in New York, "Miss Hayes is so entirely moving and credibly tragic that the photoplay takes on qualities of splendour that are hardly inherent in its plot manipulations."

Before the opening of *A Farewell to Arms* Helen had attended the ceremonies for the Academy of Motion Picture Arts and Sciences awards at the Ambassador Hotel, Los Angeles, on November 18, 1932. Although she was nominated for her performance as Madelon Claudet as Best Actress (1931 to 1932) Helen was convinced that Marie Dressler would win for *Emma*. The only other nomination that year was for her friend Lynn Fontanne in her first and only film *The Guardsman*. *Grand Hotel* was named as Best Picture; Frank Borzage was Best Director for *Bad Girl*. The Best Actor award was shared by Wallace Beery for *The Champ* and Fredric March for *Dr. Jekyll and Mr. Hyde*. Helen Hayes was named as Best Actress for *The Sin of Madelon Claudet*. The award was presented to her by her friend Norma Shearer. Helen said, *On the only other occasion when I ever felt like a superb woman, the only thing I could find to say was, "Gosh, isn't she red?"* Edwin Schallert claimed he had never seen anyone accept an Academy Award with greater simplicity and modesty or a bigger thrill. Charlie would later say, "Helen got an Oscar out of *The Sin of Madelon Claudet*. All I got was a brain tumor."

Helen became the first actress from the theatre to win an Oscar. The Hollywood press was unanimous in naming her First Lady of the Screen.

4

"PHENOMENA LIKE Helen Hayes, and to a lesser degree Katharine Hepburn, are occasion for inordinate joy. Their presence on the screen is a guarantee of something worth looking at," wrote J. C.

Furnas in the New York *Herald Tribune* (April 9, 1933). "Miss Hayes is literally role-proof. She does appear to be the only actress now on the American screen who does not need to worry about what they cast her in."

Louis B. Mayer stared at her and shook his head. "What *are* we going to do with you?" he said and clucked his tongue. "Have you any sex appeal at all?" he continued. "If only you had a face like Garbo. Then we could cope with all this great acting." He shook his head again. "Maybe if we get a dress like Shearer wore in that movie, something in white satin, then see how you look . . ." He looked none too hopeful. "Mr. Mayer," Helen ventured, "I'll still look like Helen Hayes." And Mayer shook his head again.

Several attempts had been made to invent glamorous origins for his star who could only boast a long ago relation in a little-known opera singer to make amends for a father who sold meat. There had been an effort to resuscitate the myth that she was the love-child of Charles Frohman and Maude Adams. Helen was quick to veto this as she was to discourage the story that she was really the illegitimate daughter of a playboy prince.

Nevertheless, if Mayer could not see in Helen's face the reason for her success, he could read box-office receipts and he knew that, if not a fortune, there was money to be made here. Academy Awards did not lend quite the prestige then that they do today but it must have been the source of some satisfaction to Mayer that Helen was the third successive Metro star to win the Best Actress Award. Failing to appreciate her features, he decreed that in her next movie she should have her face so altered that she be unrecognizable. The film was a piece of junk entitled *The Son-Daughter* in which the entire cast taped up their eyes, wore their hands in their sleeves and pretended to be Chinese. It proved one of the all-time lows at the studio and failed at the box office. So much for Mayer's judgment about his star. However, "Miss Hayes, the cinema's new First Actress, performs another of her wonder-works," claimed Richard Watts, Jr. "At first glance the character of the heroine so elementary in its acting demands might seem a quiet little vacation for Miss Hayes [but she] manages to steer her way through the pit-falls of the part so brilliantly that, even though the part is tricky and artificial, she is always touching and honest and entirely believable . . . Although the earlier sections of the picture are so slow-paced as to be a trifle wearying, the drama does in its extremely highly colored way, end with one of the best murders of the year, when Miss Hayes, virtually Electra-like in her cry of revenge, twists her wicked husband's queque about his neck and strangles him lyrically."

However, the picture was no *Broken Blossoms* and would not have the lasting appeal of that Lillian Gish picture. A remake of another successful Lillian Gish vehicle was Helen's next assignment. *The White Sister* is the story of two lovers separated by war. He is reported missing believed dead and she enters a convent. When he returns he wants her to marry him, but she has taken her final vows. He tries to force her to come away with him but then realizes they have both changed. Fatally wounded in a bombing incident, he dies in her arms. Ronald Colman had played opposite Miss Gish. Cast opposite Helen was Clark Gable. Her new champion, Richard Watts Jr., was not enthusiastic. "I am afraid that (her performance) is not as effective emotionally as it could have been and for this comparative coldness it is rather difficult to assign a reason . . . Perhaps the chief trouble is that the picture does inescapably recall the recent *A Farewell to Arms* and that the comparison is one that cannot well be faced." In fact it looks as though Mayer were trying to cash in on *A Farewell to Arms*. The story had been transferred from its original setting to the same wartime Italian front, with Helen's face framed in the habit of a nun rather than in a nurse's cap. Watts continued, "The similarity is so close that in the end when Mr. Gable lies dying in Miss Hayes' arms—as opposed, of course, to the last scene in *A Farewell to Arms* when it was she who died in the arms of her leading man—a recalcitrant spectator somehow expects a moment to come when she will pick her lover up and carry him to the hospital window while doves flutter around them." Watts concluded by adding that Helen was "as lovely and straightforward and moving as ever." Lyn Tornabene in her biography of Gable claims that he was hopelessly self-conscious in her presence. However this did not prevent him from making a pass at her. Gable was no Charlie-like Gary Cooper and Helen sought shelter in her dressing room. David Selznick tried to persuade Helen that Clark had only been trying to be gallant. "Sometimes, even I wonder if she's some innocent babe in the woods or a wise old grandmother," claimed Selznick. "Then I remember she's married to Charlie MacArthur. Anybody who has to play to him twenty-four hours a day has to be shrewd." Helen liked

Clark, however, and the MacArthurs met the Gables socially. Years later Helen was in conversation with the distinguished British film and stage actress, Dame Flora Robson. Flora had read a biography of Charles Laughton in which it was claimed that Gable had walked off the set of *Mutiny on the Bounty* because Charles Laughton had refused to look him in the eye. This interested Flora because, although she found Laughton a charming human being, he had proved an impossible fellow-actor who would never look her in the eye, always looking slightly downstage of her, both before a live audience and on camera. Helen thought for a moment. *I don't think that story's true. I just can't imagine Clark Gable ever walking off the set. He just wasn't that kind of person. And besides, if Charles Laughton were an honest homosexual, wouldn't he have looked at Clark Gable?*

Reading between the lines of what Selznick said above it might, correctly, be inferred that he was no fan of Charlie's. In fact, for some unknown reason they loathed one another. Whenever they met they ended up punching one another on the nose. One night Helen and Charlie attended a party thrown by Harpo Marx. Myron Selznick said to Helen, "Do you think it's all right for your husband to be talking to David?" Helen looked over and saw the two deep in conversation and said they seemed to be getting along like a house on fire. Moments later they were rolling on the floor punching the living daylights out of one another. The fight was only broken up when Irene Selznick started beating Charlie over the head with the three-inch spike of her shoe. "Now I know why I like women who wear flat shoes," said Charlie.

Selznick had succeeded to Mayer's favor when Thalberg had a severe heart attack late in 1932. Norma Shearer chose to stay at home and nurse him and Helen was rushed in as her replacement in *Another Language.* The film was from a stage play about a girl who finds she has married her husband's whole family. A matriarchal family tyrant makes her sons subservient to her and demands the quailing subjection of their wives. Louise Closser Hale was cast as the mother. It was her third Helen Hayes film in a row, the first film in which she had a leading role, and sadly it was to be the last film she ever made. In an article written during filming, Miss Hale said of Helen, "I watch her as she works, frightfully inattentive up to the zero hour of silence, and then the quick creeping into the mantle of her role. I watch her till the scene is finished, when, without affectation, she leaves her role in a heap on the floor and gallops to our card table. She wrote me a little note once and said she would like to be like me when she grows to be my age, and my note was crossing hers at that time in which I admitted, if I could ever be a young woman again, I would like to be like her! And this is very generous of me for she still owes me two cents from the last game of Russian bank."

Mordaunt Hall in the New York *Times* claimed this role to be Helen's best in films and Robert Garland went so far as to say in the New York *World-Telegram* that it placed her among the immortals of the screen. Although she had starred in four films in quick succession her stern taskmaster Mayer would not let her complete her six months without yet another. Selznick was to produce *Night Flight* with an all-star cast along the lines of *Grand Hotel* and *Dinner at Eight.* Helen would have to forgo the top billing she had enjoyed throughout her MGM films and in *A Farewell to Arms.* However she could have had no qualms about taking second billing to John Barrymore. Billed beneath her were Clark Gable, Lionel Barrymore, Robert Montgomery, and Myrna Loy. It was a rather odd screenplay, more about airplanes than people. Helen was cast opposite Clark Gable again. Although they were shown in a clinch on the poster advertising the film they actually had no scenes together! He spent virtually the whole film in the cockpit of his plane. Her best scene was an emotional one in which John Barrymore had to inform her of Gable's death. As soon as the film ended she, Charlie, and Mary with Irving Thalberg and Norma Shearer sailed from San Pedro Harbor for New York and, after a three-week stopover, for France.

Shortly after Helen was awarded her Oscar, Charlie, too, had something to celebrate. On December 29, 1932, his and Ben Hecht's brilliant comedy *Twentieth Century* had opened at the Broadhurst Theatre. Helen was longing to get back to the theatre. She was gradually forming the opinion that movies were not for her. Although she enjoyed the wealth she was able to command in Hollywood she was not enamored of the life she had to lead. *It's such an odd limited sort of life. You spend all day making films; then if you go to a dinner party you talk all the way through the meal about films; after dinner the women are all segregated, very often for the rest of the evening, so that the men can talk among themselves. About films . . .*

5

HELEN HAD ALWAYS TRUSTED Brownie's judgment in selecting her plays. One day she had tossed Brownie a manuscript and asked her to read it. It was the first act of a play about Mary Stuart by Maxwell Anderson. Brownie could not put it down. She was enchanted by it and Helen agreed to play the role. During writing, Anderson had not been able to make up his mind as to who should eventually play the role. It was between Helen and Katharine Cornell. Against Cornell was her lack of vulnerability. Against Helen was her height. Mary Stuart had been one of the tallest women in history, topping six feet; Helen was one of the shortest actresses on Broadway, fully twelve inches shorter than the queen. One day, however, Anderson had met Helen on board The Chief on his way to California. It dawned on him that it was more important to have a good actress rather than a tall one, and so it was to Helen he offered the role. In Hollywood Helen heard that Mae West, who was exactly the same height, wore specially built-up shoes, with four-inch heels and two-inch soles, which possibly explains her strange, lumbering walk on the screen. Helen had a pair made and wore them from the beginning of rehearsals. The added inches in the shoes were probably necessary at that stage because her co-stars Helen Menken and Philip Merivale, who were cast as Queen Elizabeth I and Bothwell, were both quite tall. Eventually Helen developed a way of thinking herself tall, largely for her own encouragement, which transmitted to the audience who were often convinced of real height.

When I was preparing to play Mary I was taken by a friend to the Morgan Library where I was allowed to hold in my hands and read several letters actually written by Mary. One in particular had been sent to Queen Elizabeth shortly before her execution begging for a chance to speak to her face to face. Although they met in Maxwell Anderson's play they never met in life. "Dear Cousin," the letter began. Reading that long letter one can see the gradual deterioration of her handwriting. At its close she apologizes to her "gracious cousin" explaining that the prison was so cold her fingers couldn't get a proper grip on the pen. At every performance during the entire run of the play I saw that line in my mind's eye, and it somehow made me feel the poor queen's suffering much more poignantly than all the dialogue in Maxwell Anderson's eloquent script.

Mary of Scotland, under the direction of Theresa Helburn, tried out in Washington. Helen and Brownie were thrilled to be invited to the White House to take tea with Mrs. Roosevelt. Brownie still attended rehearsals. In her book she claimed, "I attended to see that none of Helen's ingenue mannerisms crept into her characterization of Mary Stuart." The tryout performances went extremely well, but there were still improvements to be made and rehearsals continued through the tour. After the final dress rehearsal, Helen was sitting exhausted on the stage. Theresa Helburn rushed up to her. "Where's Helen?" she asked. Helen thought she was obviously so carried away by her performance that she didn't recognize her. "I'm Helen," she said. "No, not you," continued the insensitive director, "I mean Helen Menken. Isn't she wonderful?" Exactly what a star actress needs to hear the night before opening night . . .

"Never in a career that began with her childhood and has included many successes has this actress approached the quality of this particular performance," wrote Burns Mantle. "And the answer is not entirely that never before has she had so fine a chance. She has in these last few years been gaining in poise and force and understanding. It may be her picture experiences have helped her. In any event here she stands, definitely planted near the top of her profession not, I suspect, to be again shaken from that eminence." All the critics were in accord, many pointing out the illusion of physical stature, none pointing out the biographical whitewashing of Mary's character. From November 27, 1933 the play would continue at the Alvin with Helen in the role until the following June 1. Helen would have liked to continue in the role long after that but her Metro contract insisted she report back for work in California. The rest of the cast and the Theatre Guild, the producers, were shocked at her leaving, but she had no choice. Margalo Gilmore replaced Helen in the part, but without the star with whom the role was now identified it didn't last more than a few performances. However, after Helen's next MGM film she was able to tour the play.

Philip Merivale again played Bothwell. Elizabeth was played by Pauline Frederick. If anything Miss Frederick enjoyed a greater celebrity in heartland United States than Helen. She had been a great star in silent films, her most celebrated role being that of Madame X. Naturally she was accorded equal billing with Helen. Philip Merivale, who was placed beneath them, always used to make a special point of paying a visit to the theatre as soon as he arrived in each city on their itinerary to make sure his name had not been omitted. This rather absurd insistence on his importance always amused Helen. Sometimes they would play only one performance at the theatre and yet Merivale would go down to the theatre straight from the railway station to check the billing. Helen recalled with some hilarity one occasion when his name was not to be seen. "I've never heard of him," said the man responsible for the omission when Merivale protested, "and besides I haven't got enough 'I's . . .' "

As ever when she traveled through the country, Helen was constantly approached by would-be stage mothers, hoping to make of their offspring what Brownie had made of Helen herself. At one point on the tour of *Mary of Scotland* while the train on which they were traveling was stopped at a small country station, such a mother ushered a rather plain little girl into Helen's drawing-room. "Miss Hayes," the woman said. "My little girl would like to sing for you. She sings 'Momma's little baby loves shortenin' bread.' " Helen took a deep breath and then inspiration struck. "I don't have any influence with producers," she said, "so it wouldn't be any use my hearing her sing. However"—and here a twinkle danced in her eyes —"Mr. Philip Merivale, who is just along the corridor might be able to help. Why not go along and let your little girl sing for him." Helen chortled with glee fifty years later as she recalled the sound of a distant "Momma's little baby" issuing from Merivale's part of the car!

There arrives a moment during the actor's identification with a role when he steps over an unseen boundary beyond portrayal, through technique and thought and becomes the person he has been delineating. My most memorable experience is of a performance of Mary of Scotland *in Columbus, Ohio. Although I had played the part hundreds of times by then I still had a twinge of dissatisfaction about it. On that particular night I couldn't have felt drearier. I'd rather have been anywhere than in the theatre. I was waiting for my entrance "on the pier at Leith" and feeling lonely and tired and too far away from Charlie and Mary. My cue came. I hurtled onstage to a spurt of limp clapping. I faced John Knox. His long harangue poured over me. I opened my mouth to speak. Then it happened. Mary Stuart spoke through me with all her strength, gentleness, and simple dignity. I played as if I were in a trance, meeting each mounting demand of the role without effort, vaguely conscious of the startled reaction of the actors and the stillness of the audience. I changed costumes automatically and then on I went again. Pauline Frederick caught my emotional fury, and the two of us were swept along to the final curtain. They told me afterward that when the curtain fell there was a long silence and then a roar of applause. It took me an hour to summon the energy to change and when I stepped out of the stage door a crowd was still standing, waiting in the rain. No one spoke—they just applauded. I had never given such a performance of Mary in New York and I never gave such a performance again, though I brought several new points to subsequent performances. But that night was the kind of experience an actor lives for, that makes all the tedious repetition seem worth while.*

6

MAYER, ALTHOUGH he was unable to comprehend Helen's appeal, would seem to have blundered in not buying up the kind of properties in which Helen had made successes on stage. For example he might have bought *The Good Fairy*, which was eventually snapped up by Universal and filmed with the charismatic Margaret Sullavan in the lead. Helen would have loved to play the small-town girl in *Alice Adams*, the Booth Tarkington novel. Indeed someone suggested that she ask Mayer to buy the property for her, but she was too afraid of him to do that. RKO bought it for Katharine Hepburn as they would *Mary of Scotland*. However, during their trip to Europe Helen had suggested to Irving Thalberg that he buy *What Every Woman Knows* for her, and it was to film it that she had to leave the cast of the Anderson play. Perhaps her heart would not have been too heavy, knowing she was going to make a permanent record of one of her favorite roles.

How she was to change her mind! Thalberg had decided to take a poll to discover whether people wanted *What Every Woman Knows* shot in period or modern dress. Costume pieces were generally unpopular and the public decided they wanted to see Helen and co-star Brian Aherne in modern dress. Helen discovered, to her horror, that there was a scene in which Maggie visited London to beard the Prime Minister at 10 Downing Street, an action that would be quite out of character. When she protested, she was told to leave movie-making to the people who knew how to do it. Adrian, who dressed Garbo and Joan Crawford, was given the task of dressing the mousy little Scots girl of the story. Helen felt so sorry for him that when filming came to an end she sent him a French poodle with long diamond earrings. He reciprocated by making her a hat for a costume party with two live ducks on it.

Filming got under way. One day Helen had to do a scene in which she had to go into a fit of uncontrollable laughter. This is one of the most difficult things for an actor to do. Actors can laugh technically by using a kind of panting action on the diaphragm, but uncontrollable laughter must have hilarity behind it if it is to ring true. Helen managed it without difficulty. Something went wrong with the camera and the director asked for another "take." She was able to reproduce the laughter exactly. Her friend Ruth Gordon, who was staying with her in Hollywood and was visiting the set, sat by in astonishment.

The director was far from enchanted by Barrie's gentle comedy. His dire mutterings about the entire affair seemed to be borne out by what happened at the sneak preview in a rather rough neighborhood in Huntington, Los Angeles, when the audience who had come to see Jean Harlow in Red-Headed Woman *was completely bewildered by* What Every Woman Knows, *Scots accents and all. The next morning the entire company was called on the set for retakes. The director, Gregory La Cava, was well armed with every Joe Miller Scotch joke ever written. When I protested—violently, I'll admit—and said he couldn't do this to Sir James, he turned to me and said, "Miss Hayes, last night Sir Barrie laid an egg in Huntington. We'll do it my way." Of course, the jokes were not added to the picture. But it was then and there that I decided I would devote my efforts to the stage.*

What Every Woman Knows is one of the least memorable of Helen's films, though there is much that is touching and beautiful in her performance. Unfortunately a touch of cuteness was beginning to show; perhaps as a result of her disenchantment she was falling back on old tricks for support. She was devastated when she saw the film to realize that she had missed many of the little touches she had thought would be good. She could hardly bear to watch herself. It had been such a dreadful experience that she called in to see Metro's managing director, Eddie Mannix, before she left Hollywood to begin rehearsals for the tour of *Mary of Scotland*. She told him that she had decided not to return to Hollywood. She was sure they would be glad to see the last of her. Mayer, it was clear, had never been interested in her. Mannix said that, on the contrary, she would return in six months or MGM would sue her for the $96,000 already spent in preparing *Vanessa, Her Love Story*. He also threatened to take out an injunction to close the play. Irving Thalberg wasn't able to do anything to help her, suggesting she return the following summer and make *Vanessa* her last film on the understanding that she would not be held to the remainder of her seven-year contract.

The film, which was based on the fourth book of Hugh Walpole's Herries chronicles, was poor stuff. Although she enjoyed working again with Robert Montgomery, her leading man from *Another Language*, her heart was not in the film. She could think of nothing but leaving Hollywood for good.

There was an odd tradition at MGM that on December 24 all the men ran out of their offices at noon and kissed any woman who was foolish enough to be there. At the stroke of noon, Louis B. Mayer leaped out of his office, spotted Helen, and kissed her. Ben Hecht loved to recall that Helen responded by sinking her teeth into his neck.

Helen has given many reasons for hating her Hollywood years and the films she made. She had certainly enjoyed the wealth they brought and had been concerned that she might be seduced by the material comfort which subjugated so many of her contemporaries. When working on *Night Flight* she had mentioned to John Barrymore what she felt was the obligation of stage actors to return to the theatre. Helen was shocked to see him turn a deathly white. He told her he had completely lost his nerve and could never appear before an audience again. *When you work in a picture you leave everything outside—all the things you've ever learned through many years and much hard work on the stage. Your voice, your ability to sustain a long scene through to a dramatic climax, those things you can just file away for future reference when you begin a picture. One thing, however, the movies teach you is the valuable lesson of repose. You must possess that before the camera and it is good to possess that too in the theatre.* Many years later she would say of her early films, *I thought my face didn't have—I'm not talking about beauty, because I wasn't aiming for that—but the character of my face, it didn't seem to me to be expressive. Everything about me was ordinary. Ordinary—that was the word for me on the screen.*

It is the exceptional actor who can be so objective about himself that he recognizes the qualities an audience sees in him. In viewing a scene in which he appears he sees all the other actors giving exactly the performances they gave in the studio with a strange creature lumbering about doing his part as badly as an actor could possibly do. Helen saw only a face that did not compare with her vision of what a film actress should look like. She missed all the subtlety because it came as second nature to her; she was unaware of the originality in her work because that was the way she always played. Had she been given scripts of quality (for years she said the only thing that would tempt her back to Hollywood was another *Farewell to Arms)* she might have had an altogether different career and one in which she might have gained self-confidence.

In effect she was still under contract to MGM when she left Hollywood and would continue to be until the length of the original contract had run its course. They were free to call on her at any time to fulfill her obligation. However, she had no intention of returning. Paramount offered her $85,000 to play in *The Old Maid* opposite Ann Harding, but she turned it down. *Lost Horizon* was slated for her but it was made without her. Louella Parsons gave an exclusive at one point in which she claimed that Selznick wanted Helen for the part of Melanie in *Gone With the Wind*. Louella, however, let her readers into the secret that the part would eventually be played by Janet Gaynor . . .

On hearing that Helen was quitting films to return to the theatre, Katharine Cornell said, "The theatre needs Helen Hayes so much that it is good to hear she has decided to devote herself in the future entirely to our stage. I think it is most significant when an actress who has contributed what she has to the screen comes to this conclusion in regard to her art. Her film appearances have raised the standard of talking pictures."

Helen could not help but recall some of the words she had spoken as Mary Stuart, "I rot in my mind here-in what I think about myself." *Having experienced frustration and disappointment from every performance I've given on the screen, I asked myself why I was persisting in the movies. And I had to confess to myself that I had become enslaved to that great big pay check, to the neglect of my home, my family, and my own life. I don't think I'm very good in pictures and I have a beautiful dream that I'm elegant on the stage.*

FIVE

A BEAUTIFUL
DREAM

1935 – 1949

1

IN HOLLYWOOD MARY had just been Helen Hayes's daughter. Now there was a chance she could become Mary MacArthur. They had not been returned more than a few days when Ned Sheldon suggested she should become Mary MacArthur *officially*. "Isn't it about time she was baptized?" asked the man who had suggested her name. She was by this time well past her fifth birthday. Perhaps the tardiness had been due to Helen's rejection of the Church which had refused to recognize her marriage. An altar was set up in Sheldon's living room. Charlie decided that Mary should have two of each kind of godparent, as she was "extra special." His sister-in-law, Mary, Sheldon's sister, and Ruth Gordon would be godmothers and Sheldon himself and Alexander Woollcott the godfathers. Woollcott was disturbed that the minister did not heat the baptismal water before sprinkling it on Mary. "If she catches cold, I'll never forgive him," he said. *Alec was the kindest man I've ever known, but you weren't supposed to notice it. One mentioned his generosity a little furtively, in the tone of voice one might use when discussing a friend's secret vices.* As they returned to their East End Avenue apartment the doorman told

Mary that she suddenly looked grown-up. "God will do that every time," she replied.

Mary's life abounded with all the most brilliant wits and celebrities of the day. Quite naturally she saw them simply as ordinary human beings. When later a schoolteacher was invited for dinner Mary warned her father, "Don't be funny tonight." Her first birthday party had been a star-studded occasion. Charlie had decided it should be one of the high spots of the season. "But no one will want to come to a child's birthday party," argued Helen. "They'll want to come to this one," winked Charlie. Then he drew up the invitation. It read, "Helen and Charles MacArthur request the honor of your august presence on the fifteenth of February to meet Scarface Al Capone. RSVP." Everyone they invited arrived and enjoyed the joke hugely. That is, except for the opera diva Lucrezia Bori who had postponed a trip to Europe so that she might meet the notorious gangster. She refused to believe that it was all a joke and insisted that she meet Capone. Finally Charlie rang a lawyer friend in Chicago whom he knew represented the mobster. Incredible as it may seem, Capone was brought to the phone, maybe as a result of Charlie's having given him a good press in Chicago days, and spoke to La Bori. "How do I know who you are?" he snapped at her from Chicago. "You could be any broad that MacArthur's picked up." He was interrupted by the opening strains of the drinking song from *La Traviata*. "Okay, okay," he yelled, "you wanna blast my eardrums off?" So Bori had her way and Mary had one of the best birthday parties a girl could wish, even though she slept through the entire proceedings, *La Traviata* included.

"I have a very important lesson to teach you," Charlie said to Mary at the dinner table. "The time has come for you to learn how to shoot mashed potato. When you're at table and someone is talking too much or is a bit too stuffy and something must be done to prevent everyone else being bored, then there is a need for some subtle course of action. The only thing to do in the circumstances is to load your spoon with a generous helping of mashed potatoes, turn it around like this, take your thumb, place it at the back of the spoon, and . . . FIRE!" He may not have planned the potato to hit Mary's governess quite so smack in the face but when it happened he almost fell off his chair in riotous laughter, and after a pause to ascertain that the good woman was not too discomfited, Mary joined in his hilarity.

Neither Charlie nor Helen were happy that Mary should grow up in the city. She needed a backyard where she could play to her heart's content and not be dependent on having someone trail her to Central Park. Then when a neighbor's two-year-old son was kidnapped, their determination to get Mary away from Manhattan increased. Eventually they discovered a white Victorian house in Nyack, New York, upriver and across the Hudson from New York City, the tiny town in which Charlie himself had grown up. *I loved the place from the moment I saw it. It was covered with gingerbread trim and had an enclosed widow's walk perched on the roof. On a clear day you can see for miles up and down the Hudson River. There were beautiful trees and lawns that sloped down to the water. I knew the MacArthurs had finally come home.* The house cost rather more than they could afford at the time but they were determined to have it. In fact, "it cost a pretty penny," said Helen. The house had found its name and was called Pretty Penny from that day.

Helen had wanted lots of children. Ten would have been a nice number. She had been born on the tenth day of the tenth month and had ten letters in her name be it Hayes or Brown. A large family would prevent the loneliness she had experienced as a child and overdependence on a parent as a companion. But after producing Mary she found it impossible to conceive. She and Charlie went to specialist after specialist but with no result. Several years of severe migraine were diagnosed as the result of worry about Helen's inability to extend her family. Had she thought of adoption? She had, in fact, told a reporter as far back as 1930 that because it was essential that Mary have a playmate and "a character pacemaker," then she should have a brother or sister, if not of her own, then an adopted one. Now she wondered whether Charlie would be able to accept an adopted baby. However, when, in 1937, they first went to see a prospective addition to their family, the tiny boy looked straight into his eyes. "Jamie MacArthur adopted *me,*" he said.

Helen was able completely to leave the theatre behind her when she came home to Pretty Penny. Thus the MacArthurs enjoyed as normal a family life as could be in a family peopled by four such colorful individuals. Helen's memories of those days are the memories any grandmother nibbles contentedly on as she rocks in her favorite chair on the veranda, the high days and holidays of long ago. There aren't many families, be they rich or poor, who don't have special memories of Christmas, and the MacArthurs were no exception. They did Christmas as traditionally as it was possible to do. *As I look around my living room, I see a typical Christmas Past: the half-hung garlands of green, the huge red satin bows, the fat sweet-smelling tree, and Charlie risking life and limb to hang the Angel Gabriel over the eighteenth-century crèche he'd found in Sorrento. The endless boxes and wrapping paper! The sound of our laughter still clings.* Mary had decided that as the weather was so cold Santa Claus might appreciate Ovaltine and cookies, so the milky drink was made and stored in a thermos before she went to bed. Charlie, with a genius for the stage management of details left a trail of cookie crumbs from the tree to the fireplace and made sure that there was an authentic ring of Ovaltine left on the cup. Then the master stroke. Plucking a few silver-white hairs from their offended dog, Caesar, he placed them around the lip of the cup, obviously shed from Santa's beard. "Now *that* is a stroke of genius," he said. And he took a bow.

2

A YOUNG AMERICAN ACTOR had been engaged to play a cop in the play *Chicago* by Maureen Watkins at London's tiny Gate Theatre under the arches of Charing Cross Station. The Gate was a theatre where plays which had been banned by the Lord Chamberlain for one reason or another could be seen by members of the private Gate Theatre Club. As the young actor recalled, the main reason he had been hired was to teach the actresses in the cast how to chew gum. "They chewed it very daintily and then swallowed it!" he remembered. "Then I heard they were going to put on a play called *Victoria Regina* by Laurence Housman, which had been banned because many of Queen Victoria's family were still alive and in those days it wasn't considered proper to put them in a play. They needed someone tall and Germanic-looking to play the part of Albert. I convinced them that I could play the role." He opened in the play opposite Pamela Stanley as Victoria. "Within three months of opening," continued Vincent Price, "I was introduced to Gilbert Miller, who asked me what I thought of this play as a play for Helen Hayes.

126

I was incredibly flattered that he thought it worthwhile asking my opinion."

The complete manuscript of the Housman play was many inches thick. It consisted of thirty-two short plays, only ten of which had been used in the London production. Helen really wanted nothing but to rest after Hollywood and flung it to one side and forgot about it. Her rest was interrupted when she was asked by a friend, Robert Cutler, whether she would consider doing two weeks of summer theatre for him at the County Theatre in Suffern, New York, in a play of her choice. Delighted, she chose to try again with *Caesar and Cleopatra*, feeling that in the ten intervening years she had perhaps grown more biologically suitable. It was the triumph she had hoped the earlier production might have been. Also in the cast of the play were Jose Ferrer, Dan Duryea, and Joshua Logan.

There was still nothing suitable for the 1935–36 season. The project she favored the most was an adaptation of *Pride and Prejudice*, but some intangible doubt prevented her from committing herself fully to the idea. When pressed she asked for twenty-four hours to make up her mind. An urgent message came from Miller saying it was imperative she give him an answer about *Victoria Regina* as there were problems with the rights which had to be cleared up immediately or the play would be lost. Rather reluctantly Helen picked up the script. The words on the cover were forbidding. A friend had asked what they meant. "That is the archaic way of saying Queen Victoria," she replied. "Sounds very dark brown," said the friend, and Helen agreed. Listlessly she picked through the first pages. Gradually she became engrossed. Then she began to feel excited. It was wonderful stuff. Guests called and she hid from them, anxious that her concentration not be broken. She cabled Miller, terrified that she might have lost the part, but he cabled by return that it was secured. Anxious for a second opinion from Brownie, whose judgment of her scripts had always been unfailingly accurate, she received the reply, "No American audience is going to be interested in this play." Brownie's prediction continued, "If you go ahead with it make sure you have another play to fall back on. This play will not run more than a few weeks."

It was no hardship for Helen to visit her beloved London to confer with the author. With Mary and Ruth Gordon she sailed on the *Normandie*. Also on board were Fredric March and his wife, Florence

Eldridge. All of them were given a tremendous reception when the boat docked in Southampton. Helen could understand that Freddy March should receive such adulation but was taken completely by surprise by the reception she was given. Certainly her early films had been reasonably good, but since then she had appeared in nothing but flops. She was reckoning without the different mentality of the British who, when they take someone to their hearts, love them unreservedly and overlook their failures. In her native America a star is only as good as her last picture no matter what she may have done before. It was refreshing and encouraging to meet the warmth of such praise and she loved the English that little bit more. Wherever she went she was stopped for her autograph. Crowds would gather outside her hotel and wait for her, chanting her name when they knew she was inside. For many it might have been an irritation but Helen basked in it. It was the only tangible good to have emerged from her soul-destroying Hollywood career.

The one major point she wanted to discuss with Housman was the later scenes of the play. Throughout the entire piece Victoria had to age from young princesshood to the octagenarian Empress of India. Helen could easily identify herself as an actress with the early scenes but she was convinced it would be impossible for her to portray the aged queen. Housman simply pooh-poohed her arguments, telling her that anyone could act them. She insisted that a perfectly good ending for the play could be found in the moving and tragic death of Albert, but Housman was insistent that the play worked better if the whole sweep of her life were shown. Following her practice with Mary Stuart, Helen used the time in London to visit as many museums as she was able to view the history and relics of Victoria. Miller arranged for her to meet the Marchioness of Milford Haven who was a granddaughter of Victoria and could remember her grandmother well. She told Helen she was delighted that an American actress should be playing the part. Helen was relieved. "I have been terribly worried that I would be criticized for my American accent," Helen said, "but I believe that the queen spoke with a real German accent." The marchioness shook her head. "No, no," she said, "My grandmutter spoke chust as gut Anglish as I do." That was another problem solved. Socially Helen had a marvelous time during her short stay, being royally entertained by Charles Laughton and his wife, Elsa Lanchester. Helen thought to ask

Laughton for his advice on her old-age makeup. He suggested that she pad out her cheeks with large slices of apple. This seemed splendid advice as she loved apples and would enjoy the taste.

She would have enjoyed staying in London a longer time but she had previously signed a contract to broadcast a weekly radio program entitled "The New Penny" each Tuesday night for the season. When *Victoria Regina* eventually opened the Tuesday performance was given as a matinee because of this prior commitment.

Throughout rehearsals the most worrying aspect of the role remained the same, the two final scenes as the sixty-year-old and the eighty-year-old queen. Helen has said of her approach to acting that she is an "eliminator." By this she means that she begins rehearsals with a full-blown overstatement of everything the character might be and gradually through the weeks leading up to the first performance pares down the irrelevant aspects until she finds the simple through line which best expresses the personality of the character. However, playing these two scenes she used all the clichéd, obvious expressions of age and felt herself to be giving the performance of the worst kind of amateur. She needed a key to the character of the old lady. She had only once had to portray great age and that was in the film *The Sin of Madelon Claudet* in its last reel. As was so often the case, she had found the key to aid her portrayal of Madelon in an event in her memory. In 1921 when Helen had first crossed the Atlantic under orders from George C. Tyler, a fellow passenger on the *Olympic* had been Madame Curie, who was returning from the United States, where she had been presented with a gram of radium for her laboratory by the schoolchildren of America. Helen would watch in awe as Madame Curie's daughter hauled her mother up on deck and walked her up and down. The elderly lady was still beautiful, with her white hair held down by a black skimmer. When she approached Madelon Claudet's last scenes, Helen went to the costume department to assemble her costume herself. She knew exactly what she was looking for and found a black Spanish dancer's hat. With the gaudy rose removed she was able to feel herself as Madelon Claudet through this memory of Marie Curie. Approaching the ancient Victoria, she tried Laughton's apple slices but was so tantalized by the taste that she had to eat them. Cotton pads were less appetizing and ultimately more effective. The British designer Rex Whistler designed padded gowns for her which helped change her body shape, but all these aids are only so much window dressing to an actor who hasn't discovered the right feeling with which to fulfill the appearance. Helen tried to find a shake in her voice, palsied movements in her body, but the true key constantly eluded her. *Then it happened. One night as I lay in bed my Graddy Hayes marched across my vision. There she was and there was Victoria. She settled down inside me and took over. Graddy had been a devotee of the old queen. Hadn't she stood and cheered as Victoria's carriage had gone by? Later in her own life she began to affect a style of dress like her idol. I couldn't dissociate Victoria Regina in her scenes as the old lady from my Grandmother Hayes. I never saw anything but my Graddy in my mind's eye every night I played the part. And that was more than a thousand times.*

Had Brownie threatened to eat her hat were *Victoria Regina* the success she had predicted it could never be she would have been choking on felt and feathers when the play opened at the Broadhurst on December 26, 1935. "Miss Hayes succeeds with Victoria as she succeeded with Mary," wrote John Mason Brown, "in being a queen without ever forgetting she is a woman. [She] has the good sense and the artistic perception to realize that what makes a queen a queen is not the costume she wears when she rides through the streets in a gold coach to open Parliament, but the blood coursing through her veins and the spirit born of it."

There was tremendous applause between each scene, but the testing time came when the curtain went up on the penultimate scene of the old queen sitting in silence. "Who is it?" said someone in the audience. "That can't be Helen Hayes," said another. When finally she spoke and they realized it truly was she there was an even greater ovation. After the first performance Helen removed her headdress and bonnet but neglected to remove her makeup when the well-wishers began to appear. Seeing her later in a restaurant one woman completely failed to recognize the actress she had been praising in the dressing room, obviously imagining the elderly face to be Helen Hayes's own!

Lillian Gish recalled this performance: "She was wonderful as Victoria, playing her right through from being a girl of seventeen or eighteen. Afterward I went round and told her that the lighting was awful and was working against her. When I go and see someone I know in a play I always look for what's wrong. If it's a film, then it's set and nothing can be changed, but if there's a fault in the theatre, then it can be improved. There are so many people who come round and tell you you're wonderful and after a time you begin to believe it."

Sir John Gielgud recalled, "I saw her in *Victoria Regina* in which she was superb, giving the queen a slight German accent. She was so clever at avoiding sentimentality and her performance was exceedingly witty as well as touching, particularly in the scenes with Albert and the two final scenes as the old lady."

"Helen Hayes—what an enormous blessing she was to the beginning of my career and my life," recalled Vincent Price. "It was Miss Hayes's great and generous acceptance of a young actor that made the opening in New York and the subsequent three years such a landmark in my young life. However, almost more exciting than Helen's professional help and acceptance was the friendship that developed between us. I can never forget her many kindnesses to me, but even more I cherish her friendship. She is a very great lady and always a joy to be with!"

One visitor to the play was Queen Victoria of Spain. Helen was worried that the queen might be offended by her portrayal of her grandmother and her fears were increased when the lady failed to come to Helen's dressing room after the play as she had promised. In actual fact she had been terrified of the crowds at the stage door and requested that Helen take tea with her at her hotel the next day. "How ever did you learn so many things about my grandmother?" she asked in astonishment. "Why, you laugh like her and talk like her, and who told you of that impatient little shrug she made if anyone tried to sympathize with her or help her when she was old?" Helen smiled. "I guess all old people do the same things," she said, "or, at least, Your Majesty's grandmother and my grandmother had a great deal in common."

The whole town was ringing with her praises. Noël Coward claimed she was the greatest living actress, and the first issue of *Life* magazine echoed his sentiment. Percy Hammond wrote an article in which he discussed the relative merits of Broadway's three leading actresses. Katharine Cornell he described as "lofty and distant . . . a shrine in which any intelligent drama-worshipper may light his candles." Lynn Fontanne was "both artist and show-woman." Helen, he claimed, echoing his sentiments of a decade earlier, was "a democrat, distributing her esthetic wares via the radio, cinema and the Drama. [She] is the most far-reaching and influential of the three, and so, I believe, she is entitled to be known, for the present, at least, as our First Actress."

3

"THE MOVIES THEY MAKE in Hollywood are unreal," pronounced Charlie, "and besides, it's a crummy town to live in. Everybody out there is a genius and to be anybody you've got to be a head genius. Well, you can't be a head genius until you go to a story conference with a doctor in attendance. Even with all the lettuce they give you, it isn't worth it." Fond of the money that movies could bring but tired of the town they were made in, Ben Hecht and Charlie MacArthur started a two-man campaign to bring movies back East to where the American film began, in New York. They rented a studio in Astoria, Long Island, back in 1934 and commenced production. Their first feature *Crime Without Passion* was based on an original story by them called "Caballero of the Law." As well as writing and producing the film, the two boy wonders jointly directed it, with Claude Rains and Margo heading the cast. An unbilled Helen Hayes made a small guest appearance. Peter John Dyer in 1966 claimed it to be "a flamboyant, undisciplined, but compulsively fascinating film classic." One of its great merits was that it was realized for well under $200,000. Their next venture was equally successful. *The Scoundrel* was an odd and moody melodrama about a New York publisher who dies and whose shade returns to earth to discover the meaning of love. Although Noël Coward had appeared in a small role in a 1918 Lillian Gish film, this was to be his sound film debut. Woollcott had a leading role and turned in a creditable performance. Benchley was cast as a hog-caller who suddenly loses his voice. When the role was eliminated from the script he picketed the studio with a placard that read HOGS OF THE WORLD UNITE! It is an interesting screenplay and the pair were awarded an Oscar for the original story, but the film has dated badly. *Once in a Blue Moon,* their next film, was considered by a Boston critic to be "the worst movie ever made." *Soak the Rich* moved them up a notch. The same critic called it "the second worst movie ever made."

The two accepted a commission from Samuel Goldwyn when he was preparing his film of *Wuthering Heights* for Merle Oberon. It was one of Woollcott's favorite novels and he suspected that the two of them would ruin it unless they were supervised; he invited them to his island in Vermont to write the screenplay. Both of them knew Woollcott of old, guessed his reasons, and cooked up a great practical joke. They knew what a snoop he could be and left lying around where he might find it a phony page or two describing what happened to Heathcliff in the interim between his running away from Cathy a poor gypsy boy and his return as a wealthy gentleman. Their twist to Emily Brontë had him coming to America, fighting Indians and cattle rustlers with a pair of six-guns. Alec shrieked when he read it, "You vandals! You have raped Emily Brontë!" Smiling, Charlie replied, "She's been waiting for it for years." They managed to write the entire screenplay in eight days and it proved the basis for one of the cinema's all-time classics. As with many another film in those days, there was many another writer involved by the time filming was completed. Engaged on additional dialogue was John Huston, two years short of his directorial debut with *The Maltese Falcon*. The linking passages of the narrative were written by the actress who spoke them, Flora Robson.

Victoria Regina was taken off for the summer of 1936 and reopened at the end of August. "The New Penny" had now ended, but Helen signed a similar twenty-six week contract with the same sponsors, Sanka Coffee, for a new serial entitled "Bambi." In order to fulfill the new contract, Helen had to be at the Broadhurst by seven o'clock each Monday evening to make up and dress. She then covered herself in a hooded cloak and was driven to the radio studio, where she made her broadcast between eight and eight-thirty. A policeman would stand on the running-board of her car and a siren would be kept going as the car raced back to the Broadhurst. The curtain went up promptly at eight-thirty and Helen's first entrance was at precisely eight-forty. From the car she would hurry through the stage door to the wings, where she would drop her cloak, dab her face with powder, and step straight onto the stage.

One night Helen was invited to a party given by Moss Hart. Ruth Gordon called for her. They had both treated themselves to new evening dresses and felt like a million dollars. Helen told Ruth that Joan Crawford was coming to pick them up. In Joan walked in a white spangled hat, a white spangled dress, and white fox furs. Helen and Ruth looked at each other. When the three arrived at

Hart's home in Sutton Place, Joan Crawford swept out of the car. Helen stumbled out in her blue satin and Ruth followed in her black. Helen said, "It's Snow White and her two dwarfs."

Charlie and Helen had held onto their East End Avenue apartment where they holed up in the winter when Nyack was snowed in. Beatrice Lillie had taken an apartment in the same building. A former paramour of Charlie's, Miss Lillie, realizing she was no match for Helen in Charlie's affections, had not only graciously given up her claims on him the moment she met Helen but had begun a lifelong friendship with her. From the back windows of the apartments they had a good view of Welfare Island with its hospital for criminal cases. They had often seen the ferry taking visitors over to the island, and one day the three of them decided to climb aboard and spent the afternoon in exploration of the environs. Returning to the ferry in time to get back for Helen's and Bea's evening performances, they were asked to show their passes. "What passes?" asked Charlie. It seemed all visitors had to have passes. "My good man," exclaimed Bea, "Can't you see who we are? I'm Beatrice Lillie, Lady Peel. This is Helen Hayes, the First Lady of the American Stage, and this is Charles MacArthur, the playwright." The glowering guard said, "Oh yeah? And I'm Napoleon Bonaparte." Repeating their story to the officers at the local police station to which they had been hauled, they were allowed to make one telephone call. They chose to call Bea's doctor, who sometimes held a clinic on Welfare Island. All they could summon was his answering service! Despairingly Bea demanded that the answering service try to track him down and gave the number where they could be reached, preparing if necessary to spend the night there. Fortunately the doctor called in and he was able to effect their release. Both actresses had to play their respective performances without dinner. A sympathetic Charlie waited dinner too.

Although she could have commanded a queen's ransom for her role as Victoria, Helen chose to receive only twenty-five hundred dollars a week during the run of the play. Although, even today, this is a substantial amount of money, at that very same time Gertrude Lawrence was commanding a weekly salary of six times that sum. Helen preferred not to take too much money out of the theatre, thus ensuring longer runs for the other people in the cast. One day she was walking down Broadway and heard two women talking. "Isn't that Helen Hayes?" said one. "No, it can't be," said the other, "Helen Hayes would never wear such a shabby coat." Helen's vanity was aroused. She still had not learned to be the kind of star offstage that Mr. Tyler had wanted her to be. She decided to make immediate amends and ordered a fabulous sable coat. The very same day she passed an art gallery in her taxi and saw an exquisite Renoir in the window. It was the *Girl in the Lace Hat*, which seemed to suggest the way she hoped Mary would grow up. She stopped the taxi, paid off the driver, and went in and bought the painting. The sable coat was canceled and she made do with the coat the women had despised. The picture gave her much more pleasure over the years than the satisfaction of her vanity in front of strangers could ever have done.

Her friend Ruth Gordon had made an enormous impact in Tyrone Guthrie's production of Wycherley's *The Country Wife* when it had opened at the Old Vic in London that October. Helen suggested to Gilbert Miller that they co-produce a transfer to Broadway. Together they put up forty thousand dollars, and the play was a great success when it opened at the Henry Miller at the beginning of December. It closed in New York after eighty-nine performances. Miller took it off before it began to lose money. Helen, ever generous to actors, suggested he leave it to run another week to see if, in actual fact, it would begin to lose. However, the practical businessman won. It was useful experience for Helen to learn another facet of theatre.

In the summer break between bouts of Victoria, Helen had finally met George Bernard Shaw. He had not forgotten that Helen, then a mere ingenue, had once stood him up. "You're appearing in Housman's *Victoria*, aren't you?" he asked. "Yes, Mr. Shaw," she had replied. She knew that he was an admirer of the play, or at least Housman had told her he was. He got his revenge on that long ago slight. "Silly little part, isn't it?" he said.

4

Victoria Regina finally closed on Broadway on May 29, 1937, after 517 performances. The following September saw the start of a tour of the play which would last for almost ten months. There were several cast changes. Werner Bateman took over the role of Albert.

One of the new cast members was Helen's old friend from *Golden Days*, Alexander Clark, Jr. "Helen was still the lovely person she always was," recalled Alec. "She was an impulsive person. I remember a time during the intervening years when a brand-new car, a Ford I think, was delivered to her. We were going to the races, she and I, maybe it was Belmont. We got in the car. 'Do you know how to drive it?' I said. 'I think so,' said she. Without stopping to figure everything out she just started it and we were off. 'It'll be all right,' she yelled. Fortunately it was!

"She was extraordinary and wonderful as Victoria. There was one scene in the play where she had to cry. We toured altogether for nearly two years, I guess, but she shed real tears in that scene every single performance. She was a terrible giggler too. Once she starts laughing she'll laugh right through a scene. I remember Orson Welles's 'War of the Worlds' broadcast. That was on a Sunday night. The next night the whole city, the whole world was talking about it. Every actor in the play was in one scene only except for the actor who played Albert. In the scene preceding mine I was backstage waiting. Helen wasn't on and she and I were talking about the Martian invasion, how everyone was fooled. And I told her the funniest thing I'd read was some man in New Jersey who had received a phone call from his friend in New York saying, 'Hey Jim, what's happening out there?' Jim replied, 'Don't bother me. The world's coming to an end and I've got a lot to do!' Helen burst out laughing and she laughed all through the third scene. She tried to hold it in but I kept hearing this giggle. After that the stage manager made a rule that no one could talk to Miss Hayes in any scene backstage.

"There was another time in Chicago. There was a Chinese restaurant around the corner. Somehow smoke from it got in the theatre near the beginning of the play. She could see several people at the back part of the orchestra walking out. Finally, after about five minutes of it she stopped and said, 'Ladies and gentlemen, don't you want to see how the play comes out? Everything's under control'—though of course she didn't know what was wrong—'and we're going right on.' Everyone still in the theatre returned to their seats. Her quick thinking saved the show. We reached New Year's Eve in Philadelphia. In the last scene, she was wheeled on in a wheelchair. The whole court was on the stage. Charlie MacArthur was there. They were going on somewhere afterward. He'd bought one of those long tin horns, about a foot and a half long. Just before that scene began he said to Helen, 'I dare you to blow it in the middle of the scene,' and pushed it into the seat as she was being wheeled on. Well, of course she didn't blow it in the scene, but as the curtain went up on the first curtain call she whipped it out and gave it a glorious blast! The audience loved it, of course."

Afraid that she might grow stale in the part, Helen decided to mount a production of *The Merchant of Venice* with members of the company which they could present for the occasional matinee. Abraham Sofaer, who was playing Disraeli, had played Shylock in England and repeated his role, also directing the play with Helen as Portia and Alec Clark as Bassanio. It was a great success and Helen was the first actress many heard who treated the "quality of mercy" speech without the reverent solemnity with which the lines were associated. "She treats Portia's decision about 'no drop of blood'— the turning point of the trial—as an inspiration of the moment," recorded a Chicago critic. "It comes to Portia out of the blue . . . Miss Hayes pauses in her speech, opens her eyes wide, breathes an 'Ah' and then proceeds to give Shylock the works."

Another diversion was having Mary along for part of the tour in the small nonspeaking role of Princess Ena. Shirley Temple was her idol. They were both about the same age. When the tour reached Los Angeles, an introduction was arranged. At first Shirley, impeccably trained to do just that, spoke to Mary as if she were any fan. "Do you like milk?" intoned Miss Temple. "No," replied Mary bluntly. "Oh, you must drink your milk and eat your spinach," recited Miss Temple. Then she noted a hint of boredom creeping into Mary's expression and asked her a professional question. "Are you an actress?" she inquired. "Oh yes," said Mary. "In pictures?" continued Shirley. "Oh no," replied Miss MacArthur grandly, "I only play in the legitimate theatre."

After the first leg of the tour was over Helen paid another visit to the County Theatre at Suffern where she laid the ghost of *What Every Woman Knows* in much the same way as she had done two years previously with *Caesar and Cleopatra.* An unprecedented step was taken when, previous to the second leg of the tour, *Victoria Regina* was presented once more in New York, this time at the Martin Beck where it played for eighty-seven performances. Brooks Atkinson, in reviewing the play for the second time, reported, "Since she first appeared as England's doughtiest monarch nearly three years ago Miss Hayes has not been perfunctorily repeating. She has found ways to enrich her performance. She acts it more easily now; the whole range of the character is well inside the compass of her playing. She is completely relaxed . . . when Miss Hayes first played the part the two scenes of venerability seemed no better than good mummery to this playgoer . . . Miss Hayes has now got through the imposing make-up into the weary, patient heart of a simple old lady."

On the very last night in Pittsburgh she left the farewell party after only the briefest sip of champagne so that she could make the midnight train, longing to be back with Charlie and the children as soon as she possibly could. *Out in the alley there was a huge crowd waiting. The company manager pleaded with them to keep clear of my car, explaining the reason for my haste. The car had to back out of the alley, which was very narrow, and the driver had to maneuver with great caution. The crowd reluctantly spread and gave ground. But one voice began chanting, and it was taken up by many others until as we backed out of the alley all I could hear was, "You stink! You stink! You stink!" Only because I had not stopped to sign my autograph.* This was the last memory given her by her public for the greatest success of her career. Thus ended the reign of *Victoria Regina.*

5

CAROL FRINK had made a dramatic return into their lives. Not having been able to produce her great American novel, she had returned to journalism. Among other things she had reviewed films. In her review of *The Sin of Madelon Claudet* she had spent several column inches describing the film and its story. The review ended "Madelon Claudet was played by Helen Hayes." Perhaps it is unreasonable to expect that there would be any love lost for her former husband's second wife, but what took place toward the end of the thirties was entirely unreasonable in anyone's book. She brought a one-hundred-thousand-dollar alienation-of-affection suit claiming that Helen had "maliciously and willfully" snatched Charlie from her. Benchley, Woollcott, Marc Connelly, and Ben Hecht all attested in depositions that Helen had not, in fact, met Charlie until after he was separated. Helen had opted for an open trial because she wanted to be cleared in the public's eyes and for Mary to be free of the insinuations made about her parents. When Charlie took the stand the members of the public present were frequently told to stop applauding his rather flippant approach to some of the questions asked. On the third day of the trial Carol suddenly called off her suit. Later she told a reporter, "I never did want any of her money. I just wanted a chance to tell my story."

Helen's return to the theatre after *Victoria Regina* was to be in a play by Ladislaus Bus-Fekete, reworked and rewritten by Charlie and Ben. She had planned a year away from the theatre but soon became restless and was pleased when this project materialized. The play was tried out in Santa Barbara with Herbert Marshall as leading man. However, Philip Merivale was opposite her when the play opened at the Martin Beck on October 17, 1939. There were opening-night telegrams from Florence and Freddy; Lynn and Alf; Dorothy Parker wired, HELEN HAYES YOU STOP BEING SO GOOD; another read I LOVE YOU I LOVE YOU I LOVE YOU I LOVE YOU I LOVE YOU I LOVE YOU I LOVE YOU I LOVE YOU I LOVE YOU I LOVE YOU, signed Gertie Susan Skylark Lawrence; a further one read GREETINGS TO THE MOST EXCITING OF ALL ACTRESSES and was signed Katharine Hepburn. Miss Hepburn was and has remained a great fan. "I don't really know Helen Hayes," she indicated recently, "just sort of how do you do—but when I had just started she was very very nice to me. She said something which made a great impression on me—'Oh, you can say anything really if you're any good.' She has certainly been and continues to be—extraordinary—in the theatre and out of it."

She needed all the support that could be mustered. Her part in *Ladies and Gentlemen* was as a stenographer to a movie star. Many were not prepared to accept her in anything less than a queenly role. Had the play been a better piece of theatre she might have been forgiven. One critic, however, said she had never appeared in anything so trashy since *Golden Days.* It was virtually impossible to follow an act like Victoria without disappointing someone. Rather than let herself become typecast again she had chosen to go completely against type and it was rather unfair of the critics not to give her some support in this. Audiences, on the whole, were prepared to give her the benefit of the doubt and the play ran for about four months, rather longer than the five weeks notched up by *Golden Days,* and the run was followed by a tour.

HELEN HAYES

Sad news came in Cincinnati on March 1, 1940. Her father had died. *My father was a very passive man yet it was to him that I turned in times of stress over the years. Toward the end of his life I bought him a little house in Chesapeake Bay, Md. Oh, he just loved that place. I remember one time Mother was at home and she was drinking pretty heavily by then and Father went down there by himself. I wondered if he was lonely, so I called him and asked if he wanted me to bring Mother down there too. He said, "Now, daughter, don't do that to me. You keep her away now." I realized he wasn't lonely but had found his peace.*

Brownie, as Helen indicates here, had reverted to the prop which had supported that Essie of long ago when she had been frustrated in her hopes of a career for her daughter and a future for herself. Over the last decade she had gradually been eased out of Helen's life though with no malicious intent on Helen's part. To begin with, Helen had engaged a maid to help her in the dressing room, but first she had asked Brownie's opinion. She engaged the maid to make life easier for Brownie. She had engaged coaches to help her technique. After Frances Robinson-Duff had died she had moved on to Constance Collier. Brownie had continued as her manager until Helen signed with Gilbert Miller. Recently she had proved she was dispensable as a script reader. Now Brownie's place on opening nights was in the orchestra and not in the wings. In order to find activity in her life she had decided to write a book about Helen's life thus far. Ruth Gorden suggested she write it in the form of letters to her granddaughter and it was as *Letters to Mary* that it was published in 1940. To her surprise Charlie wrote an affectionate foreword. The book out of the way, there was little to fill her life. She wasn't content simply to be a grandmother though this role filled her with joy. The poison of alcoholism was already in her veins and she gave in to the bottle more and more.

As a young child I couldn't understand why she was always so extraordinarily gay. But, as I became older, I realized that if ever she allowed herself to stop laughing, she would have broken down and cried. She was a very witty person and there was always a crowd around her laughing, including myself. As the years have gone by I have understood her better and have more compassion. She was a woman who loved to meet challenges and somehow life didn't hold enough for her.

DAME FLORA ROBSON recalled, "Helen Hayes was an enchanting actress. She had the ability to see into the *soul* of a character. Just by coming downstage and tilting her head to one side she could win everyone's heart. Such sweetness could have been cloying in another but in Helen Hayes it was coupled with an insight so original, so uniquely her own, that she stood out from all of her contemporaries. How splendid that she is known as the First Lady of the American Theatre. It is an accolade she alone deserves."

You know that title bothers me so much. I made up my own title: "The Great White Goddess of the American Stage" or sometimes, when overweight, "the Holy Cow." In 1975 she claimed, *I would never like to be known as a great or important actress. I do think I could be known as a professional. I brought out in me the best I could deliver.* Life magazine, in the late thirties, did a feature on Broadway's best and gathered Helen, Lynn Fontanne, and Katharine Cornell together for a memorable photograph. *Look at Lynn, the glamorous woman of the world. And Kit, the noble. And me, the fading ingenue.*

There is in Helen's self-effacing attitude at the same time a certain charm and a somewhat irritating lack of sensitivity for those who love her. The fact that she cannot accept that she has changed people's lives and enriched their souls somehow betrays the trust audiences place in her. She once said that every time she signed a contract she believed this would be the time she would be "found out." Every actor is defensive against failure but Helen always seems to have been preparing for that day by proclaiming herself a failure in advance or, at least, to be less than others claimed. In an extremely generous woman there is here the lack of a generosity of spirit which would permit a gracious acceptance of the compliments many have felt her due.

One of her more memorable interpretations followed *Ladies and Gentlemen*. At the age of forty she essayed her first major classical role on Broadway, that of the teenage Viola in Shakespeare's *Twelfth Night*, which Burns Mantle claimed won her a definite place in the company of the great. *I had actually been moved to tears when, as a girl, I had read this story told by Shakespeare in some of his more lyrical lines. Unfortunately when it came to playing the part I was taken with an ailment common among us actors when we approach the bard—I caught the syntax jitters and the quotation blues. Finally I began to relax, to enjoy the part. I no longer trembled when oft-quoted passages of the play came from my lips in what I thought might be violations of preordained syntax. Instead I caught the essence of Shakespeare's character and reduced it further to the simplest human terms.* During the rehearsal period director Margaret Webster brought in a replacement actor for the role of Orsino. "She had me read the first scene with Miss Hayes before the regular rehearsal began," recalled Wesley Addy. "Book in hand I still managed to put my arm around her shoulder and tousle her hair. I felt an immediate acceptance of me as Orsino—I gave what she needed as Viola, recognition of her youth and assurance that her disguise as a boy was working. It was a happy company in a style which only survives today in the Royal Shakespeare Company. I have never lost over these many years my warmth and respect for this bubbling lady with an inner core of such strength. She knew what she wanted as an individual and needed as an actress. She had the energy and directness to secure them."

With a fine Malvolio in Maurice Evans, *Twelfth Night* opened at the St. James Theatre on November 19, 1940. Richard Watts, Jr., found Helen's portrayal one of "sweet and tender loveliness . . . a glowing delight . . . lyric, warm, human, humorous and incredibly moving." Brooks Atkinson was not so impressed, feeling that she dwelt on the gaucherie in the role and not the inherent breeding. Neither did he like her conversational reading of the lines; it wanted poetry, in his estimation. Helen chose to play the role as it is now always played and was one of the first to break away from traditional patterns set by Julia Marlowe and Jane Cowl. She made Viola into the kind of human being everyone knows and not a heroine on a removed plane. Cornell could play the grandeur of a Cleopatra, Judith Anderson could portray the austerity of Lady Macbeth, Fontanne could fulfill the extrovert Shrew, but in the theatre of her day only Helen could bring magic to Viola.

In order to play down some of the customary theatricality which attended Shakespeare on Broadway, Peggy Webster asked Helen to throw away "It is too hard a knot for me to untie" on her exit from Act II, Scene iii, as a round of applause on her exit would interrupt the flow into the next scene. Helen managed successfully to leave the stage in silence for several performances but suddenly, even though she had not altered her playing in any way, the applause came. One evening as she left the stage, out of the corner of her eye she saw Maurice Evans in the wings making one loud clap with his hands which succeeded in inspiring the audience to follow suit.

All of the *Twelfth Night* cast were shocked to hear the news that Middle Temple Hall in London had been devastated by a German bomb. It was in this hall that one of the earliest performances of *Twelfth Night* had been staged in February 1602. Some years later Helen would visit the restored building. Though the original had been leveled to the ground, the stage on which the Chamberlain's men had performed had remained intact. With an audience only of workmen putting the last touches to the restoration, Helen, with great emotion, recreated a part of her performance of Viola and spoke the lovely words of the "willow cabin" speech.

Twelfth Night chalked up a respectable run of 129 performances before going out on tour. During the tour the play had a profound effect on one member of its audience. "Helen was my great heroine then and now," she recalled. "When I saw her in *Twelfth Night* I was about thirteen or fourteen. Helen had a beautiful hairdo—I don't know if it was a wig or not—but I loved her little halo of curls—and went to the hairdressers in Grosse Point, Michigan, clutching a picture of Helen in the play and said, 'You must make me look like Helen Hayes.' My hair is straight and was quite long then. It was all cut off and I was given my first permanent wave. I cried when I saw the result—I wasn't Helen Hayes and it took a long time for those baked curls to grow out!" She wasn't Helen Hayes, but she *was* Julie Harris and would eventually enjoy her own particular eminence as a Broadway star.

Just before we were to close, the day before, to be exact, I came offstage and telephoned Charlie. I told him that I had finally learned the secret of playing Viola. He laughed and said, wasn't it a bit late? "I'll be able to have two more goes at it," I said. It was the willow-cabin speech which did the trick for me. Viola's life and soul were manifested to me in these few lines. The important thing to remember is that the playwright's message is not evident in the text alone. This is a happy phenomenon of all plays: the ultimate completion of the part lies in a wonderful kind of cooperation between playwright and actor.

CHARLIE REALIZED early in 1941 that American involvement in the war in Europe was virtually inevitable and volunteered his services. He and Ben scripted an immense political pageant which was staged in Madison Square Garden and entitled *Fun to Be Free*. Roosevelt's Secretary of War, Henry L. Stimson, congratulated the two of them, saying, "Our country is in your debt." Charlie wanted nothing more than to enlist as a private as he had done in two previous skirmishes.

Shortly after he and Helen had been married they were celebrating New Year's Eve in Chicago's Tavern Club. Charlie spotted Colonel Milton Foreman, who had led the Pancho Villa campaign in Mexico. "Come and meet my first colonel," he suggested, and led Helen over to his table. Hearing the name MacArthur the gentleman began to splutter furiously and marched away from them. "Can he still be angry about the victory parade, do you suppose?" mused Charlie. Spectators on Madison Street, Chicago, saw the procession headed by a battered Ford draped in a huge American flag with two whores borrowed from Madame Farrington's brothel chained to the sides as representative Mexican prisoners, with Charlie yelling at the top of his voice, "Long live Tinpants Milton Foreman!" He was placed under military arrest. Seemingly it had been a memorable experience for Foreman.

Ben Hecht claimed, "In MacArthur's odd response to war there was nothing callous. Nor was there bellicosity or avid patriotism in his penchant for the battlefields. He was lured to them as the poet is lured to sunset and moonlight. His dark friend, the ever-beckoning One, was there." One of Charlie's anecdotes of World War I ran thus, "It was on the way to Cantigny. Our battery was enfiladed by enemy fire on a railway embankment. The Heinies had drawn a bead on us and were peppering us with big shells. We'd been ordered to halt, and stand by our half-witted artillery horses. I stood watching the goddamn shells explode, each a few inches nearer my toes. Finally our officer came out of his siesta and gave the order to take cover. I let go my nag and dived off the embankment. I landed head first in an abandoned German latrine. Smothered by enemy crap, and with shells blasting all around, I got an optimistic feeling. I said to myself, 'MacArthur, this is the lowest point of your life. From here on everything has got to be an improvement.' "

Victoria and Albert. With Vincent Price in *Victoria Regina*.
Vandamm/Billy Rose Collection

Later that same evening, her Graddy Hayes impersonation in the penultimate scene.
Vandamm/Billy Rose Collection

"With me you may never be rich, but you'll never be bored," said Charlie.

Billy Rose Collection

Brownie penning one of her letters to Mary. Daughter and granddaughter look on.

Vandamm/Billy Rose Collection

With Jamie and Mary.

Vandamm/Billy Rose Collection

At forty she was disguised as a boy again. As Viola in *Twelfth Night*.

As Harriet Beecher Stowe,
with Edward Abel and
Mildred Taswell in *Harriet.*
Vandamm/Billy Rose Collection

She won her first Tony
Award as the prim librarian
who let her hair down in
Happy Birthday, here with
Margaret Irving, Charles
Gordon, Jack Diamond,
and Jacqueline Paige.
Vandamm/Billy Rose Collection

Like mother like daughter.

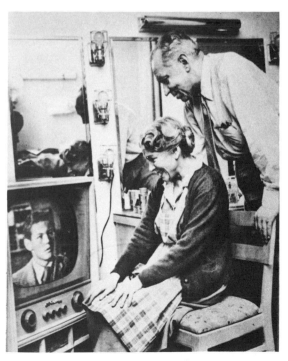

Jim's television debut watched by
two proud MacArthurs.

The role which was hers by error. In *Anastasia* with Ingrid Bergman.

Twentieth Century Fox

A *grande dame* she wasn't, but she won her second Tony Award for *Time Remembered*, here with Susan Strasberg.

Vandamm/Billy Rose Collection

Stuffy dowager turned maid-of-all-work in *Mrs. McThing.*

Louis Melançon/Billy Rose Collection

Universal

Ada Quonsett in *Airport* earned her a second Oscar. It was to prove the archetypal role of her later years.

Her Aunt Mamie impersonation in
The Show-Off, with members of the
touring company—George Pentecost,
Jennifer Harmon, Clayton Corzatte,
Suzanne Grossman, James Greene,
and her old friend Alexander Clark.

Still box office! Issuing the first tickets
at the second Helen Hayes Theatre.
The theatre means she is still
represented on Broadway more than
three quarters of a century after *Old
Dutch.*   *Courtesy Helen Hayes Theatre*

"Get me back to the trenches," he pleaded with the Army in 1941. Told that modern warfare didn't involve trenches, he said, "Now I can see how badly I'm needed. Someone has got to show you how it's done." Ultimately he was commissioned a major, later to be promoted to colonel, in the Chemical Warfare Service in what was mainly a desk job. His poor physical condition, the result of years of heavy drinking, was the cause. Helen later told a friend that being chained to a desk virtually for the duration rather than finding the active service which would have stimulated him, he began to drink even more heavily.

Helen had also responded to the war effort in a Maxwell Anderson play *Candle in the Wind,* which sought to disclose the full inhumanity of the Nazi regime by means of the story of an actress's determined efforts to have a French journalist released from a concentration camp. It was a play which dealt passionately with its theme but which was rather pedestrian in its writing. It had a moderate run in New York, where it opened under Alfred Lunt's direction on October 22, 1941, at the Shubert, followed by a tour. *The government must feel that* Candle in the Wind *is good propaganda, because we have been given priorities on transportation of company and baggage and scenery—and a lot of it.* Helen did her best to help the USO and other defense organizations by making as many public appearances as she could. However, as she said at the time, she wished she were a blues singer because then she could do so much more.

"Many years ago," recalled President Ronald Reagan, "an American patriotic poem was set to music to the noble strains of the national anthem of Great Britain, 'God Save the Queen.' Our American poem, however, lost much in the transposition because, in order to fit the music, it had to be badly phrased. During World War II a great ceremony was held in Soldier Field Stadium in Chicago. Helen Hayes was introduced to a crowd of 125,000. Looking so tiny down on the floor of the great stadium she recited the poem, the words that everyone in the crowd had sung hundreds of times. I think it was the first time we had ever heard the beauty of those words. The silence when she finished was, I'm sure, a greater ovation than any she had ever received. Perhaps others could be effective in reading that poem, but would anyone else think of it?"

About this time Helen began to realize that though her responsibilities both to her public and her country were important considerations, she had for too long been overlooking her responsibilities to her home and to her family. Weeks out on the road meant that she had little time to offer to her children and she was missing seeing them growing up. She was determined to have a sabbatical year. Brownie wrote to her: "My dearest, I do believe you will stick to that decision of a sabbatical year, for no matter how cheerfully you wrote I could sense that loneliness for your family. I know nothing could make the children happier than to know that you will be at home and reachable at a moment's notice. As for Charlie he is like a lost spirit when you are away. I won't say anything about my feelings, for I failed you so many times when you were at home. I'll just prove to you how happy it will make me."

There was soon a temporary fifth member to the family. When Helen had been touring in *Victoria Regina* a special train had been used to ferry the company to each new venue. The railroad even had a poster emblazoned with a portrait of her in color, bearing the legend, "QUEEN OF THE STAGE, QUEEN OF THE FILMS, QUEEN OF THE AIR." The queen had a drawing room entirely to herself, which was sometimes pleasant, sometimes less so. Often she would sit in lonely seclusion wishing she could join in the happy-go-lucky sing-songs she heard from the other carriages, but suspecting she might have the dampening effect she had feared from Gillette at her covert smoking parties all those years before. One night the train was halted and she saw outside a magic tapestry of snow and stars. She rushed into the next carriage and told them to turn out the lights and look outside. Everyone's eyes widened, as there stood the Empress of India in cold cream and curlers. One of the English girls in the company said in a deadpan voice, "Just one quick click for the *Pic* and I'll die happy!" The actress, Bunty Cobb, became a great friend from that moment. As a mark of her friendship, Helen persuaded Bunty to send her little boy, Charles MacNaughton, to stay at Nyack during the Blitz. He proved a great playmate for Jamie. When at the end of the war he left for home, the child "doubled up in sorrow" at leaving such good times behind him.

During 1941 Helen had a radio series entitled "Helen Hayes Theatre," which in 1942 was retitled "Helen Hayes Theatre of the Air" in which each week she performed in a single play. Several of these were versions of movie hits such as *Arrowsmith* and *A Farewell to Arms*, others celebrated hits in the theatre such as *What Every*

Woman Knows and an adaptation of *Victoria Regina* entitled *Victoria and Albert,* in which she was again partnered by Vincent Price. There were adaptations of *A Star Is Born, Mayerling* (opposite Brian Aherne), *The Late Christopher Bean, Jane Eyre, Tovarich,* and many others. It was in the second of these seasons that she finally played in Eugene O'Neill's *The Straw.* One of the great jokes of the time was that her show was the chief competitor of another, which starred Charlie McCarthy, the wooden dummy of ventriloquist Edgar Bergen, with whose name her own Charlie's was, and is still, frequently confused.

Helen appeared as herself in the film *Stage Door Canteen* which like *Hollywood Canteen* attempted to show what the stars were doing for servicemen. It gave quite a false picture. There were never many stars in attendance. Besides, the men didn't go there to have tea with Katharine Cornell but to dance with the showgirls who were always there in plentiful numbers.

When she had closed in *Candle in the Wind,* Helen had said, "I can't bring myself to think of the strain of another Broadway opening night," saying that she would retire and devote herself entirely to the radio. Charlie added, "I've heard her make that speech annually and she's always back." Should there be a return to the theatre it would have to be in a play which reflected the current situation but which did it more eloquently than the Anderson play had done. Charlie came up with an inspiring idea, a play about Harriet Beecher Stowe whose book started a war which rid America of slavery. After a short search for a script they found that the University of Syracuse was presenting just such a play for two or three performances. The young authors were astonished when the eminent actress visited their theatre. They were stunned when she bought their play.

Charlie's creative drive was petering out. One day Helen confided her fears about this to F. Scott Fitzgerald, who was paying a visit. "Helen," he said to her, "What difference does it make whether he produces masterpieces for four people around a dinner table or for four million readers of the *Saturday Evening Post?* The chances are that those people at the dinner table understand and appreciate him more than the four million. There are some people," he added, "who have to *do* in order to make their mark. They have to perform, they have to contribute. And there are some people who only have to *be.* Charlie is one of these." Nevertheless Helen remained concerned.

She also felt that seeing her too much around the house made him even more disconsolate than he might have been had she been pursuing her professional career. It dispirited him to have her see him idle. Although it was pleasant for the children to have her around they missed the energy she brought from the theatre. "Here, in beaming comedy, is proof that the hand that rules the cradle rocks the world," wrote John Anderson when *Harriet,* under the direction of Elia Kazan, opened at the Henry Miller Theatre on March 3, 1943. It played on Broadway for thirteen months and was followed by a long tour.

Charlie did eventually get to the real war. Fellow screenwriter Herman J. Mankiewicz claimed he was the secret weapon of the Chemical Corps. "They'll fly over Berlin holding him head over heels," he quipped. "Then when he breathes on the city it will fall." Charlie managed to trick a B-52 bombardier into taking him along, posing as an observer for Montgomery. Asked why Monty hadn't sent an Englishman, Charlie replied that his father was born British and added, "And I drink scotch." When they got over Berlin, Charlie produced a pile of whisky bottles stuffed with toilet tissue. "Drop them on the German high command," he ordered.

"Darling," Charlie wrote home, "We've come from Greenland's icy mountains to India's coral strands, in the words of the old hymn, and the end is not yet. I can't tell you where we are, of course, but I think the censor won't mind my saying that en route here we paused for gas near the Taj Mahal and dropped over for a visit. It's an exquisite thing, quite worthy of the legend (which you will find in my guide book on India). The priests howled prayers that echoed forever from the lovely dome, then blessed us and bestowed a love flower which I enclose. Treat it with care. It cost five rupees, along with the sandals I had to wear over my shoes. Despite war, India comes up to expectations, all jasmine and poverty, purple and rags, with the scent of sandalwood everywhere. They're nearing the end of the monsoon and warm rain falls most of the day, but flowers bloom everywhere, even from behind the ears of little children. Pony carts spank along, stopping only for the sacred Brahma cows, and turbans glow with all the colors of the rainbow. The air is heavy and sweet and damp, with insects by the trillions, cigarettes, clothing, food all slightly mildewed, but who the hell cares? They tell me it's wonderful in a month or two . . ."

When he returned to Nyack from the Eastern Theatre of War he tossed a small, heavy bag into Helen's lap. When she opened it she discovered it was brimful of emeralds. "I wish they were peanuts," said Charlie.

8

IT WOULD SEEM that Mary had always been destined to be a professional actress. When she returned late at night after her debut in *Victoria Regina*, Charlie asked how she had gotten on. "I didn't get paid," she protested. Jamie made his first stage appearance during *Harriet*, though this wasn't his official debut. Playing backstage, he heard his mother's voice. "My son! Where is my son?" Not realizing it was a line from the play, on Jamie ran. "Here I am, Mommie!" he cried.

Neither Helen nor Charlie wanted either of their children to be actors, which perhaps goes some way to explaining why both of them became just that. Most actors started out as children who were ignored or overlooked in some way and chose to pursue a career in which they could find approval. This was certainly true in Helen's case. However, actors' children who choose to pursue the same profession often do so because they see an opportunity to extend the joys of childhood play and fantasy into adulthood. From an early age they appreciate and are not afraid of the hard work which goes into an actor's life. They also see what fun it can be.

To Helen's relief Mary showed no early aspirations to the theatre. In 1935 Helen said, *Mary hasn't shown any tendency toward acting, and I think I'm just as well pleased. She's going to enjoy the childhood I missed. I don't for a minute regret my childhood. I love to look back on it. But I suppose it's quite natural that I should like to experience vicariously the happy-go-lucky life of a little girl. Mary probably won't have any more fun than I did, and I wouldn't be sorry if something caused her to fall into acting as I did. But I'm not going to nudge Destiny and point out Mary. I'll let things take their course.*

In its own time Destiny intervened and pointed Mary toward the theatre. By this time Helen was only too pleased to share her delight and share the stage with her in her professional debut. As Barrie's *Dear Brutus* had launched Helen on a major career, so it seemed would Barrie's *Alice-Sit-by-the-Fire* for Mary. Joshua Logan's produc-

HELEN HAYES

tion of the play opened at the Bucks County Playhouse, New Hope, Pennsylvania, on July 15, 1946, with Helen, Mary, and Mary's friend Bethel Leslie in the cast.

The night we opened I lost myself watching the magic flare up in Mary's eyes as she spoke to me on the stage. If you have that, you can learn the rest. If you haven't got it, nothing else counts. All the technique, all the training will do no good. Mary had the star on her forehead, I could see. I became so excited that I forgot my lines. She had to prompt me.

The following summer Mary toured with Lillian Gish in *The Marquise*. "Have you any instructions about taking care of her?" asked Lillian. "No," replied Helen, "she'll take care of you." The same year Mary appeared in Emlyn Williams's *The Corn Is Green* at Olney Theatre, in Maryland. Mary rang home to ask if Jim, as Jamie had insisted he be called, his other name seeming suddenly too babyish, could come and play one of the miner's children in the play. "It'll be such fun having him here," she said, "all smudged-up and Welsh and everything, and you know I'll take care of him." *The acting bug bit him so hard I had to put my foot down to keep him off the stage. I don't want him to run into the sort of unhappiness and maladjustment that happens when boy actors fail to bridge the gap between boyhood and maturity professionally. Girls, who don't have to face the prospect of being breadwinners for the rest of their lives, make the adjustment more easily. If Jim still wants to act when he's older, he'll get my blessing.*

Helen's own career took a new and exciting turn in 1946. Six years earlier she and Charlie had entertained his old friend Anita Loos at "21." Helen had complained of the critics' response to *Ladies and Gentlemen*. She felt they were insisting she typecast herself as grandiose queenly characters and suggested that Anita write her a really rowdy part where she could kick up her heels. Once upon a time she had almost played Lorelei in *Gentlemen Prefer Blondes* and loved Anita's brand of humor. "How would you like to play a drunk?" Anita asked. "A drunk?" asked Helen. "How about a frustrated old maid, a teetotaler who is against everyone having fun? She gets gloriously tight one evening and during a twelve-hour bender becomes an understanding and sympathetic human being?" Helen's eyes glowed. "Go ahead and write it," she said.

"It's always good news when Helen Hayes is in town," wrote George Freedley when *Happy Birthday* opened at the Broadhurst on October 31, 1946, "but it is particularly good news that she has

150

found a role quite out of the ordinary which delighted her first night audience . . . She sings a new song by Richard Rodgers and Oscar Hammerstein II entitled "I Haven't Got a Worry in the World" along with a mock-opera aria and acquitted herself well. She dances in a spotlight [and] bops her poor old father over the head with a liquor bottle. . . . In other words Our Helen had an evening for herself and audiences are going to like her better than ever." On the whole the other critics were in accord. However Robert Garland of the New York *Journal-American* wrote an extremely bitchy review. "What I'm wondering is how Helen Hayes got mixed up in it," it concluded. "Maybe she's been seeing too much of Charles MacArthur." Normally Helen never read reviews but everyone was so incensed about this one that she spared it a glance. Garland had never taken a line against her like this before, and it seemed so unjustified in the light of the other press the play had received. "What am I going to do about him?" Helen kept saying, "What am I going to do?" As usual Charlie came up with the answer. "Oh, toss him a poisoned choirboy," he suggested.

The play ran for 564 performances and Helen received the accolade of the first Best Actress Tony Award, presented to her at the Waldorf-Astoria Hotel on April 6, 1947. The play finally closed in March 1948. Four months later Helen made her debut in London's West End.

Some years later, when questioned as to which were the ten most memorable stage performances she had seen, she listed John Barrymore's Hamlet, Laurence Olivier's Oedipus, Shirley Booth in *Come Back Little Sheba*, Pauline Lord in *They Knew What They Wanted*, Marlon Brando in *A Streetcar Named Desire (He exuded a kind of animal magnetism that was exactly right for the part. Very few people can get away with an insolent performance such as Brando's, but it's nice to watch those who can, and I have a secret admiration for them. When I am on stage I find myself always trying to give the audience their money's worth and I guess I just like to see someone to whom this means nothing.),* Mary Martin in *South Pacific*, W. C. Fields in *Poppy*, Frank Fay in *Harvey*, Jane Cowl as Juliet, and Laurette Taylor as Amanda Wingfield in *The Glass Menagerie. There was a beauty about Laurette in this role—the beauty of her eyes, her hands, her smile and especially her voice—that illuminated the character with a kind of radiance, and magic that was peculiarly her own. She somehow managed to get sympathy into a part that was written in anger.*

Helen had caught Miss Taylor's performance during its second week of tryout in Chicago when she had been touring with *Harriet.* She had gone along with high hopes. Laurette Taylor had been one of her greatest idols in the theatre. Once upon a time Helen had inscribed a photograph to her, "To Laurette my guiding star." Miss Taylor, several years later, had reciprocated with a photograph bearing the inscription, "To Helen, who knew how to follow her star." When the actress's career had foundered in alcoholic depression, Helen had thought she had seen the last of her special perfection. It was a joy to see her playing again with such beauty. But Helen hated the play. Everyone around her was moved deeply by the plight of the Wingfields, but Helen could summon no identification with their pathos. After the adulatory well-wishers had cleared her dressing room, Miss Taylor challenged her, "Come on now, tell me how you really feel." Helen took a deep breath and told a lie. She was thrilled by Laurette's performance and told her so, but so as not to injure her self-confidence before the Broadway opening told her she had loved the play too. The lie was repeated with exultation to the playwright Tennessee Williams at dinner after the show. Laurette told Helen that she hoped to take the play to London if it was a success on Broadway. The play was an enormous success and established the career of one of the handful of truly definitive American playwrights of the twentieth century. However it was to be Miss Taylor's swansong. Worn out by the rigors of the Broadway run, she died. Audrey Wood came to Helen and told her that it had been Laurette Taylor's fond wish that if she were unable to take the play to London, then Helen should be the one to play Amanda Wingfield there.

Helen, caught in the trap of her lie, realized she could not back out without losing face and agreed to do it. Tennessee Williams seemed greatly pleased. In his memoirs he claimed that though he liked Helen well enough offstage he was no great admirer of her acting. He gives the rather odd reason for this that an electrician working on *Twelfth Night* had told him that she was impossible to light. However he thought well enough of her acting and her eventual performance of Amanda to recommend her to Warner Bros. for the film version of the play. Helen, her aversion to the play almost as great as her aversion to the cinema, turned the offer down and Gertrude Lawrence took the role. The question arose as to who should direct the play. Helen wanted Elia Kazan, with whom she had worked happily on *Harriet,* but Binkie Beaumont, the English manager of II. M. Tennent's, who were producing the play, told her it would be impossible to get a work permit for him. He suggested Tyrone Guthrie, who had directed Ruth Gordon's *Country Wife* or Beaumont's great friend, the actor John Gielgud. Tennessee Williams wrote to Helen, "I do not much like the idea of Gielgud as a director unless no American is available, and that does not seem to be the case. Joshua Logan is now in Rome. How do you feel about him? . . . I must say that I have a suspicion that he is inclined to lean a bit too heavily on broad comedy effects in direction . . . What he would do with a play requiring a delicate and finely balanced touch is a matter of faith and speculation . . . but I would unhesitatingly prefer him to Gielgud or any other Englishman." However, it was Gielgud whom Beaumont finally signed. "I have always been a great admirer of Helen Hayes both as actress and enchanting lady," recalled Sir John Gielgud. "I first saw her on my first visit to New York acting brilliantly in *Coquette.* When I was playing in *Hamlet* on Broadway in the 1936–37 season we made friends and I got to know her a little. Her only London appearance in *The Glass Menagerie* was not really a success, though she was most professional and expert and a great pleasure to direct. But her personality was somehow too practical to be ideal for Amanda, and I think she was daunted by the memory of Laurette Taylor whose definitive performance made such an impression on everyone who saw it."

Tennessee Williams claimed that during rehearsals her performance was honest and moving. At one of the last rehearsals before the pre-London tryout in Brighton, Helen, according to Williams, summoned Gielgud, himself and the other three members of the cast to her dressing room. "At this point in the making of a play, I know if it will or won't go," she said, and then gave a sad and meaningful shake of the head. Williams stayed for the Brighton opening and reports that her playing was flat. *I've never known such fear as I felt that night. My dread was that they'd shout, "We don't know what you're saying." Then the courage of despair seized me, and I believe I gave the best performance of my life.*

Williams flew to Paris to join his friend Gore Vidal. He became involved with a young man there and missed the London opening. Whatever he might have said in his book about Helen in Brighton, he wrote to her that it had been one of the truly deeply satisfying adventures of his life and thanked her for it from the bottom of a contrite heart. The play opened at London's most beautiful old theatre, the Theatre Royal, Haymarket, on July 28, 1948, where it would play for 109 performances. Britain's most distinguished actress at the time, Dame Sybil Thorndike, was in the audience. She wrote to John Gielgud, "I've no words I was moved intolerably—never since Duse has an actress moved me like this—Edith [Evans] is the nearest but not this perfection quite. I can't for one moment believe Laurette *touched this* performance. The funniness of her, the tragedy, the absurdity . . . She fulfils all I feel about acting—she has restored my faith—every part I've ever played I'd love to see her play. Never for one moment does she let you see the wheels working though they are oiled marvellously."

Almost a year later Helen repeated her role of Amanda at a few performances at the Nyack High School, putting something back into the community from which she derived such peace of mind. Although she still disliked the play, she had learned some enchantment in Williams's dialogue. During the London run she had always listened from the wings to the scene in which Laura, Amanda's daughter, falls in love with her Gentleman Caller only to discover that he is proposing to marry another, and had found the language exquisite. In the Nyack production cast as Laura was the young actress who had worshiped her Viola from afar and tried to become the actress by emulating her curls. Julie Harris (could there ever have been a more perfect Laura?) was now at the beginning of her own distinguished career. "Joe Sullivan and I were rehearsing the scene where Laura is left alone with the Gentleman Caller," she recalled. "I think we must have been having some difficulty with the part where we danced—and Helen couldn't bear our blundering away any longer and shot out from the wings—and said, 'For goodness sake, this is the way you do it!'—and her way was perfect. I had seen Laurette Taylor in the role in New York and that performance has always been a beacon of light and inspiration for me—she was radiant and seeing her changed my life—she was the Holy Grail. Helen is a darling actress. She is for me the perfect actress for the Barrie plays. In fact she is a perfect actress, unique, adorable of face and voice. And so lovable." Although Helen always loathed *The Glass Menagerie*, apart from *What Every Woman Knows*, it was the play to which she would most often return.

9

DURING THE SUMMER of 1949, Talullah Bankhead planned a surprise for Helen and Charlie. She commissioned English artist Brian Stonehouse, the former secret agent who had survived the Nazi death camps, to paint a portrait of Mary and Jim. Stonehouse began by painting Jim on his own, leaving a space for Mary. The reason for this was that Mary was rehearsing with Helen for a summer theatre tour of William McCleery's *Good Housekeeping*. It was intended that she would sit for the artist later. The painting was abandoned, the space next to a cheeky-faced Jim left blank. On September 22, at the age of only nineteen years and seven months, Mary MacArthur died.

Mary and Helen were closer than many a mother and her daughter. There were naturally generation divisions but they shared many similarities. One day each went out to buy a dress and returned with exactly the same model. On a less trivial level they shared a love for the theatre. During her life many said that Mary showed exceptional promise. It was a different talent from Helen's, but then she was a different woman and emanated from a different age. She had taken her approach to theatre seriously, studying at the American Academy of Dramatic Arts the theatre of which would eventually bear her name. She was full of life and energy and humor.

She was so vivacious and pretty that Charlie worried about her effect on young men. How would she defend herself against their advances? "No problem, Pops," she assured him. "When I'm going to be alone with a boy I toss some gum in my mouth. Then when I see a lunge coming, I just blow a big bubble and that kills the whole mood." Charlie looked at her in disbelief. "The poor bastards," was his only comment, suddenly having changed sides.

The end of her life began with a cold which seemed to drain her of all strength. Helen sent her home to Nyack and her understudy took over. It seemed it might be influenza and was thus diagnosed by a doctor. Charlie was in the hospital at the time being treated for an ulcer. A few days later Mary was admitted and given a room across the hall. She insisted that Helen stay with the play, saying, "We can't have two members of the family leave the cast!" Then Helen received a call from Charlie to come at once. The play was closed. Helen rushed to New York and found Mary in an iron lung. She had bulbar polio. Charlie left his sickbed and the two of them sat with her. She smiled gaily at them and showed them how she could wiggle her toes but eventually, in a spasm of pain cried, "Help me, Pops." Charlie clasped his hands and prayed. Years before, he had said, "We have given her life and we have given her death."

By the time Jim could be brought from school, Mary had died. Charlie wandered the streets, lost and alone. Helen sobbed, "Why Mary, why not me?" Death isolates us all. Charlie told Jim, "You must take care of your mother now . . ." Helen told him, "You must take care of your father . . ." The three of them stood together, holding hands, staring at one another as if at strangers. Charlie had Ben Jonson's lines inscribed on her tombstone, his last gift to her:

Underneath this stone doth lie
As much beauty as could die . . .

SIX

HOLDING UP THE UNIVERSE

1949 – 1956

1

The biggest battle of my life was forcing myself to go on with my own life after I lost Mary. But I'm a survivor and survivors don't spend their time in mourning. They fight. So I just went in there with my fists up and started working to help fight this dreadful disease. Recently Jonas Salk told me I was one of the biggest assets he had in getting his vaccine to the world. So you see Mary's death was not in vain. Sometimes when I am alone I sit around and try to visualize what Mary would be like now if she were living and I try to imagine the conversations we'd have together, and I can almost see the grandchildren she'd have given me. I guess a mother never quite gets used to the fact that she has outlived her child.

It was some time before Helen found her fighting spirit. Hers was a broken spirit for many weeks. Charlie proved a tower of strength. "I have thought many times," recalled the actor James Stewart, "of the time I met Helen Hayes and her husband Charles MacArthur in Hilo, on the big island of Hawaii, where my wife and I were on our honeymoon. As we found out later, they had just lost their daughter to polio and were traveling to do their best to decrease the sadness they felt. Gloria and I were on our way to Kona, on the other side of

157

the island, and we asked them to come with us. They did; and we drove to Kona and had several days of marlin fishing out in the very smooth waters of the Pacific. I've always felt so happy that we were able to do this with them because I like to think that it helped take their minds and thoughts off the tragedy."

While in Honolulu, Charlie was passing a sports store and saw a pair of sunglasses in the window. "They'll be just right for Mary," he thought, and went in and bought them. It wasn't until he had left the store with the sunglasses wrapped in a bag that he realized what he had done. He noticed a girl of about Mary's age, thrust the bag into her hands, and ran off. He couldn't bring himself to tell Helen what had happened. To help her recover from her grief he had suggested a return to the theatre. However she was unable to contemplate it. He had mentioned to Joshua Logan that he thought a new play might prove the best therapy and Logan was prompted to suggest a pet project of his own. Some time before, Helen had told him she would like to play Ranevskaya in *The Cherry Orchard*. Logan had suggested a novel idea, transferring the action of the Chekhov play from Russia to his native Louisiana. The parallels, he suggested, were obvious. The decline of power in the landed gentry due to the abolition of slavery took place in each country around the same period. Actually the idea was not new. John Anderson had, as far back as 1930, in an article named "Look Away Dixieland," suggested that much of Chekhov's work could, with few changes, be transplanted to the South.

Logan adapted the play and, under the title *The Wisteria Trees,* offered the leading role of Lucy Ransdell to Helen. At first she was extremely reluctant to make a return to the theatre. She had often spoken of retirement and now seemed the ideal moment to draw the curtain on her career. Eventually, however, she made up her mind to tackle the role. Several critics were delighted to welcome her back but several believed she behaved rather more like a star in the role than the character she was supposed to be playing. Indeed Arthur Pollock suggested it would have been a better play had it not been contrived with a star in mind. In fact it was an unsatisfactory adaptation of a fine play. John Mason Brown pointed out the central fault. This lay in the dissimilarity between the "souls" of the two countries. The melancholic introspection of the Russians was masked by a false gaiety. The false gaiety of the Southerners masked nothing quite so unyielding. Though he admitted that Helen made the best possible use of her material he claimed that the play seemed "no more than a chronicle of a very silly woman who deserves to lose her plantation."

The play, which opened at the Martin Beck on March 29, 1950, ran for a respectable 165 performances. Also in the cast was Mary's old friend Bethel Leslie. Almost as if to keep the flame of Mary's spirit alive Helen took a great interest in Miss Leslie, a year later producing *Mary Rose,* the Barrie play which might have given Helen a memorable role many years before, with Miss Leslie in the leading role.

Helen made her television debut in October 1950 in *The Late Christopher Bean,* following it up with *The Barretts of Wimpole Street, Victoria Regina,* and *Mary of Scotland.* Her attitude to television changed with the years. Toward the end of the forties she had said, *Television will mean the end of all art in the theatre. It strikes me as awful, reducing everything to that little breadbox. Imagine, all that rehearsal for just one performance.* Five years later she said, *I've thoroughly enjoyed all of my television work. Most of the top programs are done in relatively the same manner one prepares for a stage assignment. A little more hurried perhaps, but alive and rewarding, at least from an actor's point of view.* A further five years on she would add, *We are so darn limited by the star system in America. On Broadway I can't accept a secondary role—my fans wouldn't stand for it. On television the biggest stars play small parts. They're not trying to hold up the universe every time.*

2

Why do parents try to change their children? Why do they invade a child's life and spirit and knock the childhood out of him. I do it all the time. I yell at my son, "When are you going to grow up?" I don't even know what grown up means. Helen was talking to a reporter as part of the publicity for her next play which was to be her greatest success since *Happy Birthday.* In it she would play a mother who was punished for interfering in her son's life. However before the play she made her first return to Hollywood movies for seventeen years and the role which tempted her back was another interfering mother.

Leo McCarey had kept up a barrage of calls to try to influence Helen to make the film. She continually told him she was too busy in the East, so he flew to New York and personally delivered the script to her. It was a story written in impassioned terms of the reactions of a Catholic family on learning that their eldest son is a Communist. Helen liked the script, sensing in it a positive affirmation of the American way of life in contrast with existence under Communist domination. The film would have an exceptional cast with Dean Jagger, Van Heflin, and Frank McHugh, and Robert Walker as the son. It would be made at Paramount Studios where Helen had made her greatest film *A Farewell to Arms*. She agreed to star in *My Son John*.

One of the things she had hated about Hollywood film-making in the thirties was the hours she had to spend being scrutinized first from one side and then from the other, the false eyelashes, the shape of her eyebrows calculated to the fraction of an inch. Now she was fifty-one no one cared which was her best side and her makeup took only ten minutes. How much happier she felt!

During filming Robert Walker died suddenly after a drinking bout. His major scenes had been completed and a number of out-takes from *Strangers on a Train* were interpolated into the picture to fill out the running time. Other scenes were filmed where members of the cast played to his stand-in who had his back to the camera. Leslie Halliwell has suggested that "The lower depths of Hollywood's witch hunt are marked by this Goldwynesque family saga, all sweetness and light, in which the commie son is treated as though he had rabies." Although Helen received a fair amount of praise for her performance the film was seen to be misguided. Otis L. Guernsey in the New York *Herald Tribune* shuddered at the thought that the film might be seen outside the United States. *My Son John* would join *The Weavers of Life* and a couple of Disney movies she made in the seventies as the collective nadir of Helen's film career.

Helen was president of the American National Theatre. After every producer had, in turn, tried to interest her in *Mrs. McThing*, it eventually landed on someone's desk there. As chairlady of their Subscription Drive Helen complained that ANTA had only one projected production with which to invite subscriptions, Eugene O'Neill's *Desire Under the Elms* which was to be revived. "All right," said ANTA's producer Bob Whitehead, "cast yourself in *Mrs.*

McThing and we'll have two productions to sell." Helen had never actually read the script but she agreed on the spot.

It was an extraordinary and charismatic play by Mary Chase, the author of *Harvey*. An immensely wealthy woman is rude to a tiny female trespasser who wants to play with her son. The little girl's mother just happens to be a witch and she casts a spell replacing the charming son with a priggish child who is the embodiment of all the stuffy behavior the mother had always wanted to see in her boy. The real son finds himself in a den of thieves where he wins his spurs and is permitted to join the Mob. In time the spell is extended and the rich mother becomes a maid-of-all-work in the gangsters' employ. The moment arrives when her son is ordered to give her a stiff talking to because her work has proved far from satisfactory. Eventually everyone is returned to their proper place a little wiser. Helen was cast as the tyrant mother and Brandon de Wilde as both the true son and the pompous changeling. The trespasser's role was given to a mite named Lydia Reed.

I was sitting in my dressing room when the author, Mary Chase, under-standably worried about her play, came in with Bob Whitehead and Joe Buloff, who was directing. "We have got to get rid of Lydia Reed," she announced. "She can't project. She'll never be able to hold up her scenes." I heard an echo. "That's me," I thought. I stood with my back to the dress-ing-room door and told them of the time I was rehearsing The Summer Widowers. *I was nine years old. Ned Wayburn, the director, stopped rehearsals one day and called Mr. Fields. With no regard to my feelings and as though I were a piece of the furniture he said, "Lew, you've got to get rid of this kid. She can't project. You've got to get a replacement." Mr. Fields answered, "Now then, Ned, I guess Miss Hayes is just like me. She has to see two dollars in every seat before she can act." Wise, wise Mr. Fields. He knew that children can rarely give at rehearsal. "So," I told Miss Chase and the others, "if Lydia goes then so do I." She stayed and became the hit of the play.*

The play was a great hit too. Only the generally cynical George Jean Nathan was not enamored of it, suggesting that Miss Chase should have involved a few large rabbits. The show-stopping moment came when Helen, forced to work for the gangsters, made a pathetic attempt to sweep the floor with a broom. It joined the moment in *Clarence* ("Wash my face?") and her song and dance in *Happy Birthday* as the great comic moments of her career. "Miss

Hayes' ingenious magic is in full bloom here," proclaimed William Hawkins, "creating flecks of pathos and masses of humor. The deftness and generosity of her reactions constantly enrich the performances around her. Looking like one of the Three Bruises from the Ice Show, she is staggeringly funny, aiming to please with a broom. Young Brandon de Wilde is assured and enchanting in his dual role." The play which opened on February 20, 1952 at the Martin Beck would play for 350 performances.

It was perhaps a poetic turn of events that the last play in which Brownie would see Helen in the theatre was one in which she was supported by two exceptional child actors. She died the following summer, aged seventy-six. For all her faults of self-interest, without her ambition and guidance Helen would doubtless have become yet another Washington housewife and not the preeminent of her kind, Broadway's first and foremost actress. *Requiescat in pace*, Brownie.

3

THE TIME IN a star actor's life when old age begins to threaten middle age is often marked by a retrospective glance at former glories. The risks and nervous tension involved in approaching entirely new work suddenly seems too arduous. Truly suitable new work is hard to find, as the actor by this time has too definite an idea of his limitations, not daring as he did in his youth to shut his eyes and jump but always to look nervously and cautiously before his leap. No longer will he allow himself permission to fail, feeling that no audience will allow it either. Thus it was that from the summer of 1954 to the summer of 1955 Helen chose to look over her shoulder. She had never had to look for work, well certainly not since *Coquette*. As Ruth Gordon has pointed out, work came looking for Helen. Possibly it was that she was preparing for her final retirement yet again; 1955 would mark the fiftieth anniversary of her first steps on stage as Peaseblossom in *A Midsummer Night's Dream*.

While Helen was in *Mrs. McThing,* she played herself yet again in an appalling little piece for the cinema entitled *Main Street to Broadway,* an inauspicious return to MGM, and continued in television. Then she went to Coonamessett, Massachusetts, to the Falmouth Playhouse, where during July and August 1954 she took part in the Helen Hayes Festival in which she played Maggie Wylie, Mrs. Ransdell, Mary Stuart, and Mrs. Larue in *Mrs. McThing. I went over to Dennis to see Tallulah Bankhead in* Dear Charles. *Tallulah exclaimed to me "Dahling, isn't it terrible? How are you bearing up? That festival will kill you!" People say to me, "You must lie down now, you must get plenty of rest." They think I'm some kind of heroine. We Americans have grown so soft no one expects us to be able to take it. English stage people go to Stratford-upon-Avon and play for virtually no pay at all, on an equally strenuous schedule and think nothing of it. I don't feel tired at all. Strength in the theatre, I think, comes from joy in the work.*

Alec Clark was in the company with her again that summer as was his wife, Frances Tannehill. Frances recalled, "Helen's relationship with an audience was unique. Her performances had all the beauty of a virtuoso violin, moving effortlessly from lightness and comedy to pathos and tragedy in only the briefest moment. Always completely natural, her work was always enriched by her special humanity." When the Clarks' daughter Nicole was born in 1957 Helen became a proud, loving, and diligent godmother.

Helen was miscast in a television production of *The Royal Family* in which she co-starred with Claudette Colbert and Fredric March. She made a courageous return to New York as Maggie Wylie in *What Every Woman Knows* twenty-eight years after she first tackled the role. Further returns to *The Wisteria Trees* and *Mrs. McThing* were followed by special performances of a program entitled *Gentlemen the Queens* which included Shaw's *Great Catherine,* and scenes from *Mary of Scotland, Victoria Regina,* and *Macbeth,* as part of the 1955 University of Michigan Drama Season. With Helen in the cast were the Clarks. Alec recalled, "I played Duncan in the *Macbeth* scenes which were built around the murder of Duncan. At its conclusion on the first night Helen whispered to me, 'Well, I bet I was the cutest Lady Macbeth.' Nevertheless, she was good. She didn't howl down the wind nor did she wash her hands too soon. She didn't shake when she read the letter either."

Thornton Wilder had just completed The Skin of Our Teeth *when he rang me and said, "I have a new play I would like you to do." When I finished reading it I said to Charlie, "It's just not possible, twice in a lifetime. This role is greater than Victoria. She's the eternal mother, wife, homemaker, and thorn in the side of the world!" I was overwhelmed and immediately telephoned Thornton. After babbling on to him about how much I loved the play I finally said, "And who's going to play my hus-*

band?'' There was a long silence at the other end of the phone. ''Oh, Helen, I didn't mean for you to play Mrs. Antrobus. I want you to play Sabina.'' Sabina in the play is the quintessence of all the femme fatales of history. ''Thornton, my love,'' I said, ''I couldn't possibly play a femme fatale. I would ruin your play.'' How disappointed I was and so was he. Wilder could not offer her the role of Mrs. Antrobus. Fredric March was already engaged to play Antrobus and his wife, Florence Eldridge, would play at his side. Helen recommended the actress who would eventually create a major hit with Sabina as Helen could never have done. The actress was Tallulah Bankhead. That had been in 1942. Thirteen years later ANTA asked Helen to head the cast of a foreign tour of the play with George Abbott as Antrobus and the delightful Mary Martin as Sabina. They opened at the Théâtre Sarah Bernhardt in Paris on June 28, 1955, where the play was billed as La Peau des Dents. The French didn't like the play but were delighted by the performances of Helen and Mary Martin. *Mary Martin radiates more perfection and sheer joy per cubic foot of actress than anyone else of recent memory.* In her autobiography Miss Martin recalled the family atmosphere in the company. Her husband, Richard Halliday, was along, and their daughter, Heller, was in the cast. Charlie accompanied Helen and Jim was in charge of the lighting. The opening night was disastrous. In the part where Wilder indicates that the scenery starts to fall to pieces and Sabina starts to reassemble it, stage hands who were supposed to help her from offstage actually came *on*stage to assist her. The audience listened to a simultaneous translation through headphones. At one point, Sabina had to say, ''I don't understand one word of this play.'' When it was translated back to them the audience yelled its agreement. Miss Martin acknowledged Helen's help and support in coming to terms with her enormously difficult role. ''Listen Mrs. Antrobus,'' she wrote to Helen, ''It is girls like you who started the alphabet—with A for Acting—and I'm *glad* to say it—you *are* a beautiful woman—and you will never know what you have done for girls like me—I *have* to say it Mrs. Antrobus, you are a beautiful woman—and I love you—and that's God's truth!!'' It was signed ''Sabina Martin.'' The same cast played three weeks at the ANTA theatre, toured in America, and performed it as a television special.

On a dull, dark day in November 1955, Helen made a solitary pilgrimage to Broadway and West Forty-sixth Street. She stood alone on the sidewalk amid the indifferent to and fro of pedestrians, trying to appear nonchalant as workmen dismantled the identifying sign outside the Fulton Theatre. When it had been carted away, up went a brand-new sign. It read: HELEN HAYES THEATRE. Many of the moments of glory in an actor's life are received with a kind of numb emptiness as he strives to maintain control of his emotions; the full enjoyment is only realized in retrospect. However, alone and unobserved, Helen could give way to the understandable degree of emotion which had built up in her, and her tears began to flow. Had Brownie only lived to see this day! Like daughter, like mother. As on that long ago day when each of them had stood on the island in the middle of Columbus Circle and read in awed disbelief Helen's name for the first time spelled out in lights on the Park Theatre, so on this day, the shade of Brownie stood looking over Helen's shoulder, and both were awash with tears. Her Helen was now a theatre.

4

AT THE END OF 1955 virtually every New York theatre program carried as its cover a Hirschfeld cartoon of Helen to mark her Golden Jubilee as an actress. It was also celebrated at the First Night Ball at the Waldorf-Astoria Hotel on December 30, 1955. A glittering array of fellow actors appeared in a two-hour program of vignettes recalling her career, as Helen sat beaming with pride between Jim and Charlie. It was one of the last times she and Charlie would be seen together. By the summer he would be gone.

Charlie had been ill for some time. Although he rallied and gave Helen the support she needed to get back on her feet again after Mary died, as soon as she was back at work he crumpled. A friend said of them that at this time if Mary was mentioned, Helen's face brightened but Charlie looked solemn. He went even deeper into drink. On the whole, however, Charlie was a happy drunk, not the morose and murderous kind. He even joked about his situation. "I'm a member of Alcoholics Acknowledged," he once said. Helen's life with Charlie was no bed of roses, but from the moment they met it was inevitable as life itself that they live their lives together. Brownie had warned her, "That satire will drink too much and he'll play around with women." In her memoirs Helen claimed that her mother's more dire prophecies came true. Later she would retract this, saying that this inclusion had been in error and that if Charlie had been unfaithful to her, then she knew nothing about it. But then, had Charlie been incapable of infidelity they would never have met. It is only reasonable to suppose that in thirty years a man who had played the field would stray at some point. But he knew that home was best and he always returned. His enduring love for Helen is captured forever in the letters he wrote. In December 1943 he had written, "It's 5:30 A.M. and I've given up the idea of sleep so I might as well be writing you a letter. I've been alternately reading bad plays and thinking pleasantly of you and wishing you were here in my arms. I've been remembering so many things from our buggy ride to Fraunces Tavern on down the years—all my boobish love antics return to entertain me. I run upstairs in East 40th Street with you in my arms (I believe I could do it still without getting too much out of breath) and I see you coming down Madison Avenue in a little gray suit with a green orchid I sent you on your shoulder or wearing that awful Empire dress I bought you from Paris or that pretty postillion coat or standing on the dock when the *Belgenland* hove to when you told the newspaper boys we were engaged and I got slapped with Miss Frink's summons at the baggage pile. And the first time I ever kissed you in a cab and how you lied ever after when you said you didn't lean toward me first. And sitting up with you in Childs and going over the brow of yon hills in France and the fight about Molnar's picture and the swing at Syosset and the open fire at Otto Kahn's. And the Victrola I bought you for your birthday and the way your stomach felt at the Santa Barbara Biltmore when the embryo Mary was only a few weeks old, and how I rubbed your stomach later with cocoa butter and got my face slapped for further familiarities and how I nearly abandoned you on the street (or said I would abandon you) when you told me the waterbag might burst on the way to the hospital. And how I used to chase you around with a Leica whenever I caught you with your clothes off, and the time you posed with hat and fan. 536, Madison, with you frightening me stiff by telling me you were going to stay the night. The bed at 15 Park we were never going to sell. The time you got tight and gambled and were so gay at Barney Glazer's, and picking out the hat for Madelon Claudet and my horror the first time I went back and saw an old belle of mine in a bustle after a performance of Victoria. And my boobish names for . . . And now I'll go to work. Don't worry about me. I hope I always have this particular form of insomnia. Thank you for a very pleasant night, my dearest, only love. All this is so little of my happiness, Charlie."

Charlie and Ben had tried to collaborate on a last play together but they just spent two years talking and Ben had gone off to make money in Hollywood. Charlie would often shut himself up in the East End Avenue apartment which they still retained and try to pull a last play of his own together which similarly never materialized. Helen told Frances Tannehill, "I didn't have a menopause, but Charlie did." Every night they would dress up and he would go wander around hardware stores. But he was stalked by illness.

Ben Hecht said, "Charlie's spirit was the product of awareness of death. He was born without the illusion of permanence. He knew at the beginning the road's end." Resigned to death he looked the Grim Reaper in the face with cheeky impudence. Opening his eyes at one point he saw his sickbed surrounded with white-coated medics. "Is this a block party?" he inquired. At one particularly ominous moment a doctor asked him his religion. "I'm a phallic worshiper," he replied. Feeling his strength return he asked to be released immediately. "Okay, MacArthur," countered a waggish whitecoat, "you may leave the hospital, but only under the following conditions. You have to be carried out by four Chinese midgets, followed by a brass band that's led by Mary Martin." As soon as the doctors had left the room Charlie was on the phone to *Variety* to ascertain the whereabouts of the Long Trek Sam vaudeville troupe, to the Musicians Union to price a three-piece band, and to Mary Martin to ask her availability. Perhaps it was just as well he was released from the hospital before this vaudeville act was assembled.

However, it was only a temporary remission. Soon the hospital reclaimed him. At his bedside Helen held his hands tightly in hers. To his still and silent face she murmured, "I love you." His eyes quivered open for the last time. "You should," he said.

The last thing Charlie would have wanted was a funeral. Helen knew this but also realized that there were hundreds of friends who would want a chance to say goodbye. She asked Ben Hecht to speak the final tribute. Just before he began to speak a huge floral wreath which was suspended in midair came loose and threatened to come crashing down. There was more than one there who thought Charlie was having his last protest.

HELEN HAYES

Ben Hecht ended his tribute with the words of a song Charlie had often used to sing:

Bonnie Charlie's gone away
Out across the deep blue sea
Many a heart will break in two . . .

SEVEN

A TREE WITHOUT
LEAVES

1956 – 1969

1

TALLULAH BANKHEAD, who had been one of the first to pooh-pooh
the idea of a match between Charlie MacArthur and Helen Hayes
now said, "That merger almost restores my faith. Not only was it
made in heaven, but when He made it, God was even wiser than I
am. What sheer inspiration joining those two together."

*Charlie had an extraordinary mind. He was a great talker, a very
gregarious person and he loved to be with people. Often, in retrospect, I've
felt that I wasn't good enough for him. But then I say to myself, "I was the
object of his love, and that made me enough for him." I console myself that I
gave him an object upon which to pour his love. He had a tremendous
capacity for loving. That is a great gift which comes to people with exceptional minds.*

Charlie's passing left her bereft. There are some psychologists
who claim that grief is a seven-year illness. It was just seven years
since Mary had died and she was in mourning again with no one to
rely on but a teenage son who had to grow up very quickly. Ben
Hecht said, "There was no First Lady of the theatre here, but a little
tree without leaves."

Until Charlie died I was pretty darned arrogant. There was actually a time when I felt, why did God give me this gift of being right so much of the time? Why should I be the one who always chooses the right play, the right line of action? I literally felt infallible. I don't anymore. Charlie was always watchful and supportive and protective of me. Actually he was the one who made the decisions, and I hadn't recognized that or acknowledged it to myself. Since his death I have marked time. I haven't wanted really to be an actress since then, now I don't have his judgment.

Now others began offering their judgment. No doubt recalling how his play had helped restore her sanity after the death of Mary, Joshua Logan told her, "You can never find another Charlie; you can never have another child. But you can have the theatre and you can use that God-given talent of yours to make other people happy." Helen thought, *If only my talent had died and I had been allowed to keep Charlie and Mary. I made a big try for life. I am left with make-believe.*

There was work on offer. Before Charlie's death Twentieth Century–Fox had asked Helen to play the Dowager Empress in *Anastasia.* The film was to be made in England. Although it was an interesting part she had turned it down because she knew she was needed at home. The part was still not cast. Lillian Gish, Anita Loos, and others urged her to accept it now. She finally relented but would regret her decision for the rest of her life.

The offer of the film had, in fact, been a fluke. The role had been played on the Broadway stage by Eugenie Leontovich. On the London stage it had been played by the elderly Helen Haye. Miss Haye was an actress of great classical experience, a brilliant teacher of actors, who in later life played only small character roles in films and occasionally in plays. The role of the Dowager Empress was the great triumph of her later years. She was perfect for the part, possessing the authority of an aristocratic bearing, stature, and voice. An executive producer from Fox cabled: SIGN HELEN HAYE. The studio offices contacted Helen Hayes. It was a great loss for the British actress who would die only a year later. The mistake in identity didn't end there. There is more than one film encyclopedia in print which lists *Atlantic* as Helen Hayes's first sound film. It was in fact an early British sound feature which had Helen Haye in its cast. When in 1984 Ronald Harwood published a history of the theatre, *All the World's a Stage,* a page which bore the photographs of several of Broadway's luminaries including Katharine Cornell, featured a

photograph of Helen Haye with the caption "Helen Hayes
(1900–)."

Helen did not have Miss Haye's dignity or aristocratic authority
but she did supply the right wellspring of emotion to the woman
who had grown embittered by the procession of impostors who
came to claim their share of the Romanoff fortunes. As the undis-
puted head of that tragic family, she was the only one who could
recognize the authenticity of her granddaughter's claim. Cast as the
mysterious woman who came to convince her of her identity as
Anastasia was Ingrid Bergman, who would win an Academy Award
for her performance. "I only made the one picture with Helen Hayes
but it was a rewarding experience," she recalled. "I had once received such encouragement from her when it seemed all the world
was against me. She and Charles MacArthur had written me a beautiful letter of support. Working on the picture I felt she needed my
support but I did not know what I could do. However when she was
on the set, everyone, the cast, the crew, stopped whatever they were
doing and watched in admiration. I know I did. She symbolized that
quality which distinguishes a superb actor from an adequate one.
Garbo had it, Katharine Hepburn had it, and Helen Hayes had it.
She sat around on the set of *Anastasia* and she was a sweet little
woman. She stepped on the stage and suddenly she was six feet
tall." The high point of the film is the scene in which the unimpressed Dowager Empress confronts the claimant. Suddenly the
woman begins to cough, something she says she always does when
she gets excited. The grandmother recognizes not the history that
could have been learned or the physical proportions that could have
been assumed, but the secret personal trait only a member of the
family could have known and accepts the woman as the Grand
Duchess Anastasia. The scene is exquisitely played by each of them.

The friends who persuaded me to do the picture didn't realize I needed
that time as a quiet time, a time I could be apart. Grief is a very feeling
thing. If I had had a chance to sit still and indulge in grief, I think it would
have made my time of recovery much shorter. Instead I went over to England
and found myself doing the oddest things. I had always been so reliable and
dependable, always on the job—a real trouper, they called me. Well, one
time I took off, went to Brighton with a friend. I just took a fancy to go to
Brighton and I went, and left no forwarding address at my hotel. Heavens,
the picture company was beside itself. I had completely put it out of my mind

that I was making a movie. That's a time I flinch to look back on, because I was most unattractive. Unreliable and erratic. I squabbled with directors. I had never done that before. I took umbrage at nothing at all. I gave rather pompous and silly statements to the press. I was nutty and that's the truth.

One of her statements to the press concerned the state of the British theatre which she said was completely backward. There were no playwrights fit to be set against American playwrights and that, lacking the discipline of severe criticism, even the acting had become slipshod. In many ways she was correct, certainly in her view of playwrights. The British theatre of those days claimed a master technician, Terence Rattigan, as its first playwright, and who was he set against Wilder, Williams, Miller, and William Inge? However, several months before Helen's statement the English stage had undergone a major revolution when John Osborne's *Look Back in Anger* had been staged for the first time. Nevertheless, Helen's words occasioned a great deal of flak from both sides of the Atlantic.

When she got back to Nyack, Helen was allowed a little time to stand and stare. In Sanskrit the word for "widow" also means "empty." Along with many other women Helen understood this meaning. She suddenly felt an overwhelming urge to return to the Church. But she knew she could never agree that her joyous marriage had been a sin. She spoke to someone about it who convinced her that though she had broken a Church law it would not be considered a sin. She found a quiet moment to tell Charlie that it was going to take the entire Roman Catholic Church to replace him.

2

SHORTLY AFTER her return from England there was a telephone call one night from Jean Dalrymple of the New York City Center where Helen had made her return appearance as Maggie Wylie. She was in something of a state. She needed to borrow money to pay the New York City Opera Company's salaries and she knew the bank would only entertain such a loan if she were able to say she was staging a low-cost revival with a star name. She asked Helen if she would consider playing Amanda in *The Glass Menagerie* for two weeks. Helen groaned inwardly but heard herself saying yes. *Charlie used to say I was the head of the sucker list.* She was happy to help out such a noble institution, but did it have to be in *that* play? However, the production was well received. Naturally comparisons were made. Walter Kerr wrote, "Miss Taylor played [the part] like a scratching tree branch working on a window-pane on a night the wind never stopped. Miss Hayes plays it like a belligerent sparrow bent on marching her brood right into kingdom-come. She is a battling bantam-cock bashing at the world in an untidy bathrobe, teetering on stiff little legs with the determination of a dowdy Napoleon, waddling wildly at top speed up a short flight of stairs to collar her restless runaway son. Though there are fleeting reminders of the downcast Taylor mouth, the fiercely bright face haloed by a straggling grey bob, the soul is different. It is a bit simpler, perhaps; not so much a grinding echo of glories long lost as a foolish shining faith in glories yet to come. The tartness and the screeching are still there in honest measure. Yet to watch Miss Hayes spread her thinning taffeta and waltz vaguely about a dingy room, only to pause in sudden, death-like, but yearning stillness before the photograph of the man who deserted her is to see this 'ugly, babbling witch' in a new, and equally valid perspective. Amanda Wingfield is here a spectre to make you cry . . . the part now belongs permanently to two people."

Before Charlie died, Helen had appeared in a television production of *Dear Brutus* in which Susan Strasberg, the actress daughter of Lee Strasberg, who had founded the Actors Studio, had played Helen's original role. Now they were reunited in Helen's return to Broadway in Jean Anouilh's charming play *Time Remembered*. Helen's role was that of the knowing Duchesse de Pont-au-Bronc who decided that the successor to the heart of her nephew Prince Albert should be a little Parisian milliner named Amanda. Amanda was the role played by Miss Strasberg. The role of the moody and difficult Albert was played by the moody and difficult Crown Prince of the British theatre, Richard Burton. There was no need for a warm professional relationship between Helen and Burton as they never met on stage. Although there was a formal courtesy between them to begin with, this soon deteriorated. The three stars had an after-theatre dinner together in Washington where the play was being tried out. Helen and Miss Strasberg had rather too much champagne and all three ended up in Miss Strasberg's hotel suite. Miss Strasberg was by this time the worse for wear and, as she lay on her bed wishing she hadn't had the last one-for-the-road or two, Helen and Burton argued about which one should undress her. Memories of Mary brought out the protective mother in her. Miss Strasberg was in no fit state to blow bubble-gum at Burton and as far as his reputation was concerned she knew darn well that if she did it wouldn't make a scrap of difference. On this occasion she won but she knew as the run of the play progressed that she had lost the battle and that Burton was having his way. Consequently the run of *Time Remembered,* which opened at the Morosco on November 12, 1957, and lasted for almost 250 performances was not the happiest time of her life, even though she had a splendid role, the praise of the critics, the adulation of her audiences, and her second Tony Award.

Her greatest occasion for joy at the time was the newly emerging career of Jim. Both of them had weird hairstyles at this time. Helen had her hair bleached white for her role and Jim, more than two decades before punk, had a Mohican haircut. This was for his role in the Disney picture *The Light in the Forest* in which a teenage boy who had been kidnapped by Indians as a baby is returned to his parents only to find the white man's ways completely alien to him. In fact Helen had been offered the role of his mother in the film, but her commitments had precluded it and the role had gone to Jessica Tandy. Jim had already shown his acting ability in the role of a rebel without a cause in RKO's *The Young Stranger.* For the next few years he would be no stranger to Hollywood, making one Disney picture after another. In *Third Man on the Mountain,* which he made in Britain, Helen would have a tiny unbilled role as she had done in one of his father's pictures. Jim's career never shone with brilliance, but he had a gentle, quiet style as a young man which fulfilled the ideal Disney hero of that period. He represented all the qualities Disney chose to project to the youth of the day. Helen was justly proud of him. Perhaps the door had been opened for him by his eminent parents, but Jim was equal to the work. He was reengaged not for who he was but for what he had to offer.

Helen's next work in the theatre was for one performance only when she played Rosie the maid in *Mid-Summer* at the Tappan Zee Playhouse in Nyack. It was a neighborly gesture. Also in the cast were James Mason, his wife Pamela, and daughter Portland. However, in October 1958 she made her theatrical debut in a Eugene O'Neill play. It was also her debut at the Helen Hayes Theatre. It proved quite a contrast from her last role. From flighty aristocrat she moved to Norah Melody, the household drudge of a slovenly tavern in *A Touch of the Poet*, exchanging exquisite gowns for an uncompromisingly slatternly kitchen dress. The play concerned a braggart, tyrannical Irishman who had won honor on the battlefield under the Duke of Wellington but who had turned into a lazy drunkard who thinks everyone beneath him and yet is himself less than worthless. It was a play of character rather than a play of narrative. The British actor Eric Portman was cast as the braggart, Helen was the wife, and Kim Stanley was the daughter.

In everything he plays, Laurence Olivier does something odd to himself; he puts on some nose putty, some extraordinary elaborate makeup as if to say, "I must wipe off Olivier completely, so that when I look at myself in the mirror I'm not there at all." I have never been able to go that far; I don't take to makeup. Of course, there was Victoria Regina *but right now in* A Touch of the Poet *I'm happiest because I don't wear any makeup. I just put on a little eye shadow. I leave myself behind in the dressing room; I've got to forget about myself. I search for that other person who is my bridge to the character I'm playing. Many years ago Booth Tarkington presented me with the script of* The Wren. *"There you are," he said. "This is my portrait of you." That was all I needed to be sent flying behind a protective wall. I wanted not a remembered experience of my own but someone else's. The twenty-fourth performance brought down the final, merciful curtain.*

There were almost three hundred performances of *A Touch of the Poet* which opened October 2, 1958 to excellent notices. Eric Portman's performance on opening night was almost unintelligible. He had a rather rapid, machine-gun-like delivery which, while it thrilled audiences in London's West End, was too staccato to be easily understood by American audiences used to softer, more rounded sounds. He modified it somewhat as the run progressed. The greatest praise was heaped on the shoulders of both Helen and Miss Stanley. There was one particularly charismatic scene toward the end of the play where the two women late at night spoke quietly together, each absorbed in the other but speaking different thoughts. Few who saw that scene would ever forget it. It was a meeting of two exceptional actresses. Unfortunately it would not last the entire run. The volatile Miss Stanley took exception to the way she was treated by Eric Portman and suddenly left the cast. Portman himself was somewhat ambiguous in his memories of working with Helen, claiming that the experience reminded him of "walking barefoot on mice." Brooks Atkinson would claim that Helen's performance was one of her greatest achievements on stage. Whitney Bolton added, "Miss Hayes plays the pseudo gentleman's low-born Irish wife with lovely perception and a gift for using tiny and seemingly inconsequential things to build a creature of dimension and earthy grandeur."

3

THE FIRST CHRISTMAS after Charlie died, Helen and Jim went to stay with Helen's brother-in-law Alfred MacArthur in his beautiful two-hundred-year-old colonial mansion in Cuernavaca, Mexico, an hour's drive from Mexico City on the road to Acapulco. Helen immediately fell in love with the little city and remained behind after Jim returned to Harvard. She loved the peace she found there and the ever pleasant climate. When she learned that a little house on the Calle Victoria was up for sale, she bought it. Alfred was acquainted with an architect who transformed it into her Casa Serena (serene house). Helen has spent the best part of every winter there ever since. *Several people I know don't understand why I take off for Mexico away from all my friends. "How can you want to be there, all on your own?" they say. No one knows me in Mexico and that's a major blessing. They don't know I'm famous, don't know anything about me, and I am left blissfully alone. Cuernavaca is nestled in the hills and from my back garden and from my galeria I can see two snow-capped volcanoes— Popocatepetl and Ixtaccihuatl. I sit there by the hour watching the color on the snow change with the colors of the sky.*

As time went by, with Jim away from home, Helen began to feel that Pretty Penny was too big for her on her own and wondered about moving elsewhere. True, the house was full of memories but so often the memories were uncomfortable, reminding her too much of a time when she was infinitely happier than she was now. And as she looked around she saw a house crowded with "things." Not wishing to become a slave to them, she decided to put all but her most precious possessions up for auction, clear the house, and begin again somewhere else. The auction brought $52,000; $27,000 went to a children's home. The balance went to the American Academy of Dramatic Arts, where it was used to fund The Mary MacArthur

Theatre. But when it actually came to the point of leaving the house, Helen lost heart. The sale was almost through when she managed to terminate the deal. But she had made the change that was necessary. With new heart she set about redecorating and refurnishing. When she had everything more or less fit to be seen she invited Jim to come and take a look, more than a little worried that he might find it too fancy. He took one look, smiled, and said, "Mother, the house embraces you."

When Jim turned twenty-one Helen decided she should offer him the opportunity of knowing his real roots. She handed him an envelope which contained all the papers pertaining to his adoption. He held the envelope in his hands for only a few moments before he tossed it unopened on the fire. He had never been in any doubt as to who his true parents were. Their names were Charles and Helen MacArthur. Not long afterward he married a pretty blond actress named Joyce Bulifant. In May 1960 they presented Helen with her first grandchild. His name was Charles MacArthur. On Helen's sixty-fifth birthday, five years later, she was present at the baptism of a new granddaughter, Mary MacArthur. Jim certainly had a sense of family. *I had the feeling that the whole glorious day—that beautiful baby—writes a happy ending to my story. It took a long time to get to that. A friend of my Mary found a little gold bracelet that had belonged to her—its links spelled her name. I had it fixed up and polished and put it around little Mary's wrist.*

Some years later Jim returned to Pretty Penny after a safari in Africa. *He was reguling the dinner guests with his experiences. Suddenly it was a case of* déjà vu. *He was electrifying the table in much the same way that his father once did. I thought at the time he was worthy to sit in his father's chair.*

Ben Hecht died in 1964. His wife tried unsuccessfully to have him buried near Charlie in the cemetery at Nyack. When Helen heard about this she made a diplomatic phone call to the right quarter. In years gone by Walter Howey would have had a desk drawer full of relevant resignations. Helen had to rely on tactful charm, something she has in plenty. She was able to have Hecht buried right next to his old buddy. If life, or death for that matter, imitates art, reminded that it was these two who collaborated on the screenplay of *Wuthering Heights,* can we honestly imagine anything other than "unquiet slumbers for the sleepers in that quiet earth"? Surely they are off, heaven only knows where, raising the kind of hell only they know how.

4

HELEN HAD long cherished an ambition to work in the kind of repertory situation enjoyed by so many generations of actors in England where stars would be able to play leading roles in one play and then play small cameo roles in the next, to the enrichment of both plays and players. This she was able to do in 1966 when she joined the APA-Phoenix Repertory Company at New York's Lyceum Theatre. In the intervening years between *A Touch of the Poet* and the repertory season she had had a mixed bag of opportunities. Following a television production of *The Cherry Orchard* in which she had finally played Ranevskaya she went on tour with a stage presentation of the play. In 1960 she toured as Mrs. St. Maugham in Enid Bagnold's *The Chalk Garden.* Early in 1961 Lawrence Langner was asked by the State Department to organize a theatre company for a tour abroad. Langner asked Helen if she would care to recreate her Mrs. Antrobus in *The Skin of Our Teeth.* The only drawback was that she would also have to play Amanda in *The Glass Menagerie.* Exhilarated at the thought of the one she was in despair at the thought of the other and drew up a whole list of roles she would prefer to do from Linda Loman in *Death of a Salesman* to Mary Tyrone in *Long Day's Journey into Night.* She would even be happier playing the small role of one of the mothers in *Our Town*—anything but Amanda Wingfield. But Langner was adamant that this was the program of plays which best projected the view of American life and theatre they wished to convey and which fitted with the third play, *The Miracle Worker,* which was also to be toured. So Helen played her least favorite role in thirty different countries in Europe, Asia, and South America during 1961. In late 1965 she went on a Far Eastern tour for the State Department, spending two months in Japan, Korea and the Philippines. Most of the time she was rehearsing and playing in scenes with actor-soldiers in army camps. However, in Tokyo she made a final and somewhat unorthodox return to *The Glass Menagerie.* Helen played Amanda and Tomoko Naraoka played Laura in a televised scene from the play. Helen's dialogue was in the original English, but the Japanese actress did her dialogue in Japanese. The two dovetailed their actions and the scene worked well.

In 1962 Helen was reunited with Maurice Evans in a program of Shakespeare entitled *Shakespeare Revisited* which was originally presented at the American Shakespeare Festival Theatre at Stratford, Connecticut, on July 10, and which subsequently toured. "Miss Hayes holds us best," recorded Frances Herridge, "when she is coy and gay—as Rosalind in *As You Like It* or Katharine in *Henry V*. But she loses conviction in the more passionate roles—as the angered Anne in *Richard III,* as a fearful Juliet or fiery Lady Macbeth. Evans is best in the excerpts he speaks alone, when his acting is at a minimum. Here he relies on a voice that is vastly expressive and zestful. The two together are most successful when they are not engaged in any scene, but when they are bombarding each other with lines picked at random that make sense and humor in their new sequence."

After appearing as Miss Dove in an adaptation of the Frances Gray Patton novel *Good Morning, Miss Dove,* with students of the Catholic University of America, she appeared in an unsuccessful attempt at doing for the inmates of *The White House* what had been so successfully achieved the previous season for those who sat upon the throne of England in *The Hollow Crown.* Helen was cast as a string of First Ladies, the wives of several Presidents. The high spot of the evening was a courtroom scene in which Mary Todd Lincoln was being examined for insanity on the accusation of her son. Walter Kerr wrote that playwright A. E. Hotchner had found her a passage in which she "Very simply, very clearly and very humbly explains to a court her recent aberrations. She could not seem more plausible or more innocent—until her face becomes a spasm without warning, and a motherly, bird-like simplicity vanishes behind the talons of her lost, clawing hands." The play, which opened at the Henry Miller on May 19, 1964, lasted but twenty-three performances. During the summer of 1966 Helen toured as Lady Catherine in Somerset Maugham's *The Circle* alternating with *Lovers, Villians and Fools* (sic) as the narrator. In the program she also recited the role of Chorus from *Henry V.*

Finally, with a sense of immense relief, she settled into her repertory season. *What a beautiful thing it is, at this stage in my career, not to have to work under that terrible, terrible pressure a star feels on Broadway, none of that sense of an awful weight on you, all that money riding on your performance and all those people working with you who will be out of a job if you catch a cold or forget a line opening night. The feeling of panic. I see it in the theatre all the time, that haunted look in the eyes of the actors. That's what I like so much in the APA, the lack of anxiety. There is freedom and enthusiasm and exhilarating excitement.* There were some who thought Helen's joining the group a rather patronizing action, as though she were condescending to help out an up-and-coming group of actors. The strangeness to America of the repertory phenomenon was responsible for this. It was only to be expected that there would have to be a period of adjustment to the idea. Audiences were uncomfortable at the participation of one of their favorite actresses in the company. How were they to treat a star in the relatively minor role of Mrs. Candour in Sheridan's *The School for Scandal,* her APA repertory debut role? *No actress worth her name wants to be loved all the time. She wants to be admired for a performance and wants to excite people with her art, to be respected for her craft. It seems like cheating just to want to be loved. It's not the true actor's aim. When I came on in* The School for Scandal *the audience, impressed I suppose because I was playing a secondary role in a repertory company, well, they wouldn't stop applauding. This terrible long reception went on and on, and I remember standing there facing the other actors in profound embarrassment. On the applause went. I was just miserable. A critic who, for some reason, had something against me, suggested that all I had to bring this company was the love I inspired in the audience. There I was, according to him, in a fixed pose, letting all that love pour over me. Such scorn, such contempt as I've never felt. He thought I couldn't act at all.*

Her next role was as the anguished mother in Pirandello's *Right You Are if You Think You Are,* and as the mother figure in an odd piece about Walt Whitman entitled *We Comrades Three.* A fleeting few performances in midrun of *You Can't Take It With You* completed her assignments for her first season.

During 1967 she agreed to play alongside Jim, who was recently divorced, in an episode of the long-running television series "Tarzan." *They lured me into it and when they had me hooked they told me I had to make my first entrance on an elephant. A baby elephant, they said, and very gentle. Well, a few days later they led in this enormous beast —ten feet high literally, the biggest elephant I had ever seen. My elephant. The first thing he did was swipe Tarzan (Ron Ely) with his trunk and send him flying. Ron got up and whacked the beast with a board and it bolted. The trainer finally arrived and controlled the beast and I announced I couldn't possibly ride it. But actors are crazy. They talked me into it and next morning I was lifted on top. It was like riding the Empire State Building with a great, heaving, rocking motion. Well, it started out at a decent pace—and then it started to run. I had no idea elephants could run that fast! Pretty soon we had passed everyone in sight, and there was just me and the elephant. I hung onto the rope for dear life, and I heard myself talking to the elephant as one might do to a horse, imploring sweetly, "Steady, Rocky, steady." When we got to the set the elephant saw his trainer and calmed down instantly. They filmed my entrance, but it wasn't over yet. They hadn't told me there was more. I heard the director yell, "Hang on tight, Helen!" and to my horror the elephant began lowering himself for me to get off—first on one elbow and then on the other. I slid down over his head and fell off. It was a complete mess!*

5

I see where Long Beach bought the Queen Mary. *If they wanted a venerable old relic they could have gotten me a lot cheaper.* Helen's career was to undergo its last major sea change. Since the O'Neill play her career had been uninspiring. Even her venture into repertory had not produced the kind of results it might. She had tended too much toward the *grandes dames* to which a First Lady might be expected to gravitate rather than appear in roles which challenged her own individuality. In this last phase of her career she would return to the puckishness of youth. It was almost to be a second childhood. The description "cute," which as a girl she had always loathed would now frequently be applied. Many of her roles would seem to be those of flappers who had grown into indomitable old ladies. Her professional life would tend to disprove her 1940 statement: *Actors should be a little extraordinary—they should be the color in the crowd. Of course, I'm a fine one to talk—I'm about as eccentric as bread and butter.*

The new Helen Hayes found her birth in her next APA assignment. The *Show-Off,* by George Kelly, had first been presented in 1924 and filmed in 1934 with Spencer Tracy in the title role. A girl's loudmouthed new husband alienates his in-laws and nearly wrecks his brother-in-law's career. Clayton Corzatte had the title role and Helen the supporting role of his mother-in-law. However the way

Helen took hold of the part made it almost the leading role. In this she did not betray the ensemble or stand apart from them as many had thought she did in *You Can't Take It With You*. She was very much a part of this company and this family. But if a performer and a part meet as they did so brilliantly here it is impossible to subdue the effect. The director gave Helen rope and it was to the ultimate good of all that she stretched it to its limits.

As with Queen Victoria, Helen found her mind wandering back to early Hayes days. *I used Aunt Mamie mercilessly. I could hear the Hayes sisters, Mamie and Essie, sitting around the table at home in Washington as they reported their encounters with hapless friends. These victims were always portrayed as fools or fishwives. My dear Aunt Mamie always came off as a figure of great dignity and compassion. All I had to do was let Aunt Mamie move in. But so completely did she take over that at rehearsals, alarmingly near our opening, I was still expressing myself in her words instead of the author's. When I was supposed to prophesy tartly of my spoiled and demanding daughter that she would be "sadly left," instead, out popped Aunt Mamie again, with "She'll have another think coming." Because I was married to a playwright, the author's own words mean a great deal to me. And so, in exasperation, I called up to the peanut gallery which is the nearest in theatre to Heaven, "Okay, Aunt Mamie. Thanks for all your help, but will you kindly leave the stage so I can get on with it." The rest of the cast thought I'd gone mad!*

There was general accord among the critics when the play opened on December 5, 1967, that the mother-in-law stole the show. But it wasn't, as Richard Watts, Jr., pointed out, that Helen was playing the famous star but that her delight in what was her best part for years lit up the stage. The play would run an unprecedented thirty weeks. After a summer break it reopened the following September at the same theatre before taking off on the road for fourteen weeks where it broke the house record in every town it visited. Although a picture of Helen in her role graced the playbill, Helen's name was in her alphabetically ordered place as a member of the company. When the play opened in Chicago a standing ovation was led by Alfred Lunt and Lynn Fontanne. Years before all three had been setting out on their careers together. Helen was now overwhelmed that such eminent actors should honor her in this way. She turned to Alec Clark and the other actors with her and said, "Do you see? Alfred is standing for *me!*" When they came backstage Lynn Fontanne pointed an accusing finger at her. "That isn't acting," she said. "That's *memory*. Memory!"

It was a very easy move to make. As at the Mad Hatter's tea party, she moved up one place at the table and sat in Essie's seat rather than in Aunt Mamie's. *The Front Page* had been revived in May 1969 with Robert Ryan and Bert Convy as Walter and Hildy for a limited engagement. It had a splendid press. Clive Barnes called it a "positively great bad play." It was bad, he considered, in that it was twenty times life size, but was one of the funniest and most exciting of all American plays. The play would win new celebrity all over the world around this time. There would be a most notable presentation of the play by the National Theatre of Great Britain. Helen, some years earlier had seen a tremendously successful production in Paris. There had been two film versions of the play, one in 1931 with Adolphe Menjou and Pat O'Brien, the second in 1940, renamed *His Girl Friday*, with Cary Grant and Rosalind Russell as a female Hildy. Even more liberties would be taken by Billy Wilder in his 1974 version with Walter Matthau and Jack Lemmon. Helen was invited to a preview. She was outraged by it and wanted to walk out, but sat mesmerized, wondering if it could get any worse. *After the show was over they were all waiting for my word, as if it were golden. I never said a thing, just left like a streak.* She was happier with a musical version, *Windy City*, which she saw in London in 1982, claiming that Robert Longden in the part of the escaped prisoner gave the best interpretation of the role she had ever seen.

To return to 1969. The only fault in the revival had been the casting of Mrs. Grant. When the revival was restaged in October at the Ethel Barrymore Helen joined the cast for six weeks. Here she was speaking Charlie's (and Ben's) words and playing Brownie! It was certainly the end of some kind of journey. Director Harold Kennedy has remarked on Helen's ability to disappear into the scenery at moments when he wanted the focus of the scene to be on the other players. However when he wanted attention to return to Mrs. Grant he noted "those ten million candles" lit up behind her eyes. Kennedy found her attitude to herself rich in humorous self-awareness. On one occasion she told him, *One night when I was with the APA, a young actress came to me in my dressing room. She was in great distress as she had been fired from one of the shows we were rehearsing. "Look," I told her, "at this stage of rehearsal I'm not one bit better than you are," I was doing my best to console her. "The only difference is," I went on, "they wouldn't dare fire me. That would be like spitting on the American flag . . ."*

Toward the end of 1968 she went to stay with some friends. Ross Hunter, the film producer, asked her hosts to remove all the books from her room with the exception of just one. It was Arthur Hailey's *Airport.*

EIGHT

ECCENTRIC AS
BREAD AND
BUTTER
1970 – 1985

1

I'm trying to kick the theatre habit by doing an odd job in films. Thus claimed Helen Hayes when shooting began on *Airport* on February 8, 1969. Ada Quonsett, her role, was the archetypal role of the latter part of her career. She would pursue a similar persona through a string of cinema and television films though never quite succeeding to better her original attempt. The role was that of a little old lady whose only means of visiting her grandchildren lies in stowing away on airplanes. Caught red-handed in the middle of one such adventure she explains to the airport staff how she has got the whole system taped. Placed under constant supervision she manages to give her guard the slip and finds herself sitting next to Van Heflin in the role of a suicidal maniac carrying a bomb in his attaché case with which he intends to blow up the plane, thus letting his unsuspecting wife collect a large insurance dividend.

The film, which was the first of a whole genre of "disaster movies" that would dominate the cinema of the next decade, was mounted along the lines of the old *Grand Hotel* formula in which an all-star cast play characters whose lives are changed by the events of the action. The last such picture in which Helen had appeared was, oddly enough, *Night Flight,* though this time she actually managed to board the plane! In a ploy to snatch the attaché case, one of the air hostesses, played by British actress Jacqueline Bisset, feigns an attack on Helen, who has a fit of hysterics and clings to Van Heflin, thus isolating the attaché case, which Miss Bisset grabs. Jacqueline Bisset was rather wary of giving the sixty-eight-year-old First Lady of the American Theatre too hearty a slap, offering only a deferential pat on the cheek. "You'll have to whack me a bit harder than that, dear, if the scene's going to work," said Helen. So she took the full force of the slap and then, scorning a stand-in, did her wrestling scene with Heflin herself. The ploy is in vain, for Heflin retrieves the case and rushes into the toilet where he detonates the bomb. Part of the plane is blown away. At a preview of the film with many of the stars present, Dean Martin said, "Golly, Heflin, when you go to the bathroom you sure as hell go!"

"AND WHO STEALS THE SHOW?" asked critic Wanda Hale. Her answer was Helen whom, she assured us, we would love to pieces. Louise Sweeney described her as a kind of "larcenous Whistler's mother." Audiences were delighted by this performance full of quirky little touches of humor—her logical "I don't think it would be good publicity if a big airline such as yours prosecuted a little old lady simply because she wanted to visit her daughter," her beaming self-satisfaction as, heroine of the hour, she is ferried across the airport on her own transporter. A retrospective viewing of the film, in the light of Helen's subsequent reexploration of similar roles, shows Maureen Stapleton's exquisitely modulated performance as Heflin's wife to be the more interesting, especially in her shamed, impotent apologies to the passengers emerging from the shattered plane. But, at the time, Helen sparkled originality.

I was sitting in Radio City Music Hall in New York soon after Airport *opened and when my name flashed on the screen a man behind me gasped, "Helen Hayes??? My God, she must be a hundred!" I turned around and gave him a dirty look, but my God, he looked a hundred! And I don't sass my elders.*

Airport would not be premiered until March 1970. After filming she went straight into a television performance of *Arsenic and Old Lace*. She had already performed in this on television alongside Billie Burke in 1955, with Boris Karloff, Peter Lorre, and Edward Everett Horton also in the cast. On this occasion her co-star was, in fact, the actress for whom the role had been written, Lillian Gish. Miss Gish recalled, *"Arsenic and Old Lace* was written for my sister Dorothy and me to appear in together. We were both about to sign contracts for something else but we were asked to wait because of this play. Dorothy said, 'Well, can you tell us what the play is about?' The reply came, 'Murder and insanity.' We promptly signed our contracts. When I eventually played it with Helen on television I wanted to play it differently from the way it had originally been played—like a little child. Perhaps wisely they chose to have us play it as it had been done on the stage." Some location shots for the program were filmed in Brooklyn Heights. Momentarily forgetful of the fact that she was dressed in Victorian lavender with a poke bonnet, Helen wandered about between shots absorbed in examining the architecture of the street. Suddenly an open sports car pulled up. "Do you always go around dressed like that?" inquired the driver, obviously not accustomed to New York eccentrics. Helen was too surprised to answer and bounced into character. "You'd better buzz off, young man," she snapped, "I'm a killer!" At which he hastily departed.

One of the ten great performances she had earlier been asked to nominate was that by Frank Fay in the original production of Mary Chase's *Harvey*. *It is exceptionally difficult to make a drunk attractive. Fay, however, was able to portray that nebulous, contented state that is between sobriety and out-and-out drunkenness and the audience was on his side all the time.* During the original run of the play Fay had taken a break and was replaced by James Stewart who repeated his interpretation of Elwood P. Dowd in the 1950 film. On both occasions he was rather too young for the role though his amiably gangling self was put to good use. It was not until the ANTA revival at the Phoenix Theatre which opened on February 24, 1970, that he truly came to terms with the part, winning great and affectionate praise. With him this time as Veta Louise was Helen. "It's always a pleasure for me to talk about Helen Hayes," recalled Mr. Stewart, "because she is a very, very special person. Appearing with her in *Harvey* was a wonderful, heartwarming experience for me. She is all the best things you can say about a human being, and I'm proud to call her my friend."

"Equally as delightful and charismatic as Mr. Stewart was Helen Hayes," noted Clive Barnes. "She epitomizes flustered charm almost as if it were a style of acting—and in her hands, in her face and in her public, it, of course is. She is one of those actors—Laurence Olivier is another, for she keeps the grandest company—where to watch how she is doing something is almost as pleasurable as what she is doing. Her technique is so close to the surface of her acting that it gives it a special blush. She makes a particularly neat partnership with Mr. Stewart—he ruggedly and rangily immobile and she prancing all round him like a bantam champion looking for a knockout glance. It added to the fun." Helen recognized that it was, however, Stewart's play and refused to take a solo call. The play was originally supposed to run only six weeks in New York but it was extended by a further month.

Helen watched on television as the Academy Awards for the year 1970 were presented. The presenter read the names of those nominated as Best Actress in a Supporting Role, "Karen Black for *Five Easy Pieces*, Lee Grant for *The Landlord*, Helen Hayes for *Airport*, Sally Kellerman for *M*A*S*H*, Maureen Stapleton for *Airport*." Then the envelope was opened. "And the winner is Helen Hayes!" Tumultuous applause, some cheers. *I thought they had made a mistake. I am absolutely stunned, on the verge of tears. God bless those people in Hollywood*, she told reporters over the telephone. The first stage actress to win an Oscar became the first performer to win Oscars in both acting categories.

2

WHEN, IN 1929, Helen had been touring in *Coquette* she was hospitalized in Boston because of breathing difficulties. It was not the first time this had happened. Theatres are notorious dust traps, particularly the backstage area. Paint and size flake off canvas flats and backcloths. Numerous feet tramp in and out. Curtains come swooping down and stir up the atmosphere. Helen often found that the dust irritated her throat and nostrils. Common house dust was often the cause of a sneezing fit. The Boston attack was rather worse than any other had been. Charlie had been very worried and suggested she give up acting in the theatre altogether. Helen was still very ambitious in those days and wouldn't hear of it. She learned to flare her nostrils to avoid the irritation leading to a sneeze. When she inadvertently let one enormous sneeze escape she quickly ad-libbed, "There are so many of these wicked colds going around. I guess I've caught one. Don't let me pass it on to you."

Fourteen years later she had another bad attack. *I made it through the opening night of* Harriet *and was immediately hospitalized for one week. We thought it was the paint at first, because they had tried to freshen everything up for me. But the doctor finally determined it was the dust. Charlie offered to buy me a tent. He said Sarah Bernhardt went around in one once.*

In 1971 she was invited to play Mary Tyrone in Eugene O'Neill's tragic autobiographical family play *Long Day's Journey into Night.* It is a taxing play for actors—immensely long and emotionally grueling. Helen's role as the wife who is losing the battle with morphine addiction was one she had always hoped to have a chance to play. Florence Eldridge had created it in the theatre and Katharine Hepburn had made a memorable film. During rehearsals, however, the dust bug struck. Helen was hospitalized yet again, ostensibly suffering from bronchitis. The cause was quickly ascribed to theatre dust but for the first time the doctors actually realized it was an allergy and not just a susceptibility to irritation. She was warned that she must give up the play as a return to the theatre could lead to pneumonia.

I was afraid if I didn't go on they'd say she's too old to remember her lines so I went back and did the show. How glad I am that I did. I came as close as I ever wanted to complete fulfillment in my acting when I played Mary Tyrone. It was a very rare feeling to realize a character that much. Then Walter Kerr said so in print.

Kerr was not particularly looking forward to seeing the play when he made his way to the Hartke Theatre in Washington on May 13. He had "done battle with it recently, and four hours is four hours." But he would claim that Helen brought the play alive for him in a way he had never thought possible. "Most actresses who play Eugene O'Neill's drug-ridden mother come on as wraiths, ghosts," he wrote. "The first thing that we see about them is that they are hopeless addicts . . . [But] the play is built toward a discovery that her addiction is hopeless . . . Now if *we* spot the truth at first sight, the other members of the embattled clan can come to seem a shade obtuse . . . [Helen Hayes] came on as nearly normal or as other nearly normal people are, tugging her skirt tightly about her, moving through the room as though its well-being depended on her, head high, spine firm, spirits pleasant . . . Her affection for her sons was open; her husband could still take her in his arms and kiss her; he had no need to keep her at arm's length as a freak . . . The family began as close-knit. The unraveling was to come later, despairingly . . . [making] the disclosure, the turnabout, the surrender to fact, all the more heartbreaking when it comes. There is a wrench to watching a facade crack, especially when the facade has seemed reasonably sturdy. By first creating the facade and by making it halfway plausible, Miss Hayes gained suspense to begin with and a heart-sinking sympathy when, inevitably, the foundation gave way . . . The standing ovation she received was in order and not simply because she had spent a lifetime being Helen Hayes. It was Eugene O'Neill she was working for, first to last."

It was perhaps fitting that she made her final stage appearance in Washington sixty-two years after her professional debut in the same city in *A Royal Family*. Only one month before, the Actors Fund Of America had honored her upon the sixty-fifth anniversary of her debut as an actress as Peaseblossom in *A Midsummer Night's Dream*.

I look back on my career with gratitude. If my stage-struck mother hadn't catapulted me into the theatre I'd never have had the opportunity to encounter all the richness in my life—my husband Charlie MacArthur, all the people I've known, the world I've inhabited as an actor. But as for the actual work, I don't think I was ever really happy acting. I lived in deathly fear, wondering if I could make it and after I got to be famous, the expectations got worse. So for years before that doctor told me to quit I wanted to.

The day I really retired from the theatre was the day I saw some tapes I had done of scenes from Victoria Regina. *These were scenes that had had people crying from coast to coast in the late 1930s, but I was appalled by my work. Totally phony, totally overdone. I think it was the touring that did it. All those Shrine Auditoriums where you worked so hard to reach the balcony. A star had to stay with a role in those days, you couldn't drop out after six months. I think overconscientiousness kept a lot of us from developing into real artists.*

I was in Denmark once and they wanted me to meet this old actor, the doyen of their theatre as I was supposed to be the doyenne of ours. He asked

*me how many plays I'd been in. I said I'd never counted them. Then I asked
him how many he'd been in. He said 368. I thought to myself, well, I'll
just keep quiet about my 40.*

A painter's worth is never measured by the number of canvases
he covers in paint but rather for the ones he has invested with
inspiration. The same must be true of the actor. In some societies an
actor may spend his entire life playing but one role, year by year
peeling off the layers which will lead him to a core of perfection or
the hollow realization of a lifetime's failure. The fact that the Dan-
ish actor had notched up almost four hundred play credits says
nothing of his acting ability but rather more suggests he must have
been in a hell of a lot of flops. Otherwise he worked in a theatre
repertory situation which played only short runs. Helen should not
have felt chagrined by her forty credits (though she is being overly
modest, as her play credits number more than eighty, not to men-
tion her roles in radio, television, and films) but proud that the
smaller number indicated several successes.

She is similarly not being fair to herself when she suggests that
she played Victoria badly. We have seen that she never liked her
work on film, particularly that which she did in the thirties. It is not
surprising that she should not like recordings of work meant to be
seen in a theatre where the character had to be projected larger than
life to an auditorium and not to the sensitive lens of the camera.
Stage performances never photograph well, always looking phony
and overdone. Even the immensely successful televising of the
Royal Shakespeare Company's production of *Nicholas Nickleby* was
guilty of overtheatricality in its performances. We accept them simply because we are aware that we are eavesdropping on an essen-
tially theatrical event. Helen is being unfair both to herself and her
audiences in suggesting that they were moved by something unwor-
thy.

It has been mentioned earlier that sometimes Helen puts herself
down before she is put down by others. This is her own particular
vulnerability. At times, however, in her disarming frankness she
hits upon elements of truth. In her memoirs she claimed of her
career, *I was to go from gingham virgin to the Statue of Liberty in a
Mother Hubbard. I would become sacrosanct to the general public and
saccharine anathema to the cognoscenti.* Because the cognoscenti has the
louder voice through the columns of newspapers and in the me-

chanical media, Helen's work appears to have been dismissed. For these she has never been the First Lady of anything. She herself considers Katharine Cornell to have been the First Lady of the American Theatre and the smart theatre set would be quick to agree. Nevertheless the title has always been meaningful to the general public who found Cornell too distant and forbidding. Superior theatre types consider that Helen pandered to public tastes rather than aiming somewhere over the heads of the public in order to bring them up to her level. This is and is not true. After her first initial stabs at theatre, Helen never appeared in out-and-out bad work. She did appear in Barrie, Shaw, Eugene O'Neill and Shakespeare. She was not afraid to tempt providence as Mary Stuart or as Addie Bemis in *Happy Birthday*.

The dilemma lies in the theatre snob's being able to neatly categorize actors. They like to be able to say, "Oh, Cornell was this kind of an actress, Ethel Barrymore was that kind, Tallulah Bankhead was something else . . ." Helen does not neatly fit into any category. This is because she never had any definite idea of the kind of actress she wanted to become. Indeed she had never reached a point where she actually wanted to *be* an actress, because she always was one. Her main ambitions lay in continuing to be an actress, in being able to make a living and not letting anyone down. Thus she was dependent on the work offered her—in the right play turning up at the right moment. Although many actors follow a similar pattern in their careers, there are others who have a clearer idea of the kind of actor they wish to become, often making a career out of playing in classical revivals, in proven successes in great roles. Thus the gifted actor can establish a firm reputation and a through-line of work which is easily recognizable. Such an actor then attracts new work which fits into the category in which he has placed himself. Helen never did this, although her career began to take such a course with Shaw's Cleopatra and Barrie's Maggie Wylie. Had she doomed herself, as at one point she claimed she had, to being the ever-fading ingenue, her career would have foundered. But as she faced each new challenge as it arose, seldom making do with the tried-and-true, but facing the different and unknown, she created new areas for her work throughout her life.

Whatever roles an actor takes, ultimately viewed over a period of time the actor's personality shines through. No actor can do anything about this. It is completely unwitting and this colors history's view of that actor. When Pope John Paul II celebrated a papal mass at Yankee Stadium before eighty thousand communicants, Helen read the lesson from Genesis. Afterward she told Marc Connelly, "That pope's goodness shines from his entire body. The moment you see him it becomes apparent." Connelly smiled at her. "So does yours," he said. And so it does. Helen's goodness and humanitarianism is immediately evident and she exercises no control over it. Thus audiences were never able to accept her as a villain, as in the case of *Mr. Gilhooley.* The theatre snob tends to celebrate that which glitters—all the sharp, brittle qualities—stature, crystal clarity, authority, wit, elegance, style, camp flippancy. Helen had none of these. She had warmth, charm, gay humor, lightness, sweetness, puckishness, human insight, deftness, loving good nature, reserve, accessibility, vulnerability. She was a democratic actress in that she didn't bestow her gifts from on high but invited an audience into the warmth of her own delight and experience. Over sixty-five years they told her they enjoyed being there.

I find I am so vague about dates and so forth in connection with my career. In fact there are so many plays I have completely forgotten even having been in. It only proves what I have long suspected, that my theatre life was got through in a state of semiconsciousness. The one thing I can remember vividly is the struggle for perfection—the perfection that always eluded me, but lured me on.

3

HELEN'S SUCCESS IN *Airport* led to several offers, mainly, to begin with, from television. She was only one of a generation of elderly ladies with distinguished pasts. Many like Bette Davis, Olivia de Havilland, and Joan Crawford still battled to keep their faces before cinema cameras in increasingly ghoulish guises. Grand Guignol was certainly not Helen's forte. Her own particular talent for light comedy would be her stock in trade throughout the seventies. Her first assignment co-starred her with two of the great Hollywood stars of the thirties, Myrna Loy and Sylvia Sidney, and that clever actress from the theatre, Mildred Natwick. Helen had previously worked with Miss Natwick in 1951, playing Mary to her Elizabeth in a television version of *Mary of Scotland.* Although she had been co-starred with Myrna Loy twice, in *Arrowsmith* and *Night Flight,* they had met on neither. This had been a source of great unhappiness for Miss Loy, she claimed recently, as she had always admired Helen more than almost any other actress. Their eventual meeting, unfortunately, was not the occasion of distinction it might have been. The television film entitled *Do Not Fold, Spindle or Mutilate* was about four old ladies who, with nothing better to do, decide to enroll with a computer-dating agency using a fictitious persona and name and sit back to see the results. Their busybodying leads an innocent girl into being entrapped by a homicidal maniac. It is a bad joke. The characters are unsympathetic and are cast with four extremely sympathetic actresses. Though each handles the dreadful material with an expertise it does not warrant, it is embarrassing to hear them reduced to talking in near lewd terms.

The film aired on November 9, 1971. During the next few months Helen made a guest appearance on *Here's Lucy* with Lucille Ball and re-created her Veta Louise opposite James Stewart in *Harvey.* They were delighted to be back together again in this play. After the Broadway success they had hoped to take the play to London but British Actors Equity had forbidden two American actors to appear in the West End production and Stewart had gone alone. After an appearance in *Ghost Story* Helen joined Mildred Natwick once more in a feature-length television movie intended as the pilot to a series as *The Snoop Sisters.*

I don't like to throw away the whole work of a lifetime. After I made that first television movie (Do Not Fold, Spindle or Mutilate) *I was bombarded with scripts for* The Snoop Sisters. *Finally Mildred Natwick and I agreed to do it. They broke down our resistance, I guess. But I'm not sorry. It's an adventure. I think now I've tried everything—except, perhaps, burlesque, and I don't think I'd be any good at that. I want to make it clear that I've never felt superior to the television medium. I just haven't been able to feel comfortable in it. If you want to see a portrait of a frightened woman just look at me when a television director says, as they often do in this show, "Just say anything you want to here." Blank. Nothing.*

The subject of the movie (which had Paulette Goddard and Art Carney as guest stars) and the series involved two elderly lady mystery writers who, to the annoyance of their policeman nephew, investigate and solve murder cases in real life, getting themselves and him into a great deal of bother. The fun came from seeing two seemingly timid little old ladies setting foot where Starsky and Hutch might fear to tread. They are fearless and ingenious. Unfortunately the scripts weren't. An originally delightful idea petered out, and although the playing of the two actresses was consistently charming and imaginative, the idea began to pall. As it did, so Helen's enthusiasm waned. *I was miserable doing it. It was like a jail sentence. The hours that we had to work were terrible, not only for Mildred and myself, but everyone. I felt petulant, angry, and sorry for myself. Oh, it's easy to sit on the sidelines and say, "Why should television stars complain when they're getting paid $125,000 a show?" But something inside you feels put upon when you are required to work under such miserable conditions.*

When Disney director Bill Walsh approached Helen and said, "I've seen you so much as a lady, I don't know whether you'd be willing to undertake low comedy," Helen's answer was straightforward enough, "Don't you think I've earned the right to play hokum?" And hokum she would play in *Herbie Rides Again*. Herbie had ridden before in *The Love Bug,* which was the story of an unsuccessful racing driver who discovered that his Volkswagen had a mind all of its own. In Herbie's second movie (later he would go to Monte Carlo and then go Bananas) he co-starred with Helen, who played a nice little old lady who was campaigning to prevent her home, an old firehouse on top of a San Francisco hill, from falling to the wreckers. Apart from talking to a Volkswagen she had conversations with a retired San Francisco cable car and an antique music box. In fact, though Disney had moved from feature-length cartoons to live-action films the difference was scarcely noticeable. However, this kind of whimsy appeals unerringly to children and Disney knew his market. Helen was delighted to be working for the studio, following in Jim's footsteps. Another Disney feature followed twelve months later. This was shot entirely in England. *One of Our Dinosaurs Is Missing* was set in the 1920s and concerned a strip of microfilm being smuggled out of China and hidden in a dinosaur's skeleton in the Natural History Museum in London. Helen was cast as an English nanny who eventually leads a battalion of nannies against the villains of the piece. Although her co-star was Peter Ustinov, as an all-too scrutable Chinese spy, and the rest of the cast was made up of experienced British comedy actors, the film was something of a turkey. The film Helen had designated, for thus she had, the last film she would make, was a poor end to her career. Fortunately she would change her mind and return to England the following year and make the marginally better *Candleshoe* for Disney with David Niven and Jodie Foster.

After *Dinosaurs* she followed once more in Jim's footsteps, appearing with him in his long-running television series "Hawaii Five-O." *I'll go on any show that asks me to appear with Jim. He's such a delight to work with, and he's very much beloved. All through the business of being a television celebrity and being highly admired, he's carried a great urge to serve and to please. He is so caring and really yearns to do for people. I think that's a most gratifying trait.*

Helen claimed that this was to be her last public appearance and perhaps in deference to this Jack Lord, the series' top star, allowed his jealously guarded last-frame freeze to go to Helen. However this was not to be the end of her career. She appeared in the mini-series *The Moneychangers*, co-starring with Kirk Douglas, and played the vanishing Englishwoman in the television film *Victory at Entebbe*. In 1977 she paired up with another legend when she appeared in the film *A Family Upside Down* about a deeply loving couple who are forced to live apart as a result of ill-health. Her co-star was Fred Astaire. Charlie had always wanted her to act with Astaire. "It's taken all these years, but finally we made it kid," Astaire told her. Helen said she was glad it hadn't happened earlier. "Then I would have been expected to be your dancing partner," she said. "With these two left feet that would have been impossible!"

In 1981 she appeared in an Agatha Christie mystery, *Murder Is Easy*, filmed in England. She played a tweedy English spinster with her own approximation of an English accent. She had one scene only at the beginning of the film with Bill Bixby, before becoming the victim of a hit-and-run driver. It was enough for Agatha Christie's sister and the solicitor in charge of her estate to see that Helen was the ideal actress to play one of Dame Agatha's most famous creations, the inimitable Miss Marple. The inimitable Margaret Rutherford is the actress most affectionately associated with the part. However, it seems Dame Agatha did not appreciate Dame Margaret's performance as greatly as did the audiences who flocked to the four MGM films she made in that character. Indeed Margaret Rutherford simply moved her catalogue of comic mannerisms into the rather dull Agatha Christie plots which were not a million miles in format from the plots which the Snoop Sisters had enjoyed. *I decided I had to get rid of my negative feelings about not working again. I was frightened at the thought of playing Miss Marple remembering how wonderful Margaret Rutherford was in the role and how much I enjoyed her. However Marple is a plain little woman who knits all the time. But behind that façade wonderful things are going on in her mind. But how do you show that? Dame Margaret hoked it up and I don't know how to do that. I played her straight.*

A Caribbean Mystery, in which she co-starred with Maurice Evans, was filmed and aired in 1983. It was certainly a long way from Rutherford but it was fair Agatha Christie. Unfortunately Agatha Christie's work needs hoking up in some way as it otherwise seems unduly pedestrian. The director in this case seems to have thought it would play itself and the result was that it was rather dull. After making it, Helen claimed that it would be her last starring part, that a major role such as Miss Marple was too exhausting. She was, after all, eighty-two years of age when she made it. However she was making the same claims at the age of eighty-four when she was back in the studios making her second Miss Marple movie, *Murder by Mirrors*, in October 1984. For the first time she worked with Bette Davis, who had a cameo role. At the party upon the film's completion Miss Davis spoke warmly of the admiration she had felt for Helen all her life.

It is sad that Helen's work during the last decade has seemed to undervalue her talents. Her friend Ruth Gordon who had also developed a line in charismatic elderly ladies, in her middle seventies made what is surely her masterpiece on film, *Harold and Maude*. Though any actor is dependent on the right script materializing at the right moment, it does seem unfortunate that there is no such masterpiece to landmark Helen's later career in films in the way that *A Farewell to Arms* did so brilliantly her early years. There again, perhaps that performance is yet to come. She shows no signs of stopping just yet . . .

4

It might at first have been anger that made me dedicate myself to the National Foundation and its crusade to wipe out polio. But then I met one of the medical heads whose own children had been afflicted and who was determined to see that others would not be. I was struck by the fact that, if there is any divinity, it is in man's willingness to help alleviate suffering in others. I knew without the slightest doubt that it would please Mary's happy spirit.

At first Charlie had not been happy about it. "I will not let Mary be used as a tambourine!" he protested bitterly. But he would come around. Shortly after Mary's death there had been a telephone call from a stranger, asking if Helen would speak to his wife. They had recently lost a son to polio. At first Helen had refused, distraught at the idea. Charlie was being strong for them both at the time and invited the couple over. The way that each wanted comfort for the other reflected their own need.

The March of Dimes Foundation asked Helen if she would be their national chairman of volunteers. She accepted and for her first assignment with them addressed a polio conference in Washington, D.C. She spoke quietly with moving conviction and was given a standing ovation when she concluded with "We won't stop until polio is eliminated everywhere!"

The Mary MacArthur Fund, which had been created in her memory by some of her theatre friends, had endowed a twelve-bed respiratory ward in Boston's Children's Hospital. Once Jonas Salk had isolated the microbe Helen was to be of immeasurable value to him in helping the public overcome its fears of inoculation. Indeed Salk claimed that she proved his greatest asset in this difficult task which helped rid the world of a killer disease.

Helen has never let herself be tardy in aid of a cause. During the time of the McCarthy Communist witch hunt in 1947 she was one of the Broadway contingent of actors who protested the hounding of the Hollywood Ten. She is not a natural orator. Unlike the character she played in *To the Ladies,* it is not in her nature to be able to stand up and make an impromptu speech. She needs her script. When Joe Papp was trying to bring his concept of free Shakespeare to New York he ran into unexpected difficulties. Having managed one short summer season on a makeshift stage near the lake in Central Park he knew he needed funds to continue the project. One particular New York City councilman opposed Papp's application for no apparent good reason. On the strength of his wife's having been a classmate of Mary's at the Academy of Dramatic Arts, Papp telephoned Helen and asked if she would stand for him as a character witness when he appeared before the Board of Estimate to make his appeal. She agreed when he told her she would not have to speak.

On the hour-long journey to City Hall he briefed her on the relevant points. Though she would not be required to speak she would perhaps like to say a few words to the television and press people afterward. Not wishing to sound uninformed, she said she would need more information. To assist her, Papp read her his presentation. When it came their turn to make their application the mayor announced, "Our next speaker will be Miss Helen Hayes." Blank horror masked each of their faces as Helen stumbled up to the podium. Somehow the words came and not just a gabble of ill-conceived phrases but succinct and well-ordered thoughts. But she realized before she was halfway through that she was reciting Joe's speech, which somehow she had miraculously committed to memory as Joe had read it to her. She even achieved a round of applause when she had finished and a word of commendation from the Mayor. Joe Papp was left to do the ad-libbing! He must have done it well, for free Shakespeare got its grant and is alive and well and living in Central Park.

When she had played Queen Victoria in Washington she was invited to a small dinner party at the White House. "And how is Your Majesty?" asked Franklin Delano Roosevelt as he entered the room. Later the two of them were alone and F.D.R. chatted about the State of the Union message he was to deliver a few days later. "What do you think I should say?" he asked. *"You are asking me?" I replied. "Miss Hayes, you have no axe to grind," he said. "I'd like to have your thoughts." For the next thirty minutes the President of the United States listened to a suddenly tongue-tied actress try to offer ideas.*

When asked her opinion as to what was the difference between Republicans and Democrats Helen replied, *I think the Republicans have what I have—a strong, enduring respect for the American business-man and financier. I believe with all my heart in American business and free enterprise. Every tycoon I've ever known I've admired.* Her brother-in-law John MacArthur, who came from one of the most impoverished of backgrounds, chose as his alternative to the path of his father's religion a career in real estate and insurance to become one of the richest men in America with assets believed to be in the billions.

In 1982 Helen was asked to speak before the U.S. Senate on behalf of proposed legislation for home care for the elderly. *There I was on the floor of the Senate at age eighty-two, making a big noise and telling everyone that my generation has got to be noticed. Later on I thought, "You'd better watch yourself and be careful that you don't get too demanding and cocky."* Since 1980 over two hundred radio stations throughout the United States have broadcast her daily two-and-a-half-minute radio message to the nation's elderly. "The Best Years" always opens the same way. *Hello, this is Helen Hayes . . .*

Recently, on being honored by the National Theatre in Washington, Helen was entertained at tea by Nancy Reagan at the White House. When photographs of the occasion were published in the press the caption naturally read, "First Ladies Meet."

5

Sometimes in the morning I pretend I'm still a great star of the theatre and I carry my breakfast to my room on a tray using my best breakfast china and my best tray cloth. Everything is exquisite. I put it on the little table by my bed and crawl in, putting on a very pretty bed jacket, the tray on my lap— and I'm a star in bed having my breakfast. It's fun and it brings me back to the old rhythm and feeling. I try to swim five laps every day. I swim very slowly and with great dignity—no thrashing about. I don't miss anything at all about work. It's glorious in youth but you are worn down after a while by the work of a career, by the nerves and the anxiety that you need to be free of when you get old. We all have to pull in and do less, and I guess I've always wanted to do more. There's so much going on in the world, and I want to watch; I've got greedy eyes. I planted two lovely trees in the garden a couple of years ago and I look at them and think, "Oh, how I'd like to see them get tall . . ."

To mark her eightieth birthday, the town of Haverstraw, New York, up the Hudson from Nyack, dedicated a new hospital to her. *That's some birthday present isn't it—a $38,000,000 hospital! That's better than Richard Burton ever did for Elizabeth Taylor.* At the opening, the governor of New York State went down on his knees to her proclaiming her to be "Queen of the Empire State." She decided to spend her eightieth birthday at a party given by the Actors Fund Home in Inglewood, New Jersey. Instructions have been left with Jim that should she ever prove unable to manage for herself she should be moved there.

When I published my biography of the distinguished British actress Dame Flora Robson, I recalled my first meeting with Helen at lunch at Dame Flora's home in Brighton. "I felt privileged to be sitting at table with Queen Elizabeth I, Mary of Scotland, Mary Tudor, Victoria Regina, the Dowager Empress of China, the Dowager Empress of Russia, and two of the most charming women I have ever met. Each in her lifetime had been honoured by having a theatre named after her, as well as numerous other honours." The Flora Robson Playhouse had already been rased to the ground to make way for a road-widening scheme. Almost twenty years later the project has still to be realized. Ironically, shortly after the book was published plans were announced for the demolition of the Helen Hayes Theatre. Helen seemed publicly indifferent to the news. Although she had been sensible of the honor at the time it had originally been renamed, she had always been slightly embarrassed by it, always referring to it as "that theatre" rather than appear self-obsessed in announcing its name. Wherever she traveled there by taxi she always gave the street intersection location. The theatre world on the other hand was up in arms at the threatened closure. The loss of a theatre, whatever its name, threatens the livelihoods of actors. Protests were lodged, petitions drawn up, but all in vain. A last stand by several Broadway celebrities against the oncoming bulldozers failed, and Colleen Dewhurst, Celeste Holm, Richard Gere, and several others were arrested.

Although she had said nothing in the theatre's defense Helen was quick to veto an idea that another theatre on the same site within the rebuilt complex should bear her name. She very much more happily agreed to the idea that the Little Theatre at 240 West Forty-fourth Street should be renamed in her honor. She made one condition to this that the theatre would outlive her. When the Little's identity was officially changed to that of the Helen Hayes Theatre, Helen told those assembled at the ceremony, *When the other theatre was torn down I pretended very hard that I didn't mind, but I really did. Even though I couldn't be on the stage anymore myself I took comfort in knowing that I was still represented on Broadway. The theatre has been my whole life. It has given me every great thing I ever had. I hope this theatre will have many long runs and outlive me. I don't want any more tragedies. I don't want to be reduced to bathroom weeping any more. In the theatre we learn that you only cry onstage and in the bathroom.*

Was Brownie, I wonder, again looking over her shoulder when in 1984 the Helen Hayes Award was inaugurated? The first award, which recognizes excellence in the theatre in Washington, was presented by Helen in May 1985. Brownie's daughter—first an actress, then First Lady, then two theatres, then an award. Clee O'Patrick had come a long way.

The little tree without any leaves has found a whole springtime of new foliage. She is bright and alert and always on the lookout for new challenges. Sometimes simply standing and staring isn't enough and off she goes on new adventures, using her time to travel. If the offer of a job and the chance to buy a new item for her collection of paintings of the Hudson River coincide, then the cost of the one is offset against the effort of the other and she plunges back into work. Sometimes commitments overcrowd her life and she rushes back into seclusion. Her companion, Vera Benlian, blocks the telephone calls of even her most persistent best friends and she sits and stares at the Hudson, that grand old river where once upon a time the boy Charlie MacArthur skinny-dipped with his schoolfellows. She has never felt any inclination to remarry. *I'm still waiting for my reunion with Charlie, waiting eagerly and happily for it.*

An old house like hers has many memories and shares them with its treasured occupant. Like that long ago Thanksgiving which echoes in her mind, when she decided to cook the turkey with all the trimmings herself. "We can always go up the road and eat if it doesn't work," grins Charlie. "I want no cracks," says Helen as she proudly carries in her done-to-a-turn offering, only to find a grinning father and son dressed in their outdoor clothes ready to go out and eat. The spirits of dogs race round the garden, leaping on the rose beds only to be warned off by the memories of long ago threats. Remember the day Charlie learned to get his own back on the wild poodle Turvey who attacked him every time he touched Helen. Charlie thumbed his nose at the dog, who understood and barked himself crazy. Then the day a taxi drew up and out stepped Mary's poodle, Camille. She had followed her mistress to school and was sent back in style. And the day Turvey, lovesick for Helen, had howled unceasingly, it just happening to be the day Charlie came home from war, and Helen had gone to the drugstore for a measure of saltpeter to cool Turvey's ardor, and how the ladies in the store had gone suddenly, blushingly silent. "That damn dog has done me in again," said Charlie. And those peanut emeralds he had brought back that were made into the necklace which disappeared in the burglary. And is that Turvey howling again or Charlie playing his saxophone? And the time the great John Barrymore was on a bender with Charlie and they decided the water in the pool wasn't cold enough and ordered two truckloads of ice to be dumped there. Remember them both, hung over, staggering to the pool and Barrymore floating amid the ice and crying, "I feel like a fly in a highball!" And the times Helen was naked and Charlie chased her around the house with his camera. And a whole spoonful of mashed potato leaps high in the air . . .

So much past, so much still present and so much still to come. An unambitious woman who made her mother's dreams come true. The triumph, in her own words, of the familiar over the exotic. An actress of remarkable talent who has never understood her own worth. A legend in her own lifetime. A simple soul. Wife, mother, grandmother who, in or out of the theatre, always was and ever will be first and last a lady.

APPENDIX

THEATRE

Holy Cross Academy, 1905, *A Midsummer Night's Dream* (Peaseblossom)

Belasco, Washington, January 22, 1909, *Jack the Giant Killer* (Gibson Girl, Nell Brinkley Girl). Also at Columbia Theatre, February 2, 1909.

Columbia, Washington, May 24, 1909, *A Royal Family* (Prince Charles Ferdinand)

Chase's, Washington, May 25, 1909, Children's Dancing Kermiss (Nell Brinkley Girl)

Columbia, Washington, May 31, 1909, *The Prince Chap* (Claudia, aged 5)

Columbia, Washington, August 16, 1909, *A Poor Relation* (Patch)

Herald Square, New York, November 22, 1909, *Old Dutch* (Little Mime) (88 performances, then toured)

Broadway, New York, June 4, 1910, *The Summer Widowers* (Psyche Finnegan) (140, then toured)

Columbia, Washington, July 10, 1911, *The Barrier* (Molly)

Columbia, Washington, July 17, 1911, *Little Lord Fauntleroy* (title role)

Broadway, New York, October 5, 1911, *The Never Homes* (Fanny Hicks) (92, then toured)

Columbia, Washington, May 20, 1912, *The Seven Sisters*

Columbia, Washington, June 10, 1912, *Mary Jane's Pa* (Mary Jane)

Tour, September 21 to October 12, 1912, *The June Bride*

National, Washington, April 4, 1913, Flood victims benefit (Bessie Clifford impersonation)

Columbia, Washington, April 21, 1913, *The Girl with Green Eyes*

Columbia, Washington, April 28, 1913, *His House in Order* (Derek Jesson)

Columbia, Washington, May 5, 1913, *A Royal Family* (Prince Charles Ferdinand)

Columbia, Washington, May 12, 1913, *The Prince Chap* (Claudia, aged eight)

Columbia, Washington, June 16, 1913, *The Prince and the Pauper* (title roles)

Empire, New York, September 7, 1914, *The Prodigal Husband* (Little Simone) (42, then tour, to January 9, 1915)

Poli's, Washington, January 31, 1916, *The Dummy* (Beryl)

Poli's, Washington, March 13, 1916, *On Trial* (Doris Strickland) Also at Academy of Music, Baltimore, April 10, 1916.

APPENDIX

Poli's, Washington, February 19, 1917, *It Pays to Advertise* (Marie)
Poli's, Washington, February 26, 1917, *Romance* (Suzette)
Poli's, Washington, March 5, 1917, *Just a Woman* (The Hired Girl)
Poli's, Washington, March 12, 1917, *Mile-a-Minute Kendall* (Beth)
Poli's, Washington, March 19, 1917, *Rich Man, Poor Man*
Poli's, Washington, April 2, 1917, *Alma, Where Do You Live?* (Germain)
Poli's, Washington, April 9, 1917, *Mrs. Wiggs of the Cabbage Patch* (Asia)
Poli's, Washington, April 23, 1917, *Within the Law*
Tour, from September 17, 1917, *Pollyanna* (Pollyanna Whittier)
Globe, New York, September 2, 1918, *Penrod* (Margaret Schofield) transferred to Punch and Judy (42 total)
Empire, New York, December 23, 1918, *Dear Brutus* (Margaret) (184, though Helen left the cast midrun)
National, Washington, June 2, 1919, *On the Hiring Line* (Dorothy Fessenden) (8)
Nixon's Apollo, Atlantic City, July 7, 1919, *Clarence* (Cora Wheeler)
Nixon's Apollo, Atlantic City, July 28, 1919, *The Golden Age* (Mary Anne)
Hudson, New York, September 20, 1919, *Clarence* (Cora Wheeler) (300, though Helen left after three months)
Park, Taunton, February 13, 1920, *Bab* (title role), then extended run in Boston. Opened Park, New York, October 18, 1920 (88, then tour)
Gaiety, New York, October 10, 1921, *The Wren* (Seeby Olds) (24)
Gaiety, New York, November 1, 1921, *Golden Days* (Mary Anne) (40)
Liberty, New York, February 20, 1922, *To the Ladies* (Elsie Beebe) (128 and tour)
Tour, from November 2 to 24, 1923, *Loney Lee* (Appolonia Lee)
Gaiety, New York, March 11, 1924, *We Moderns* (Mary Sundale) (22)
Woodstock, Summer of 1924, *The Dragon*
Empire, New York, June 9, 1924, *She Stoops to Conquer* (Constance Neville) (8)
Booth, New York, August 11, 1924, *Dancing Mothers* (Catharine Westcourt) (312, though Helen left after three months)
Henry Miller, New York, December 16, 1924, *Quarantine* (Dinah Partlett) (151, though Helen left after three months)
Guild (ANTA), New York, April 13, 1925, *Caesar and Cleopatra* (Cleopatra) (48)
Ritz, New York, November 24, 1925, *Young Blood* (Georgia Bissell) (73 and tour)
Bijou, New York, April 13, 1926, *What Every Woman Knows* (Maggie Wylie) (268 and tour)
Maxine Elliott, November 8, 1927, *Coquette* (Norma Besant) (366 and two tours)
Broadhurst, New York, September 30, 1930, *Mr. Gilhooley* (Nellie Fitzpatrick) (31)
Empire, New York, December 15, 1930, *Petticoat Influence* (Peggy Chalfont) (98)

APPENDIX

Henry Miller, New York, November 24, 1931, *The Good Fairy* (Lu) (151, then toured)

Alvin, New York, November 27, 1933, *Mary of Scotland* (Mary Stuart) (248 and later tour)

County, Suffern, August 21, 1935, *Caesar and Cleopatra* (Cleopatra)

Broadhurst, New York, December 26, 1935, *Victoria Regina* (title role) (517 and several tours)

Henry Miller, December 1, 1936, *The Country Wife* (produced only) (89)

Shubert, Chicago, January 14, 23, 28, 1938, *The Merchant of Venice* (Portia) (3) Also at Curran, San Francisco, May 27, June 3, (2), and Biltmore, Los Angeles, June 19, (1)

County, Suffern, August 29, 1938, *What Every Woman Knows* (Maggie Wylie)

Martin Beck, New York, October 3, 1938, *Victoria Regina* (title role) (87, and further tour. Grand total of performances in this role: 969)

Martin Beck, New York, October 17, 1939, *Ladies and Gentlemen* (Miss Scott) (105 and tour.)

St. James, New York, November 19, 1940, *Twelfth Night* (Viola) (129 and tour)

Shubert, New York, October 22, 1941, *Candle in the Wind* (Madeleine Guest) (95 and tour.)

Henry Miller, New York, March 3, 1943, *Harriet* (Harriet Beecher-Stowe) (377 and tour.)

Bucks County Playhouse, New Hope, July 15, 1946, *Alice-Sit-by-the-Fire* (Mrs. Grey) (toured)

Broadhurst, New York, October 31, 1946, *Happy Birthday* (Addie Bemis) (564)

Ziegfeld, New York, January 18, 1948, Scene from *Victoria Regina*, First ANTA Album.

Olney, Olney, May 28, 1948, *Alice-Sit-by-the-Fire* (Mrs. Grey)

Theatre Royal, Haymarket, London, England, July 28, 1948, *The Glass Menagerie* (Amanda Wingfield) (109)

Nyack High School, July 15, 1949, *The Glass Menagerie* (Amanda Wingfield)

Cape Playhouse, Dennis, August 15, 1949, *Good Housekeeping* (Mrs. Burnett)

Martin Beck, March 29, 1950, *The Wisteria Trees* (Lucy Andree Ransdell) (165)

ANTA, New York, March 4, 1951, *Mary Rose* (produced only) (16)

Martin Beck, February 20, 1952, *Mrs. McThing* (Mrs. Howard V. Larue II) (350) also at Central City Opera House, Colorado, Summer 1953, return to New York and tour.

Falmouth Playhouse, Coonamessett, Helen Hayes Festival, July 3, 1954, *What Every Woman Knows* (Maggie Wylie) July 12, 1954, *Mrs. McThing* (Mrs. Larue) July 19, 1954, *The Wisteria Trees* (Mrs. Ransdell) July 26, 1954, *Mary of Scotland* (title role)

Huntington Hartford, Hollywood, September 27, 1954, *What Every Woman*

APPENDIX

Knows (Maggie Wylie) and West Coast tour, then at City Center, New York, December 22, 1954 (15)

City Center, New York, February 2, 1955, *The Wisteria Trees* (Mrs. Ransdell) (15)

Palm Beach Playhouse, March 14, 1955, *Mrs. McThing* (Mrs. Larue)

Solebury School, Solebury, May 7, 1955, *Gentlemen, The Queens* (Catherine the Great, Mary Stuart, Queen Victoria, Lady Macbeth) (1) and at Lydia Mendelssohn, Ann Arbor, May 16, 1955.

Sarah Bernhardt, Paris, France, June 28, 1955, *The Skin of Our Teeth* (Mrs. Antrobus) also at ANTA, New York, August 17, 1955 (22)

Theatre de Lys, New York, October 23, 1956, *Lovers, Villians and Fools* (narrator and Chorus from *Henry V)* (1)

City Center, New York, November 21, 1956, *The Glass Menagerie* (Amanda Wingfield) (15)

Morosco, New York, November 12, 1957, *Time Remembered* (Duchess of Pont-au-Bronc) (248)

Tappan Zee Playhouse, Nyack, July 1, 1958, *Mid-Summer* (Rosie, the maid) (played only the first performance)

Helen Hayes, New York, October 2, 1958, *A Touch of the Poet* (Norah Melody) (292)

Tour from July 20, 1959, *A Adventure* (Lulu Spencer)

Tour from January 25, 1960, *The Cherry Orchard* (Ranevskaya)

O'Laughlin, Notre Dame, May 10, 1960, *The Skin of Our Teeth* (Mrs. Antrobus)

Tour from August 8, 1960, *The Chalk Garden* (Mrs. St. Maugham)

International tour from February 28, 1961, *The Skin of Our Teeth* (Mrs. Antrobus) and *The Glass Menagerie* (Amanda Wingfield) to June 16, 1961, and further tour to South America, August 7 to October 28, 1961.

American Shakespeare Festival, Stratford, July 10, 1962, *Shakespeare Revisited: A Program for Two Players* (Several Shakespearean roles) and tour under title *A Program for Two Players* (21 weeks)

University, Washington, January 21, 1964, *Good Morning, Miss Dove* (Miss Dove)

Henry Miller, New York, May 19, 1964, *The White House* (wives of several Presidents) (23)

Tour from April 8, 1966, *The Circle* (Lady Catherine Champion-Cheyney)

Lyceum, New York, APA-Phoenix Repertory Company, November 21, 1966, *The School for Scandal* (Mrs. Candour) November 22, 1966, *Right You Are if You Think You Are* (Signora Frola) December 20, 1966, *We Comrades Three* (The Mother) *You Can't Take It With You* (Grand Duchess Olga) (occasional performances)

Lyceum, New York, December 5, 1967, *The Show-Off* (Mrs. Fisher) (30 weeks), reopening September 30, 1968 at same theatre and then tour.

Ethel Barrymore, New York, October 18, 1969, *The Front Page* (Mrs. Grant) (159, Helen played only for six weeks midrun)

ANTA, New York, February 24, 1970, *Harvey* (Veta Louise Simmons) (79)

APPENDIX

Hartke, Washington, May 13, 1971, *Long Day's Journey into Night* (Mary Cavan Tyrone)

CINEMA

Jean and the Calico Doll—U.S. (released August 30, 1910) (Miss Doyle)
Followed by several two-reelers, titles unknown
Weavers of Life—U.S. (November 1917) (Peggy)
The Sin of Madelon Claudet—U.S. (October 30, 1931) (GB title: *Lullaby)* (Madelon)
Arrowsmith—U.S. (December 7, 1931) (Leora Tozer)
A Farewell to Arms—U.S. (December 8, 1932) (Catherine Barkley)
The Son-Daughter—U.S. (January 1, 1933) (Lien Whà)
The White Sister—U.S. (March 17, 1933) (Angela Chiaromonte)
Another Language—U.S. (August 4, 1933) (Stella)
Night Flight—U.S. (October 6, 1933) (Madame Fabian)
Crime Without Passion—U.S. (August 30, 1934) (unbilled guest appearance)
What Every Woman Knows—U.S. (October 26, 1934) (Maggie Wylie)
Vanessa: Her Love Story—U.S. (April 12, 1935) (Vanessa)
Stage Door Canteen—U.S. (June 24, 1944) (Herself)
My Son John—U.S. (April 8, 1952) (Lucille Jefferson)
Main Street to Broadway—U.S. (October 13, 1953) (Herself)
Anastasia—G.B. (December 13, 1956) (Grand Duchess)
Third Man on the Mountain—G.B. (November 11, 1959) (unbilled cameo)
Airport—U.S. (March 5, 1970) (Ada Quonsett)
Herbie Rides Again—U.S. (June 6, 1974) (Mrs. Steinmetz)
One of Our Dinosaurs Is Missing—G.B. (August 6, 1975) (Hettie)
Candleshoe—G.B. (August 3, 1978) (Lady St. Edmund)

RADIO (SELECTED CREDITS)

"The New Penny" (series) 1935–36
"Bambi" (series) 1936–37
"Helen Hayes Theatre" (series) 1940–41, *Victoria and Albert, Bachelor Mother, Comstock Queen, The Straw, Mayerling, Manslaughter, The Lady with the Lamp, Within the Law, Bid for Happiness, Distant Drums, Love Affair, The Late Christopher Bean, A Farewell to Arms, To the Ladies, The Young in Heart.*
"Helen Hayes Theatre of the Air" (series) 1941–42, *Jane Eyre, The Young in Heart, Let the Hurricane Roar, Kitty Foyle, The Old Lady Shows Her Medals, The Last of Mrs. Cheyney, Arrowsmith, This Is Our Destiny, A Star Is Born, Tovarich, The Lady with the Lamp, The Lady Eve, The Outsider, The Brave Die Once, Accent on Youth, Night Raid, What Every Woman Knows.*
Mary of Scotland, April 28, 1946, Theatre Guild of the Air.
Angel Street, September 8, 1946, Theatre Guild of the Air
What Every Woman Knows, March 2, 1947, Theatre Guild of the Air

APPENDIX

Alice-Sit-by-the-Fire, June 29, 1947, Theatre Guild of the Air
Victoria Regina, November 9, 1947, Theatre Guild of the Air
The Corn Is Green, December 14, 1947, Theatre Guild of the Air
Still Life, November 13, 1949, Theatre Guild of the Air
Another Language, January 15, 1950, Theatre Guild of the Air
The Glass Menagerie, September 16, 1951, Theatre Guild of the Air
Remember the Day, June 1, 1952, Theatre Guild of the Air
The Wisteria Trees, September 14, 1952, Theatre Guild of the Air

TELEVISION (Selected Credits)

The Late Christopher Bean, October 27, 1950, "Pulitzer Prize Playhouse"
The Barretts of Wimpole Street, December 5, 1950, "Prudential Playhouse"
Victoria Regina, January 15, 1951, "Robert Montgomery Presents"
Mary of Scotland, February 16, 1951, "Pulitzer Prize Playhouse"
Not a Chance, October 5, 1951, "Schlitz Playhouse"
The Lucky Touch, November 2, 1951, "Schlitz Playhouse"
Dark Fleece, December 21, 1951, "Schlitz Playhouse"
The Twelve Pound Look, November 23, 1952, "Omnibus"
The Christmas Tie, November 30, 1952, "Omnibus"
The Happy Journey, March 1, 1953, "Omnibus"
Battle Hymn, November 7, 1953, "Medallion Theatre"
Irish Linen and Mom and Leo, December 20, 1953, "Omnibus"
Side by Side, January 26, 1954, "Motorola TV Hour"
Welcome Home, March 16, 1954, "U.S. Steel–Theatre Guild"
The Royal Family, September 15, 1954, "The Best of Broadway"
Chance for Adventure, October 24, 1954, "Light's Diamond Jubilee"
Arsenic and Old Lace, January 5, 1955, "The Best of Broadway"
The Skin of Our Teeth, September 11, 1955, "CBS Special"
Dear Brutus, January 8, 1956, "Omnibus"
Mrs. McThing, March 9, 1958, "Omnibus"
Ah, Wilderness!, April 28, 1959, "Hallmark Hall of Fame"
The Cherry Orchard, December 28, 1959, "Play of the Week"
The Bat, March 31, 1960, "Dow Hour of Great Mysteries"
The Cradle Song, April 10, 1960, "Hallmark Hall of Fame"
The Velvet Glove, October 17, 1960, "Play of the Week"
"Tarzan" (episode), November 17, 1967
Arsenic and Old Lace, April 2, 1969, ABC Special
Do Not Fold, Spindle or Mutilate (TV Movie), November 9, 1971
"Here's Lucy" (episode), January 3, 1972
Harvey, March 22, 1972, "Hallmark Hall of Fame"
Alter Ego, October 27, 1972, "Ghost Story"
The Snoop Sisters (TV movie) December 18, 1972, and series
"Hawaii Five-O" (episode), November 7, 1975
Victory at Entebbe (TV movie), 1976
A Family Upside Down (TV movie), 1978

APPENDIX

Murder Is Easy (TV movie), 1981
"Love, Sidney" (episode), October 2, 1982
A Caribbean Mystery (TV movie), 1983
"Glitter" (episode), 1984
"Highway to Heaven" (episode), 1984
Murder by Mirrors (TV movie), 1985

INDEX

(Page numbers in italics denote direct quotations from the persons indicated)

INDEX

212

INDEX

INDEX

INDEX